THE ANGEL OF THE PENNY ROSE

THE ANGEL OF THE PENNY ROSE

LINDA SAETHER

NEW DEGREE PRESS

COPYRIGHT © 2021 LINDA SAETHER

All rights reserved.

THE ANGEL OF THE PENNY ROSE

ISBN	978-1-63676-790-1	*Paperback*
	978-1-63676-791-8	*Kindle Ebook*
	978-1-63676-792-5	*Ebook*

I dedicate this book to my daughters,
Nicole and Ingrid,
and to my angel mother,
with all my love.

CONTENTS

———

AUTHOR'S NOTE

The Angel of the Penny Rose is a historical novel about Anna Caldwell's journey to the Americas, where she discovers the only way to survive is to have the courage to trust that the unlikeliest choices might be the best ones.

My inspiration for this book was one sentence I recalled from a historical tour of old St. Augustine, Florida, a long time ago, which was related to the treatment of widows without means.

Although this was the seed that started the book, it blossomed into a heart-wrenching adventure as my protagonist delved into challenges that are still relevant today.

My hope is that you will enjoy reading this book and transport yourself into Anna's world, where she met obstacles she never could imagine, found herself in places she never thought she would be, and found love where she least expected it.

CHAPTER ONE

———

London, May 1763

The first time I saw Mr. Edmund Ashton come through the oak door of my father's apothecary on St. Katherine's Wharf, he seemed no different than any other man, but there was something curious about him. He was of middling stature, handsome, and finely clad. A gentleman, surely, but he took no note of me as my brother Robert darted in front to greet him.

"We'd be pleased to be of service," Robert said after they had exchanged a few words I couldn't decipher.

It would be tempting to eavesdrop, but Robert would tend to whatever ailed the man, so I took to sorting through deliveries, hoping that my order of chalk would be among the day's supplies. Without it, Father's heartburn would leave him ailing until midday.

Lost in my thoughts, I barely noticed Robert and Mr. Ashton until they stood across the counter from me, but I looked up just in time.

"Mr. Ashton," Robert said, "may I present to you my sister, Mistress Anna Caldwell. She can procure the quantity of supplies you need for your voyage to the Americas and compound anything you may need."

"The Americas!" I stammered before I could stop myself. "I mean, how do you do, Mr. Ashton?"

If he had noticed my unrestrained outburst, there was nothing to suggest it. The thought of an adventure had been haunting my dreams of late, but the Americas had not entered even the most ambitious of them.

It would certainly be more interesting than marrying a prominent widower as my father wished.

The thought of being a richly gowned captive, flaunted for my youth, always made me feel ill, especially knowing I would no longer be allowed an occupation of my own. Robert would be the one in the laboratory formulating remedies for our patrons, and I would seethe with envy.

"Pleasure to meet a young woman of such accomplishments, Mistress Caldwell," Mr. Ashton said.

"Thank you for the kind words, Mr. Ashton. You shall certainly have my full attention."

He cocked his head and looked at me intently before his lips turned up into a pleasant bow, giving me a surprising thrill. "I have no worries, Mistress Caldwell. Robert spoke so highly of you that I have no doubts."

"Mr. Ashton is a mighty fine surgeon," Robert said before I could utter another word. "I have told him he is sorely needed here in London, but his mind appears to be made up."

Mr. Ashton chuckled and gave Robert a pat on the back the way men do. There is often a distrust between physicians and apothecaries, but in these two, there appeared to be no such thing. It would make my task easier, for advising a physician of treatments they both administer can be a daunting task.

"Alas, lad, I have been here long enough. It is time for a new challenge." Mr. Ashton smiled as he spoke, but there was an air about him that left no doubt he was certain of his cause. "I cannot argue with that, sir," Robert said. "I wish you the best, and we'll meet again before you leave, no doubt." "That, we will," Mr. Ashton said before turning to me. "So, where shall we begin, Mistress Caldwell?"

I glanced about. Customers crowded the counters, and those seated clung to their uncomfortable chairs while two small children squirmed on a bench and begged their mother for honey drops. The clunking of glass bottles and jars against wooden surfaces and metal shelves rose above a steady murmur of conversation from all corners of the room.

Turning back to our new patron, I stepped up beside him. "It's perhaps better that we talk in a quieter area, Mr. Ashton. I should not like to miss any detail of your order."

Leading him into the laboratory, a scent of cloves and lemon oil wafted toward us, but Mr. Ashton said nothing of it. I left the door open for propriety so we could be seen but not heard as we settled by the wooden table where I kept my ledgers and inkwell.

Hopefully, my mind would stop conjuring up visions of herbs sifting through my fingers into hemp bags and of the tinctures and tonics that he would request, while regretting I would not have the thrill of learning what maladies he would use them for.

"So, tell me, Mr. Ashton, what is calling you to the Americas?" I asked, hoping my sudden envy wasn't evident.

He looked at me as if he were deciding whether I was worthy of his true reason or the quip he had dealt Robert. The moment drew long, but just when I was wondering if I had overstepped, his shoulders dropped and his face softened.

"I've lost a great love, someone very dear to me," he said. "It's been years, but mulling about here makes the memories no less painful."

"I'm sorry," I said. "It was not my place to ask."

His smile was wry, but it was a smile all the same. "It does me well to say it. Do not apologize."

I smiled at him. "You are wise to seek a new adventure."

His eyes lit as he leaned forward with an informality that startled me at first, but there was nothing improper about the way he spoke of East Florida.

He was to work in St. Augustine with a doctor by the name of Mr. Catherwood. Our forces were quickly populating the region after the Spanish had left for Cuba, once the Treaty of Paris had been signed only months ago, so surely one physician was hardly sufficient.

"I am to tend to our soldiers and the English families who have settled in the area," he said, "but as of now, I know not what their needs are, so I plan to be well equipped."

"Are there no Spaniards left, then? Not a single one?"

He looked amused. "Hardly, but perhaps there are a few."

"Peculiar how a few strokes of a quill in a faraway land can cause such upheaval for so many," I said, "but it was probably less than what the natives had to endure."

He sat back, studying me for a moment. "You have a curious mind and a soft heart. Fine qualities in a woman."

And not in a man? I wanted to ask, but I managed to refrain with some difficulty.

Taking the top off the inkwell and opening my ledger, I looked up at him. He was smiling at me as if he were thoroughly entertained that I had a brain to use at all.

"Perhaps you will learn the remedies of the native tribes, who were there even before the Spaniards and who know the land and plants better than anyone."

The thought intrigued me greatly, but Mr. Ashton's pleasure in our conversation seemed to vanish.

"Perhaps we could trade remedies, but I am not at all certain they have accepted our presence there."

I nodded. "I hadn't considered that. They must wonder how we believe we have the right to arrive at their shores and help ourselves to their land. I shouldn't like that either, but if per chance they are of the friendly sort, and you do discover what they use to treat their ill, could—"

He chuckled. "Could I inform you?"

I smiled up at him. "Yes, something like that."

"You are a curious one. It will be my pleasure, Mistress Caldwell."

Our eyes locked for a second.

"Thank you. I would be most grateful."

I slid my inkwell forward and dipped my quill into it, blotting it before I wrote Mr. Ashton's name on a fresh page of my ledger. "We should begin," I said, quickly lowering my gaze and shifting in my chair.

He cleared his throat. "Yes, indeed. At first, I should want a quantity of dried herbs. Lavender, feverfew, bergamot, and mint. And of course, rosemary and sage."

"Perhaps pennyroyal, thyme, nutmeg, and musk too?" I added.

Mr. Ashton nodded without looking at me. "Yes, yes, of course."

"And should you need laudanum? Probably a good measure of elixir of asthmaticum, and paregoric as well?"

His silence made me look up from my ledger.

"Mistress Caldwell, do not question my needs. I know what I have come for. You can add ten kegs each of elderberry tonic, elixir of infinitium, and valerian."

He didn't seem angry—well, not exactly—but he started tapping his fingers on the armrest of his chair with the same sentiment as a cat whipping its tail about.

"Of course. Please pardon me, Mr. Ashton. The thought of your travel intrigues me more than I expected," I said, looking directly at him.

He shrugged. "From what I have been told, life in St. Augustine is quite harsh, far from what you are accustomed to in London."

"I should think much could be learned from seeing the world outside of one's birthplace," I said, hoping he would tell me more about the Americas.

To my surprise, he chuckled, and as he shook his head ever so slightly, a twinkle lit his hazel eyes.

"You are a most unusual young woman, Mistress Caldwell. Women far beyond your age have not the adeptness to do an apothecary's work, nor do they seem to spend more than a moment thinking of the world outside of their own social circles."

I sighed. "Robert and I worked by our parents' side from an early age. So, when our mother died three years ago and Father drowned his sorrow in drink, it was the two of us who kept the shop going, although I was barely fifteen and Robert only a year older. There was little time for frivolities."

Edmund's face became solemn. "I didn't mean to—"

I lifted a hand and smiled, disguising the sadness that always came about when I spoke of my mother. "When must your order be due, Mr. Ashton? My unusual self should like to order what is needed at once so I can begin our work."

Mr. Ashton sighed. "I meant no offense."

"None taken, Mr. Ashton. What is the date of your departure?"

Hat in hand, he rose and paused before he spoke. "The twelfth of June, but my order must be boxed and sent to the docks in Liverpool no later than the first of the month."

I stood and reached my hand out to him. "Then it shall be so, Mr. Ashton."

"I hope I haven't been cross." He lifted my fingers to his lips and kissed them. "It was not my intention."

"You presented yourself as a true gentleman," I said, looking up into his eyes.

"Then I thank you and bid you farewell, Mistress Caldwell."

"Farewell, Mr. Ashton."

He walked down the hallway, but before he reached the shop, he turned, and when he saw me standing there, watching him, he smiled.

I felt my cheeks flush. How silly of me, but he was an interesting sort. He was an even more pleasant-looking man than I had first thought. It wasn't just the well-tailored clothing that accentuated his shoulders and long limbs, or his auburn hair that had as much shine as the silk ribbon he had used to tie it, but the manner in which he walked that gave him the confidence expected of a high-ranking person, not just a mere doctor headed for a land barely civilized.

* * *

Before I had the time to consider Mr. Ashton's order, Robert was at the door.

"Father wants you to entertain a guest this afternoon. He expects a gentleman friend to call at four o'clock."

I sighed, suddenly irritated. "Did he ask if it suited me?" Robert looked at me with empathy. "No. He was merely informing you."

Our guest arrived not a minute past four o'clock, just before supper. The cook had apparently been alerted, for there was a place for a guest at the table, and the aroma wafting from the kitchens smelled exquisite.

"There you are, darling girl," Father said as I entered the parlor where he and a rotund gentleman with large furry brows were enjoying the evening's first glass of claret. His greeting was suspiciously endearing and certainly for the benefit of his friend, a man named Cecil Bertram, recently widowed and wealthy, from what I had been told.

He was a "gentleman caller," if ever I had seen one, for now that I was of age, Father would rather see me as a bride than an apothecary. So far, I had warded off all of his attempts. Certainly, this one would have to be swatted away too, for there was nothing enticing about him.

"Good afternoon, Mr. Bertram," I said as he rose and eyed me intently.

"My, how lovely you have become," he said, taking my hand and planting a wet kiss on it. "You are a delight to behold."

"Thank you." Suppressing the urge to wipe my hand in the folds of my skirt was impossible. Thankfully, neither he nor my father took note of it.

Before I could be asked, I slipped down into a chair opposite of Father and Mr. Bertram and reached for the glass of claret placed in front of me.

"Cecil was just telling me how he has become a master angler," my father said. "It's apparently the best of pastimes."

My father seemed genuinely interested, but I shuddered.

"I would not have the patience for such a thing," I said. "It's far better to send the maid to the fish market than stand by a pond, waiting for one's supper to hook itself to the bait." Cecil chuckled, though I refused to hide my disdain. "How it would please me to have a woman with such spirit," he said. "I have become quite forlorn in my great house."

Father looked at me as if an opportunity were presenting itself.

"Well, I hope you find one," I said, attempting to smile.

"I think I have," he answered, making my father grin.

I probably laid that trap for myself, but thankfully, before more could be said, our maid announced that supper was about to be served.

Fish was our main dish this evening, so I could probably steer the conversation back to his angling skill, if that were a skill at all.

"Penelope can cook trout like no other," my father said, referring to our cook. "I should raise her wages."

"Exquisite, indeed," Cecil said, and fortunately the conversation did turn back to his angling, but I could not envision myself by a river's edge with a bucket of bait and dying fish flopping at my feet.

Supper lingered long into the evening, and the flow of wine made my father and our guest as rowdy as unrestrained boys, amusing only themselves. Robert had closed the shop and snuck away to the tavern, as he usually did, so he'd be no help at all. Thankfully, the one glass of claret had left me numb and allowed me to escape to my room by claiming to have fallen prey to the vapors, something men saw as an acceptable excuse of the feminine sort.

* * *

By morning, I was back in the laboratory, crushing herbs. The pestle fit my hand as if it were made for me, and each crunch of the mortar's contents tickled my nostrils with fragrant scents, making me feel that all was well with the world, despite my father's latest attempts to marry me off.

Edmund, as Mr. Ashton asked us to call him, had stopped in several times since we first met. We had become friends of sorts, but the days until his departure approached with staggering haste.

Robert and I worked feverishly to complete his orders, and although I was eager to come to the apothecary every morning, it saddened me to think that Edmund would no longer come by. He would no longer tease my senses with his scent of sandalwood and musk, his odd humor, and the most intriguing stories, but knowing he would soon be gone only made us laugh with more abandon.

"Anna, this is ghastly!" Edmund said, after tasting my Elixir of Devil's Claw. His horrified face made me giggle.

"Then pray you won't be needing it, and be kind to your patients who do," I said.

He shook his head, but his smile warmed me. "Never have I met a woman like you—"

His words abruptly ceased when one of the apprentices came into the laboratory carrying a crateful of empty kegs.

"As you requested," he said, turning to go back to the shop.

I noticed Edmund eyeing them with curiosity.

"These are for the tonics you requested for the stomach flux. Best you not sink that ship with the weight of your remedies, for the fish would not fare well."

"Good God!" he said, trying to hide a chuckle as he reached for his hat. "I must take my leave, you silly thing. There is much to be done before this journey of mine."

Then he was gone, leaving me to my fantasies of what it would be like to set out on an adventure such as his and become part of that new unsettled territory. If I were to marry a wealthy widower, my world would be nothing like that.

* * *

A week after introducing me to Cecil Bertram, Father announced that marriage between Cecil and me would be an advantageous union and that a wedding would take place in the autumn. Imagining it gave my stomach a jolt. Surely, I would have no say in the matter, and as a girl I could hardly become an apothecary in my own right, although I was as good as any.

Stepping into the laboratory after hearing the news, my thoughts twisted in my mind and must have worried the breath out of me, for I felt my chest tighten.

Gasping for air, I felt the room spin, and my knees weakened. As my sight blurred, I heard my name ring out, and I felt the touch of hands before everything went black.

I don't know how long I was lost in time, but when I opened my eyes, Edmund was on the floor with me, holding me in his arms and stroking my hair as if it were the most natural thing to do, leaving me feeling both stunned and sinfully indulged.

"It's good I arrived when I did, or these stone floors would have made a mess of your lovely head."

I sat, allowing him to steady me, and hoped no one would find us like this, for it would appear highly improper.

"I fainted," I mumbled, "but I'm better, much better."

"You gave me a fright, dear woman. Did you forget to eat?"

"Probably… but I'm fine now," I said. However, my attempt to stand left him doubtful. After making me wait for several long minutes, he gently pulled me to my feet and held me while I steadied myself.

We had never stood so close before, and the sensation of his nearness was unnerving.

He was still watching me with the vigilance of a physician, but as I looked into his eyes, I forgot to be nervous or proper, for something wondrous came to mind.

It was at least possibly wondrous and certainly immensely exciting. I should think it through, shouldn't I? But what if there isn't enough time?

Releasing myself from his grip, I rushed to the door, shut it behind us, and glanced back at him. His brows furrowed, and he looked puzzled, but I kept my resolve.

"Something is amiss," he said.

"Not at all. It's…" I hesitated.

"It's what?"

Stepping closer, I looked up at him, plucking up my courage. "You'll be departing in a matter of days."

"I know this." He tilted his head, studying me as if I had suddenly become a loon, but I couldn't stop now. I didn't care if he found me impertinent.

He crossed his arms as I reached out for them, startling him.

"Take me with you. Please, I beg you!" I said, looking up at him.

He stood back, staring at me with more disbelief than I expected and not a hint of joy. "You've taken leave of your senses! How can I take you with me? I have no need of an apothecary!"

He turned away, leaving me aghast, but then he swiveled back and looked at me with such utter confusion that I could only cringe, and I feared that my hopes would be shattered in an instant.

"You have gone mad. I am certain of it," he said.

I couldn't give up, though there was nothing inviting in his tone. Taking a deep breath, I paused before I gazed into his eyes. "Could you not need a wife?"

He gasped. "What say you?"

I stepped closer. "How many unmarried women are there in that small garrison town, Edmund? Might you not become lonely?"

His brows furrowed again, and he started to pace. "Can you not stop yourself? Do you always speak your mind?"

I nodded. "I try to, though it's cost me a time or two."

He turned away again, and my heart sank. I watched as he raked his fingers through his unbound hair, but then he stopped and turned, looking at me pensively. Before he could say a word, I took three steps toward him, and to my surprise I raised myself to the tips of my toes and kissed him, awakening sensations I had never felt before.

Still, when I stepped back, I had to know. "So, will you marry me, or will you not?"

CHAPTER TWO

——

London, June 1763

Spring in London is usually a dreary experience. Cold, wet mists seep in from the river, and rain as predictable as the passage of time renders the cobbled streets slippery and the earth sodden. This is my London.

But on this day, the heavens smiled. The sun shone brightly in the sky, and its rays brought a twinkle to the calm waters of the Thames, pleasantly warm too, and the air free of the putrid vapors of sewage and horse manure we must endure more days than not. It was the perfect day, and with Father's blessings, it was the day that would change my life forever.

Edmund and I married in All Hallows Church by the Tower that afternoon. Father, Robert, Aunt Fiona, and several of my cousins were there, as was Edmund's elated father, his beautiful sister, Edwina, and several of his brothers.

Farewells were painful but swift, for we could not delay leaving for Liverpool, where we would embark on our journey within days.

Arriving late to our lodging that first night, Edmund's tenderness and patience with me on our wedding night made me hope I would learn what was expected of me. Our first attempt at lovemaking was clumsy at best, so there had to be something missing, unless the hushed tales I had been told were greatly embellished.

Laying silently in each other's arms, he kissed my forehead, and after wishing me a good night he turned his back to me. Still, I couldn't resist the temptation to touch him. I let my fingers glide along his finely contoured muscles and ever so gently kneaded his back until he moaned.

"I could come to love you," he murmured, still not asleep. "But rest now, wife. It will be long before we will lie in a bed as fine as this again."

His words echoed in my mind.

Could he love me, or was it my nimble hands that inspired him in the moment? Still, the thought that we could someday become a love match was too intriguing not to explore.

Nudging him, as if accidentally, he awoke and looked at me. "Husband... I didn't mean to awaken you! I was clumsy."

"You are forgiven," he said, drifting off again.

"Edmund?"

"Yes. What keeps you awake at this late hour?"

"I must know... Why did you marry me?"

His eyes shot open, and he rose to lean on his elbow, looking at me with a certain amount of wonder. "Did you not ask me to?"

"I did, but why did you oblige me?"

"Because you asked."

He seemed to find humor in taunting me, but I could hardly help myself.

"I don't believe you. Please do tell me. I can't sleep unless I know."

The possibility of a sleepless night may have dawned on him, for his grin gave way to somber reflection. "You are indeed pleasing to the eye, so any man would be proud to have you, but more so, you have skills well suited to mine... and your fingers give a pleasing rub."

I waited, but he seemed lost in thought, too long for my liking.

"So, you married me for my skills?"

He chuckled, and the grin reappeared. "Your golden tresses are quite fetching, and you have the most inquisitive and beautiful blue eyes." He looked at me as if he had only now noticed me. "You have a natural grace, if I may say so, but I married you because there probably isn't anyone in St. Augustine who is anything like you. Now, please close those lovely eyes. I will not answer another question."

* * *

The next day, we would leave England, possibly forever. Oddly, neither of us spoke of it, but it was perhaps better left at that. Missing Father, Robert, and our dear apothecary would be my burden to bear alone.

My husband became quiet when we arrived at the massive dock in Liverpool.

We strolled past more than twenty ships before the vessel that would take us to the Americas came into view. My husband absentmindedly patted my hand as if I was the one who needed to be consoled.

"From this point on, our lives will change," he said. "Anything can happen."

"Anything can happen wherever we are," I said, trying to be cheerful.

"Indeed, but this will be our home for the next few months; that is certain."

The *Penny Rose* wasn't as large as some of the ships at the port, but she would be my first ship to board, and a far cry from the river barges of the Thames.

As I looked up at the towering masts, the imposing hull shifted, tugging hard on the lines that secured her to the pier. The sails that were tightly furled, and wider than I had thought, would be marvelous to behold once we were at sea.

Around us, the excitement was palpable, and I began to yearn for the enormity of what lay ahead.

"It's time we board, Anna."

I nodded and smiled up at my husband, happy to see that the twinkle had returned to his eyes.

As we approached the gangway, the pungent odor of newly tarred wood and caulk, blending with sea air, distracted me. It would take time to become accustomed to it.

Commotion surrounded preparations for departure. Loaders and dockers shouted to one another while wooden crates and barrels were brought onto the ship, and the bleating of doomed young goats in pens and the clucking of chickens in cages stacked along the pier filled the air with a sense of urgency.

"The captain's fare," Edmund said, following my gaze.

Around us, passengers scurried, some counting their trunks, others gathering their children. As I looked at their faces, I wondered what they felt, what had made them pack up and leave everything behind to set out on this journey.

As the wind quicken around us, I overheard workers say the cool, crisp weather was just right for starting a voyage.

We would be off within hours, and after that, there would be no turning back.

"Are you ready, Mrs. Ashton?" Edmund asked when we reached the wooden gangway.

I looked up to the deck above us, feeling a stir of excitement within me.

"The ship wouldn't wait for me if I were not," I said.

We held hands as we climbed up the wobbly gangway, and I felt a flutter of anticipation that made me smile.

The moment we stepped onto the thickly caulked deck of the *Penny Rose,* the captain came toward us. He was a short, stout man with the wide stance of a seasoned sailor and the piercing gaze of someone to whom nothing passed unnoticed. He wore a blue jacket with gold trim and shiny brass buttons over a white waistcoat and breeches. His first mate and quartermaster were similarly dressed, though less gilded.

"Might you be the doctor headed for St. Augustine?" Captain Hatfield asked, glancing at our documents.

"I am," Edmund said.

"Welcome aboard, Mr. and Mrs. Ashton." The captain gestured to a ship-boy nearby. "Take the good doctor's case and stow it securely."

The lad stepped forward, but Edmund held back. "No, thank you. This bag contains fragile glass rods from France. I will not burden you with caring for them."

The captain nodded, and the boy rushed off to pull a plump little girl from the railing while a loader helped her mother haul a trunk on board. The girl's laughter made me smile, but the captain's voice startled me to attention.

"Since your fare is paid and I expect to be in need of your services during this voyage, I have given you a cabin to yourselves near my own."

As he spoke, he looked directly at Edmund, as if I wasn't there at all. "Some of the passengers will be sleeping on deck but most below."

He gestured toward the steady stream of people making their way on board, many with wide-eyed children in tow, carrying everything they owned as well as food and drink in the hope that it would sustain them during the voyage.

Thankfully, our trunks were already on board, along with the supplies from the apothecary.

"Has there been much illness?" Edmund asked.

"Aye. On the last voyage, twelve dead children were thrown into the sea, and half as many older folks. All struck by pestilence."

I gasped, but Edmund squeezed my hand and held it tightly, stopping the flow of questions about to roll off my tongue.

"Let's hope we fare better on this voyage," he said, casting me a glance.

"And pray we do not hit gale winds off the shore of the Americas. This vessel has endured enough." With that, the captain walked away.

His words made me shudder.

Watching Edmund survey our surroundings, I couldn't tell if he was worried.

"Is the ship as you expected?" I asked, glancing up at him.

Edmund hesitated and continued to look at everything around us. "She appears to be a fine ship," he said after a while. "But from the number of passengers streaming in, and some still left on the dock, I fear we shall not be able to move about as freely as I thought, and tempers will surely run short, living in such close quarters for months."

"As long as we can find each other among all these travelers, I shall have no complaints. And, I shall promise you I will keep my mood pleasant."

"That certainly puts me at ease!" he said, chiding me, as his mood suddenly lightened.

I didn't have time to ponder my reply before a young ship›s boy sought us out.

"I'm Joshua McGhee," he said, grinning at us. "I've come to take ye to yer cabin."

The boy, with his auburn locks and freckled face, could not have been more than ten, but he seemed sure of himself as he led us in the direction of the stern, toward the officer's quarters. We entered a narrow passageway behind the helm, lined with cabins on each side. At the end of the passageway, a door opened, and I caught a glimpse of an ample parlor as a servant rushed by.

"The captain's quarters," Joshua explained. "Yer's is nothin' like that."

His grin became wider, and I noticed a mischievous glint in his eye.

Ours was the third on the left, small, cramped, and damp. The floor, walls, and ceilings were clad with wide plank. A built-in cot had fresh bedding, and next to it our trunks and valets had already been stacked and strapped down. The ceiling was so low that Edmund could barely stand up without crouching, and there was little room for the two of us to stand between the cot and the door.

"I wonder what the other cabins look like," I said, remembering the passengers making their way down from the main deck to quarters below. "They can't be smaller?"

Edmund looked around as if he were truly grateful. "They are. The deck below us is likely just a vast room partitioned into tiny spaces, where some couples are assigned a cot and nothing else. We stand a better chance of staying well here on our own."

"Could we take a look?" I asked, longing to go back outside and immensely curious to see the living quarters that we had been fortunate to escape.

"If you wish, but I imagine it's already getting crowded down there."

Making our way toward the bow, we joined the line of passengers heading into the ship's belly. Carefully threading our way down the stairs, I wondered how anyone could manage those steep steps when the ship rocked.

The lower deck was as Edmund had described. I took in the long row of tiny rooms closed only by canvas sheaths that stretched from one end of the ship to the other. Some had hammocks suspended from beams above them. Others had four bunks built into the walls between them or the hull of the ship. These were intended for a family of eight or four couples, who would be huddled together as the boat rocked and creaked in the dark of night, with only a sheet of canvas separating them from all the others.

Suddenly, I felt less dismayed with our cabin, for there was no place to retreat to here and even less room to move. Edmund pulled me to him and out of the way of passengers continuing to stream in, led by the quartermaster assigning them bunks. There was much grumbling, but most settled in without disturbance.

Next to us, a little boy and his sister sat staring out from their hammock while their parents secured trunks, barrels, and satchels below them. Both studied me with guarded curiosity, reminding me of Robert and myself when we were that young.

In the small common area, a table had been built around the mainmast, and the passengers who had settled there already looked weary. For a moment I wanted to sit, but the thought of getting back up to the deck and into open air became surprisingly urgent as I started to feel chilled and damp at the same time.

The ship shifted, and I stumbled against Edmund, suddenly lightheaded and nauseated by the stale air and the enclosed space. My view of the children in the hammock became a blur, and their faces faded in front of me.

"Edmund!" I gasped, feeling my knees buckle under me as everything turned black.

CHAPTER THREE

The *Penny Rose,* June 1763

When I came to, I was lying on a narrow bench and looking up at the masts, with their furled sails and web of rigging against a cloudless blue sky. I took a deep breath and tried to sit up, but the dizziness still loomed, leaving me unsettled. Edmund was next to me, coaxing me to be still, but the worry in his face had lifted.

"This is no way to start our voyage, Mrs. Ashton," he said, grinning at me.

"I must not have received proper instructions," I quipped, looking past him at a plump young woman with a small child in her arms, peering down at me over his shoulder.

"You might want this for the missus to put on her brow," she said, handing Edmund a wet cloth.

The woman wore a simple brown dress that fit snugly over her ample breasts. Her red hair was tied in a matronly bun, but her face was youthful and her eyes bright and kind. The little girl in her arms was the one the ship-boy had pulled from the railing as she had ventured to climb, but now she watched me with waning interest while intently sucking her thumb.

Edmund took the wad of fabric and placed it on my forehead.

"That's very good of you, Mrs...?"

"Blackwood. I'm Mary Blackwood, and this is Muriel." She boosted her daughter in her arms, smiling at the child and pinching her cheeks as her little girl grinned back at her.

"I'm Edmund Ashton, and my fainting bride is Mrs. Anna Ashton."

With Edmund steadying me, I managed to sit up and hand the cloth back to the woman. "Thank you. It's most kind of you, but I feel better now."

A ship's boy handed me a tin cup filled with cider, and as I drank, strength started to return to my limbs and my head began to clear.

"So," Mary said, "you are newlyweds. Much happiness to you. How I remember those days."

"Thank you. I am the most fortunate of men," Edmund said as I felt my cheeks turn crimson.

"What brings you out on this journey, Mrs. Blackwood?" I asked, eager to move the conversation from our personal lives.

"Oh, call me Mary, my dear. My husband is waiting for us in St. Augustine. We didn't want to set out together with a child so young before he knew what we'd be going to, but now we can make the journey without that worry, for he earns good money in St. Augustine."

"What is Mr. Blackwood's profession, then?" Edmund asked.

"Oh, Harry owns the Matanzas Inn. From what I hear, it's lovely. We had a tavern in London, but it burned down. After that, my Harry wanted to try his luck elsewhere, so off we go!"

I wondered if she was afraid, but she seemed sturdy, happy, and looking forward to the adventure.

"You're brave to travel alone," Edmund said. "We shall be near should you need us."

Mary smiled, looking not the least bit worried. "Thank you, Mr. Ashton. I'm not fearful for us. I'd worry for those who haven't the money, for they will be sold into servitude for not having the fare."

"Sold?" I asked, uneasy at the thought.

"Oh, yes, ma'am. I'm surprised you haven't heard. When we arrive at port, farmers and merchants come aboard and pay the fares for those who haven't the means to. Then the passengers are worked to the bone until their fare's paid."

Upon seeing my startled expression, she smiled. "There is some hope that Lieutenant Governor Moultrie or Major Peavett may be coming aboard a-lookin'. They've got some fine houses, my Harry wrote. Couldn't be so bad to work for them."

"I would imagine it could take some time to work off the debt," Edmund said.

Mary was suddenly serious. "One never knows. Some people have sold off their children in their despair and not seen them for six or seven years. I can't imagine."

"That is no better than—"

The subtle squeeze of my husband's hand on my shoulder silenced me.

* * *

Passengers started to gather at the balustrade, some pensive, others excited over what was to come. High above, riggers unfurled the sails and darted across the ratlines as if they were on solid ground. As an unknown world unfolded before us, the captain and his first mate stood at the helm, directing others to ready the ship.

"Burns, to the main! Henley, to the mizzen!"

The orders droned on as young ship's boys scurried across the length of the ship, carrying out their duties with the agility of ship cats. For a moment, I wondered about their mothers and the longing and worry they must have for these boys, but there were probably more mouths to feed back home, and times were hard for many.

A shout from the dock announced the release of the last line that bound us to shore, and then the vessel broke free, gliding from the pier a foot at a time, then yards.

Youths yelped jubilantly, thrusting themselves against the railing while their mothers watched with weary eyes. Some of the men stood with clenched jaws, taking a long look at the land they were leaving behind.

I felt a quiver rise from within me, and I wasn't certain if it was excitement or fear. Whatever it was, we were headed toward the Americas, and the ship would not turn back if I asked it to.

When the *Penny Rose* sailed out from the River Mersey and into the Irish Sea, Edmund and I stayed on deck and watched as every gust of wind carried us farther from the shores of England and toward the open sea.

"Do you think we will ever return?" I asked, uncertain of what I should wish for.

"I don't know," he replied. "I just don't know."

"It would be grievous to never see those we left behind, but it might behoove us not to think of it just now," I said, nestling closer to him.

At nightfall, when we were alone in our cabin, Edmund helped me out of my clothing and pulled me onto the cot, wrapping his arms around me.

"It's been a long day," he said. "We should get some sleep."

* * *

At first light, families gathered on the main deck, weary from awakening to the unfamiliar sounds around them after a night crowded uncomfortably in their hammocks or braving the elements on deck. The salt sea air and steady rays of sun seemed to invigorate us, and spirits lifted with the promise of a warm meal. With still seas, the cooks could fire up the great ovens. We were all given a morning meal of oatmeal and cider brought up to deck by ship's boys running back and forth from the galley.

After eating their fill, each family staked out a place to gather for the day. From sunrise to sunset, they tried to pass the hours sewing, mending, talking, playing cribbage, or singing old shanties that would be brought to the new land and sung for generations to come.

Sometimes Edmund and I sang with them, but often we sat alone, talking about the life we would have in St. Augustine. Other times, Mary Blackwood joined us, sharing the little she knew about this new land of ours.

Within a week at sea, Captain Hatfield came looking for Edmund as we idled in the shade of the mast shroud.

"Greetings, good people," he said as we bolted up.

"And a good morning to you, Captain," my husband replied.

The captain's face became somber as he looked up at Edmund. "The lad in the cabin across from you has a festering leg wound. I'd be obliged if you looked in on him."

Edmund startled. "Do you speak of Charles Rushmore, son of Admiral Rushmore?"

"I do."

"We will see to him," Edmund said, pulling me to my feet. "I hadn't heard he was injured."

The Rushmore cabin was larger and lighter than ours, making it easy to see the flush of fever on Charles's face as we walked in, but the putrid scent of decaying flesh made me wonder if we were called here in time.

While his uncle, a handsome man named Thomas Wingfield, quickly undressed Charles's left leg, I took the boy's hand in mine and held it. He looked young for his fourteen years, small and still a child.

"I'm Anna Ashton, and the good doctor is my husband, Mr. Ashton. We will do all we can to help you."

"Thank you," Charles said. "It pains me greatly."

"Whatever caused this?" Edmund asked, looking down at the long tear on the boy's leg. From where I stood, I could see it was oozing and the margins were red, swollen, and turning dark.

"A sword," the boy said as if it were a common occurrence.

"A sword?" Edmund's brow rose.

"My cousin and I were fencing. He meant no harm. I saw it was deep, but I kept it wrapped until I was well aboard so my grandfather wouldn't keep me from sailing."

Charles looked shamefaced as Edmund shook his head.

"Poor boy," I murmured, thinking of the pain he must have endured.

"Does this hurt?" Edmund asked, palpating the area around the wound.

Charles braced himself and cried out, "Yes! Please stop!" Tears flooded his eyes, and he was left whimpering as Edmund lifted his hands.

"Why didn't you call for me earlier? This has festered for a while." Edmund looked from the boy to his uncle.

"My nephew deftly kept it hidden until he could no longer bear the pain," Thomas said. "He is as stubborn as any of us."

"I thought it would heal," Charles said, "or at least that it could wait until we were back in St. Augustine."

"Your delay may have cost you your leg, child," Edmund said.

"No, please, no!" Charles's grip on my hand became tighter as he pulled himself up.

Edmund looked at him with surprise.

"Husband, please. Let me care for him," I said, unable to stop myself. "If he is no better in a fortnight, you can proceed."

"Pray tell, what do you think to do?" Edmund asked. "We haven't any leeches."

From the look on my husband's face, I would be wise to silence myself, but the thought of this boy hobbling along with only one leg tore at me.

"I will fill the wound with maggots, for they are as greedy as leeches," I said, trying to sound pleasant, if not confident. "There is still time."

Charles and Thomas exchanged a glance and looked to my husband for clarity.

"And from where would you harvest them?" Edmund asked, doing me no favor.

"Trust in me, husband," I said, fearing I had challenged his authority in front of this boy and his uncle, but I couldn't stop myself in time. "There are maggots on every ship. I shall find them, and when their work is done I will apply balms of honey myrtle and hyssop and salves of willow bark and sage. His leg must be spared. Edmund, he is only a boy."

"He might be dead in a fortnight," Edmund said.

"Let her," Charles said with a sudden command about him. A Rushmore, indeed.

Edmund ignored him. Instead, he looked into my eyes for a painfully long moment as I tensed in anticipation.

"Two days," he said, "but no more."

"Four if he shows steady improvement, two if he worsens," I said, hoping Edmund would forgive my unseemly public behavior.

Edmund turned to Charles and his uncle. "My wife is most stubborn. It may be fortunate for you."

"We are grateful," Thomas Wingfield said, reaching a hand out to Edmund.

Turning to Charles, he looked as relieved as I felt. As I started to clean his wound with the supplies near his cot, I heard the door shut behind us as Edmund and Mr. Wingfield left the cabin.

CHAPTER FOUR

———

The *Penny Rose,* June 1763

There were days that the sea became rough. Passengers stumbled across the decks, struggling to maintain their balance, and anything that was dropped could not be retrieved without a valiant chase. Many became well acquainted with the wooden railing, where they bowed down and spewed into the sea.

Some of the ill below were too weak to ever come up into the fresh air. The stench they had to endure was gruesome, much worse than the most overcrowded areas of London, but many were too sickened to care. Edmund said I shouldn't waste time coaxing them to take the ginger tonics they had refused but instead tend to those who at least had a will to live.

"But how can they have a will to live if they feel so awful? Shouldn't they be well to know what their desires are?"

Edmund flung his head back as if the answers were above him somewhere. "They are dying, Anna. Don't bother them."

Being outside was my only refuge.

"What's the long face for?" Mary asked me when we met for cider near the forecastle.

"It grieves me that so many have sickened or been injured," I said, pulling Muriel into my arms and tickling her until she giggled and squirmed away.

"I've heard," Mary said, "but there is much talk that your maggots are as good as leeches, although they are not as well received by their hosts."

"What was I to do, Mary? There wasn't a leech on board, but you can always find maggots."

"Indeed. There is no lack of vermin."

"At least I saved Charles an amputation."

Charles had already been on deck for a while, seated with his leg propped up on a spool of rope. When I waved, his face lit and he waved back, making me smile.

"He's a sweet boy," I said.

Mary followed my gaze.

"That was no small feat, taking care of that lad," she said, giving my hand a pat just as Edmund came up from below and joined us.

"Mornin' to ya," Mary greeted him.

"Not a good one," he said. "There is going to be a funeral."

I felt my chest tighten. After weeks on board, there were no unfamiliar faces among us.

"So, it's come to that," Mary said.

Edmund nodded.

"Who?" I asked, not sure I wanted to know.

"A ship's boy..." Edmund paused, interrupted by the commotion of the captain and members of the crew gathering portside just yards from us. Two sailors held a bundle between them, clearly a body wrapped in a hammock, its cords tightly secured around it.

"Somewhere a mother's heart will break." Mary sighed as we watched the solemn group gathering before us. "I couldn't bear it."

We sat quietly and listened as the captain read from the Scriptures and prayed along with several officers and a scraggly bunch of sailors. Then the boy's body was lifted above the railing and dropped into the sea. The sailors and a group of passengers leaned over to watch, but then they dispersed, and the *Penny Rose* moved steadily forward, leaving the boy behind.

I felt a wave of nausea well up, but Mary was right; this was only the first burial at sea.

As the weeks passed, passengers began to bicker over food as they watched their supplies dwindle or spoil. More succumbed to seasickness and other ailments, and funerals became common. There was no hiding from it, and I struggled with the horror of each sad story.

Even the nights were not without worry.

"I didn't expect to see so much misery on board," I said, running my fingers through Edmund's salt-laden hair as we lay entwined on our narrow cot, listless from the toils of the day. "The despair is difficult to behold when there is so little we can do to help."

Edmund sighed. "We are more fortunate than many, but we must stay well. I would prefer that you stay on deck and not venture into the pestilence below."

"I can't, Edmund. Who should see to you while you are tending to the sick on every deck of this ship, if not me?"

It pained me that I was starting to wonder who would be next. It hadn't escaped me that the ship was no longer as crowded as it had been and that there was more room for the captain to let livestock wander about. Several of the passengers I had come to know were lined up for watery graves or packed down into the sandy ballast of the hold, awaiting burial in the Americas. We were becoming a ghost ship, with many of the living so tormented by grief that they wished they, too, were dead, and there was nothing anyone could do to change it.

* * *

As weeks faded away, July came, bringing hopes it would be our last month at sea. After the Captain's services that first Sunday in July, I saw Edmund coming toward me from the other side of the deck.

I smiled, but he didn't. He just kneeled in front of me, his face so morose, that it gave me a sinking feeling in the pit of my stomach. Mary had not felt well, of late, but certainly this wasn't about her.

"What is it?" I asked, bracing myself.

"My dear," Edmund blocked the rays of the sun as he leaned closer to me. "I want to take you to see Mary. I don't believe she will ever see the shores of St. Augustine."

I stiffened, realizing the absurdity of wishing my husband was lying to me or just wrong, but wishing it still. "No, Edmund...."

It can't be Mary. What would become of Muriel, and that wondrous bear of a man who was waiting for them in St. Augustine?

I sat for a moment, searching his face for a flicker of hope that wasn't there. He sighed, as if waiting for my thoughts to settle.

"I'm sorry, Anna. She has been a good friend to us."

I couldn't dismiss Mary so quickly. Surely something could be remedied? "Are you certain? Certain she is dying?"

"It would take a miracle to save her, and I have none," he said, pulling me to my feet.

"But you could try another treatment. You have—"

"Stop, wife! I have tried it all, and she is no better!"

I felt numb. Mary and I were to explore St. Augustine together. We were going to feast at the Matanzas with our husbands and, in time, raise a brood of children.

Edmund disrupted my thoughts. "Come with me."

I tried to steady myself as he took my hand. My legs shook, but I pressed forward as Edmund led me below to a section close to the stern. The stench was worse than the most overcrowded areas of London. Passengers huddled together, some visibly ill, many exhausted and emaciated.

Edmund brought me to a row of hammocks in a small enclosure. Mary lay in one of them. She was limp and sweating, and her skin ashen. A faint smile flashed across her face when she saw me.

I reached for her hand. "What has happened, Mary?"

"My journey is soon over," she whispered.

"Don't say such a thing. We will be in St. Augustine in just a few weeks." I winced at the futility of my own words, while Edmund stood grim next to me.

"Anna," Mary whispered, "take care of my daughter, please. Bring her to Harry. Tell them I loved them."

"I will Mary. I promise." I bent over to embrace my friend, but Edmund pulled me away.

"Go back on deck, lest you become ill."

I tried to conceal my tears as I backed away, returning to the main deck where I took a moment to settle my thoughts before I set out to find Muriel. I felt dazed as I walked past passengers huddled on deck. There were mothers picking nits out of their children's hair, some with infants suckling at their breast, others asleep with their children nestled against them, looking like a pile of arms, legs, and angelic faces.

I hoped Muriel was still too young to feel the depths of her loss. The poor child would grow up without her strong, quick-witted mother, but for Mary, I will always look after her, even if only from a distance, for who knows what Harry Blackwood envisions for his little girl?

Muriel was at the far end of the ship with several other children and their mothers, who had become accustomed to care for any child around them. With considerable effort, using both hands to steady herself, she stood up and took a few unsteady steps toward me.

"Where is Mama?" she asked, breaking my heart.

I hesitated, hoping my voice wouldn't betray me. "She's asleep, little one. Mama is sleeping."

Muriel seemed to accept that.

Settling down on the deck, I distracted us both with pieces of cheese and stale bread dunked in cider. After a while, she fell asleep as I rocked her, but our sheltered corner soon became over-run by sailors bringing the dead up from below and lining them up along the railing all wrapped in their own hammocks, and as with that poor ship's boy, the cords were tightly bound.

The captain blessed them before they were dropped into the sea, one after the other. Families wailed, and some stood with glazed faces, staring ahead with empty eyes, too numb for tears. I tried to look away, aching for every grief-stricken person.

My gaze shifted starboard, where two young sailors came up from below, carrying another body. When they reached the captain, the hammock it was wrapped in slipped. I gasped as it unraveled, and long red hair caught the wind before they tucked it back in and secured the hammock around the body, tying the cords tightly. It was Mary. No one on board had hair like Mary, so red, so lush, so alive, in spite of salt and wind. Forgetting to breathe, I watched as the sailors stopped in front of the captain. He uttered a brief blessing, and then Mary was lifted over the railing and dropped, just as the others. There was no time for long goodbyes on a ship plagued by illness, leaving me sickened by the thought.

* * *

"Feel that shift in the wind?" Edmund asked later in the day. "I never paid much attention to the wind before now."

"It is colder," I muttered.

The sails were still billowing, and the *Penny Rose* forged forward, steadfast as always, but the sudden chill in the air puzzled me. Were we not approaching the Americas? Were we off course?

"There's rain on the wind!" a sailor called out to Captain Hatfield, who stood at the helm with his first mate. "The air's gone cold!"

"Rain before wind, take 'em all in," the sailors aloft started to chant.

Passengers who had made a home for themselves on deck grabbed their belongings and scrambled below, while the rest of us were told to go batten down the hatches and remain in our cabins.

Edmund and I sat on our cot with Muriel between us, neither of us speaking. Muriel sucked on her thumb, looking forlorn as she twisted a strand of her hair with the fingers of her other hand.

Within the hour, the stillness of the last few days gave way to a furious battle building between sea and air, testing what remained of our seaworthiness after so much time aboard. Frenzied waves started to rock the *Penny Rose* in every direction, flinging us from our cot, and slamming us against the hull.

I tried to keep from throwing up everything within me as the ship heaved and dropped, but my head spun, and Edmund's efforts to brace us against the sudden shifts that kept pummeling us against unyielding planks gave us no reprieve.

When gale winds blew in, the ship seemed flung aback, and it felt as if her sails inverted. Frozen with terror, I looked at Edmund, noting his pallor even in the faint sliver of light from a lantern swinging as the ship rocked.

I held Muriel tight in my arms, and she clung to me, leaving me to wonder if she understood the gravity of the peril we were in.

CHAPTER FIVE

———

The *Penny Rose,* July 1763

"The course is blown to ribbons, but the rest are furled!" a sailor shouted as crew burst in and out of the passageway, their voices loud and alarmingly urgent.

"Drop the main!" another ordered.

I looked at Edmund, but he shook his head, unable to make sense of it.

Screams tore through the *Penny Rose,* but the wind became stronger and the voices drowned in the storm. Waiting, and silently praying, I tried to be strong and not frighten Muriel more than she already was.

The ship continued to heave and drop. Suddenly, with a thunderous sound, she spun, laid down on beam's end, and water rushed in through every crevice of our cabin. Each time the ship slammed into a wave, the water rose.

"God, help us! We have to get out!" I screamed, no longer able to contain myself as water gushed over us.

"There is nowhere to go," Edmund shouted above the pounding water. "Just hold on!"

He had said hold on, but we were standing on the wall of our cabin, with the floor behind us. *Hold on to what?*

With a snap, another hatch tore open, and water poured in, hard and relentless until it reached our shoulders. Each wave pulled us under and heaved us up.

"Edmund! The water—"

"Pray," Edmund said. "Just pray!"

When the ship shuddered, I lost my footing, and Muriel slipped from my grasp, plummeting into the dark waters, beyond the reach of my flailing limbs, but Edmund lunged for her, pulling her from the water.

Coughing, she clasped her little arms around his neck. The glance she sent me was full of reproach as she pressed against Edmund, as if her life depended on him alone. I found myself hoping we would live so I could make it up to her.

She turned her head away from me and started to cough again. With the crashing of the waves I couldn't hear if she was wheezing between bouts, but she looked dusky even in the fading light. I dropped her, and it was my fault. If this storm doesn't kill us all, I could already have drowned her.

After a while, the ship heaved violently again, and the *Penny Rose* flung herself up. The wind shifted and came over the stern as we felt the jolt of the main filling and shifting our course. The water in the cabin started to recede, leaving us gasping and tense, still not knowing what to expect or daring to hope.

When the gale tapered off, leaving us battered and weary, Edmund put Muriel into my arms and pried the door open to water tearing through the passageway and out to the deck. Wading through the stream, we made our way out, sinking down on the planks to catch our breath.

After a while, Edmund stood. "I must see how the others have fared. Can I leave you?"

I nodded and settled into a quiet corner with Muriel. The storm caused much damage, but crewmembers dove into repairs with astounding speed and vigor. Some of the women started to wring out clothing and bedding, hoisting it up into the shrouds for the wind to dry it out, while their children huddled around them, their eyes still wide with fear. Too weak to think, I tried to quiet my nerves.

Making it to St. Augustine alive was a gift, I realized, more so than having one's fare paid.

When Edmund returned he looked tired and disheveled, but he sat down and pulled me close. Muriel snuggled between us, but her lips still looked pale and her hoarse cough worsened.

"Mama," she whimpered, tearing at my heart.

She sat up and climbed into Edmund's lap as her gaze darted to every woman on deck, seeming more distraught as she realized that none of them were Mary.

Edmund whispered into her ear. Looking at him with big eyes, she hesitated, but then she settled, at peace for the moment.

After a while, Thomas came out through the breezeway, smiling wearily at the sight of us. "Who have we here?" he asked. Squatting down, he took Muriel's hand and kissed it as if she were a grown woman, much to her glee.

"How have you fared?" Edmund asked.

For a moment, Thomas looked into Edmund's eyes, not uttering a word, but my chest tightened.

"Nothing has befallen Master Charles?" I asked, feeling my heart race.

Thomas turned to me. "Only what has befallen us all, but we have both come through it, no worse."

"Good to hear," my husband said. "This ship shouldn't have to suffer more losses."

By nightfall, most of the passengers gathered on the main deck. In clothes half dry but with full bellies, families sat closer together, the quarrelling and tension of the past weeks forgotten.

I just wanted to sleep. I would do anything for a warm dry bed and a good night's rest. We retired to our cabin while other passengers were still singing shanties on deck, trying to lift their spirits. Edmund helped me out of my dress and tucked a quilt around Muriel and me as she snuggled closer, her eyes closed.

"Why is it that you seem to weather every storm without as much as a bruise, and when people fall ill around you, you remain as strong and sound as before?"

Edmund smiled. "I've wondered too. I've always had the constitution of a horse, and now I rather expect it not to fail me."

"Well, I think you are a rather fine horse, if you must know."

Muriel's cough worsened during the night and fever set in, with her little body battling shaking chills and sweats that left her weak and delirious.

After a while she started to wheeze again, slight at first, then worse, her chest tugging and her nostrils flaring at every breath. Edmund gave her drops of eucalyptus from the captain's coffers, but it did nothing to soothe her.

There was no sleeping that night as we watched over her, praying and wiping her sweat-drenched brow. We offered her cider but she pushed it away with the little strength she had left.

"She can't take this much longer," I said, watching Edmund lift Muriel into his arms and prayed he would utter something of hope.

"No, she can't," he said. "It will soon be over, if that's God's will."

At mid-day, Muriel took her last breath.

"This beautiful child is dead because I dropped her into the floodwaters, Edmund. Mary would never forgive me. This is my fault!"

For once, I didn't bother to wipe my tears.

I clutched Muriel tighter in my arms, willing her to live as I stroked my fingers through her red curls.

"Blame the sea, blame the storm, Anna, but you are faultless in this."

He let me cry until my shoulders stopped heaving and the sobs left me listless. Muriel lay peaceful in my lap, like a sleeping child in her mother's arms, but the sight of her sent daggers through me.

After a while, Edmund stood and reached out a hand for me. "It's time, Anna. We have to let her go."

"Why the haste, Edmund? She won't be any more dead if we wait just a moment longer."

"There is no good reason to wait," he said, making more sense than I wanted to hear.

I didn't resist when he pulled me to my feet and guided me out into the sunlight with Muriel clutched against my chest, although everything about it felt horribly wrong.

I turned to Edmund, pulling him back, slowing the inevitable.

"This is God's will,» Edmund said, looking at me. Something in his gaze told me to quiet myself, and I realized how much he too struggled with this.

"Got another one for burial, Doc? The captain is at the stern with today's lot." The sailor who asked looked bruised and battered, as many on board.

I let Edmund take Muriel, trusting that her little body would be handled kindly in his care. Reaching into my skirt for the pocketknife he had given me, I cut off a lock of Muriel's curls before giving her cheek a final kiss. The strand of bright red hair would be a bittersweet treasure for her father someday.

Winding the lock of hair around my fingers, I struggled to steel myself for what was to come. Nothing has prepared me for this, and there was no escaping it.

"Mrs. Ashton has become quite fond of this child," Edmund said to the captain, when we reached the stern. "She promised Mrs. Blackwood she would deliver her to her father."

"Now we must deliver her to her mother," the captain said, looking across the waves. "At least she won't be motherless."

A woman sitting nearby rushed up to Edmund where he stood with Muriel cradled in his arms and pulled at Muriel's brown leather shoes.

"She won't be needing 'em where she's goin'," the woman said, tucking the little shoes into her skirt pocket before scurrying away.

Edmund looked over at me. I wanted to scream, but my voice failed me. I sank down and watched from a distance as Edmund handed Muriel over to a sailor who stood ready to wrap her in canvas and bring her to the railing.

Edmund came back to me where I sat, draping his arms around me as the captain blessed the tiny body and gestured to the sailor to let her go. I covered my face, tormented by the vision of the little girl falling into the sea.

* * *

The next few days became a blur in my mind. Edmund and I tended to the injured and sick. We rose early, and we ate, but in our state of fatigue we rarely spoke. When the night found us together on our narrow cot, we welcomed nothing but the reprieve of sleep. Sometimes, though, sleep wouldn't come.

Late on a Sunday in the last week of July, I lingered on deck after most had retired for the evening.

Edmund was playing cards with Charles and Thomas, allowing me a quiet moment alone under the starlit sky. The wind was gentle, and I felt comforted by the familiar creaking of the ship. For a long time, I just sat, my hands limp in my lap, drawing in long slow breaths to calm my frayed nerves.

Turning my face away from the moonlit horizon, I caught a movement, realizing that I was watching Thomas and my husband at the far end of the deck,

For a moment, my heart came to a halt as Thomas stroked Edmund's cheek, and Edmund pulled Thomas into his arms and kissed him. A long passionate kiss, it was one unlike any kiss that had ever happened between us.

Fortunately, the wind muted my gasp, but the sudden gallop of my heart thundered in my ears as I tried to convince myself that my imagination had run off with me and that there wasn't something undeniable between them. But there was.

I wanted to be the one who could make him feel such passion, not Thomas!

As shock and rage swelled from the pit of my stomach, my thoughts started to tumble over one another.

Was I just part of a masquerade Edmund used to hide his true inclinations? When he said he had lost a great love that first day we had met, had it been a man and not a dear lady as I had assumed? Was our marriage conveniently shielding the life he genuinely wanted but couldn't have? Were we so seldom intimate because he truly didn't want a woman?

The thoughts stung, for surely a regular man would learn to love me, would he not? How could I not have seen this? Why would I even have thought it possible? Not my Edmund...

It took all I had to hold myself back from lashing out, from confronting them, screaming at them, demanding explanations where there were none. My mind descended into darkness before I realized I could make myself a widow, for if this secret sin were to became known, they could both be hanged.

My poor Edmund. How difficult it must have been for him to hide his longings and spare me the knowledge of the danger that constantly loomed over him.

My life in the Americas depended on Edmund, and now his life could depend on my silence, but I owed him everything.

CHAPTER SIX

St. Augustine, East Florida, July 1763

In mid-July, land appeared on the horizon as gulls heralded our approach to the Americas.

When the *Penny Rose* sailed into the Matanzas Bay, youths clambered for a place by the railing to catch the first sight of St. Augustine. Their sea-weary elders, so many of them still cored with grief, stood quietly with their eyes fixed on the shoreline.

"I shall be grateful to put a foot on solid ground," I said.

Edmund loosened his collar. "Indeed, but it's damned hot."

Without the cooling breeze of a ship in full sail, the damp heat took us by surprise. Many stripped down as far as could be considered proper, while others tried to shield themselves from the scorching sun by covering themselves.

The first structure to come into clear view was Fort St. Marks. It was a massive star-shaped fort with imposing bastions, along with two landward sides where a large swell of earth was probably meant to deter attackers. But, from what I could see, the bayside path to the fortress was a favored spot for couples to stroll. Someday we would take walks there, unless Edmund preferred the company of the soldiers idling by the seawall.

"We would hardly have been able to overpower the Spanish in battle with a fortress as staunch as this," Edmund said, unaware of my bleak thoughts.

I nodded. "But with the treaty, it has all been handed over peacefully, it seems." I realized that the houses becoming visible in the distance were those the Spanish had been forced to abandon.

Across the inlet, St. Augustine looked sparse. It couldn't have been more than a mile wide, but beyond the city walls the vegetation was lush and green. From the look on my husband's face, he was already eager to claim land of our own.

As we came closer, we could see narrow streets fanning out from the harbor, lined with whitewashed houses, some with overhanging second-floor balconies and walled-in gardens. A larger building stood near the harbor, also white, with large porches and second-story balconies. It could be a hospital or perhaps the inn that Mary had talked so much about. The thought saddened me, but I couldn't be sad on this day. Bringing my gaze to the opposite side of the bay, I gazed at a vast expanse of farmland with grander houses dividing it.

"That's Anastasia Island," Edmund said. "I've heard that some of the finest plantations are there."

"I see," I said, hoping that Edmund wouldn't be tempted to buy land before we were well settled, for we knew nothing of farming.

My thoughts were interrupted as the sound of chains thundered through the hawsehole when the anchor plunged into the bay.

"My lovely little wife, we made it through!" Edmund shouted, picking me up and twirling me around until I was dizzy and had to hold on to him to steady myself.

"We prevailed!" I said, beaming up at him. "Thank you for bringing me here."

My words were heartfelt, but he stayed true to his role.

"You are most welcome. Surely, I would not leave my wife behind."

I will have to tell him that I take my vows to heart. For better or worse, I will honor him, even if it includes accepting inclinations I do not understand. I owe him that.

While we waited, riggers aloft furled the last of the sails. They bantered among themselves with newfound exuberance likely brought on by the promise of idle time ashore before the *Penny Rose* would set sail back to Liverpool.

Finally, loud shouts from the coxswain ordering the long-boats to be lowered in preparation to take us ashore seemed to awaken even the weariest among us.

As the flurry onboard increased, I caught sight of barges heading toward us, swiftly driven through the water by oarsmen rowing in perfect unison.

Some were empty, apparently ready to haul goods ashore, but another was crowded with paunchy, loud men competing for the best view of the *Penny Rose.*

Their voices billowed across the water, reaching our shipmates at the railing, many whose faces started to reflect their dread. These were the merchants and the plantation owners who would pay their fare, tear their families apart, and subject them to servitude and an uncertain future before there would be any promise of the bounty of this new world.

Nauseous at the thought, I turned away, unable to witness the glee of the approaching men so ready to enslave those who had already endured so much.

After a while our names were called, and for a second I hesitated and looked around one last time. I would never forget the *Penny Rose*. She had challenged us and buckled us with sorrow, but now she had brought us here. This was what I had asked for, and there was no turning back.

"It's time, my dear," Edmund said. "St. Augustine awaits us."

"Indeed," I said, taking the hand of the boatman and stepping into the longboat before him.

After putting both feet on solid ground, I nearly toppled over. My legs wobbled as if I was still swaying with the movement of the *Penny Rose,* and my head swirled.

Edmund chuckled and reached for my hand, stumbling like a drunkard himself.

"Sea legs," he said. "It will take a while to become earth creatures again."

"How odd! I never thought of myself as such," I said, walking gingerly with my hand firmly gripping the crook of Edmund's elbow.

While others were laughing and wobbling, I noticed a man walking briskly in our direction. He smiled at our unsteadiness, but when our eyes met an unexpected flurry went through me as I tried to steady myself.

My gaze followed him as he strode down the pier, nodding occasional greetings to those he passed. He wore no jacket or hat, only a loosely buttoned white shirt that revealed a cluster of medallions on gold chains against his taut, sun-drenched chest.

His chiseled face, framed by a mane of black hair and the crimson kerchief he had tied about his head, made me unable to look away, and his arresting dark eyes kept mine engaged for far longer than was accepted for a married woman. Even worse, I could tell he knew exactly what effect he was having on me.

Smiling, he stopped in front of us. "Good people. Might you know Mary Blackwood? She is traveling with a child."

Edmund nodded, while I struggled not to stare, for the man stirred something in me that drew me to him.

"It is a great misfortune; they both died during the journey," Edmund said.

The man's eyes saddened.

"Are you Harry Blackwood?" I asked.

He backed away. "No, but I must find him. We shall meet again."

I exhaled and tried to clear my mind of him. We had been in this new land for mere minutes, and already my mind was causing havoc.

As Edmund and I waited for our papers to be perused and our names registered, young Master Charles approached with Thomas and an older, distinguished-looking man. Charles flung himself into my arms before introducing Edmund and me to his father, Admiral Simon Rushmore, who greeted us warmly.

"My gratitude has no boundaries, and I see my boy has a great fondness for you, Mrs. Ashton."

"And I for him," I said. "It's my great joy to see him start to walk."

"Indeed," Edmund said. "He was near to losing his leg, but my dear wife was relentless in his care, and it is her doing that he walks today."

"On board, she was called the Angel of the *Penny Rose*," Thomas said, smiling at me as I stifled a laugh.

"I see, and well deserved," Admiral Rushmore said.

"Thank you, sir," I said.

Edmund and Thomas locked eyes for a brief moment, and then the Rushmores were gone, leaving me to wonder what distance would be separating my husband from Thomas Wingfield.

* * *

A coachman, sent from the infirmary, stood waiting for us beyond the pier, smiling brightly when we approached.

"The name's Lofton," he said, stepping forward to greet us. He quickly ushered us into the carriage while dockworkers loaded some of our trunks onto the back of it.

I sat back. Beside me, Edmund glanced about. Most of his glee from earlier was gone, but he took my hand and squeezed it, reminding me that I was still of value to him.

Pulling away from the pier, a towering, dark-haired man holding a large bouquet of flowers caught my eye. He was in a deep and seemingly unsettling conversation with the captain.

I saw the man's expression turn to anguish before he staggered and dropped the flowers about him, as his shoulders heaved in heartbreaking sobs. Harry.

"Stop!" I cried out to the coachman, who pulled his horses to a halt. "That is Harry Blackwood, is it not?"

"Sure is. Somethin' bad's hapenin' from the looks of it. He's been awaitin' for his wife and child. Guess they didn't make it. A cryin' shame."

I rose, but Edmund pulled me down beside him. "This is not the time."

I sat. My husband was right. We would call on Mary's husband when we were settled, if he didn't find us first.

"Poor Harry... Looks like Captain Ortega's got a handle on 'im, though," Mr. Lofton said, more to himself than us. He slapped the reins, and the horses moved along.

Captain Ortega. It was he whose gaze had given me such a startle, hindering my thoughts of anything else on our first moments in British St. Augustine.

But the name Ortega... and his stunning, golden complexion, raven-black hair, and smoldering eyes... Certainly he wasn't English, but what was a Spaniard doing here now?

I took a deep breath, trying to expel the maddening sensations his mere glance had caused me.

Looking back at Harry Blackwood once more, my mind fixed on him.

He probably had difficulty containing his excitement, waiting for the moment he would catch sight of Mary's red hair gleaming in the sun as she approached in the longboat with Muriel perched high in her arms. Now he was told he wouldn't even have their bodies to bury.

Lost in thought, I barely noticed the carriage had stopped in front of a two-story house on George Street.

"Here's the doctor's house," Mr. Lofton announced. "There's coquina from the King's Quarry on Anastasia Island under that plaster," he continued, pointing to the walls of the first floor. "It will keep ye cool in summer and warm in winter. Sitting room's downstairs, and there's a room upstairs with a balcony on each side. The kitchen and privy are out back."

He jumped off the wagon and spit into the dusty road.

"It's a fine house, Mr. Ashton. Most here got rundown after the Spanish left, for the soldiers tore at 'em for firewood, the fools! Good houses, they were!"

"It's more than we expected," Edmund said, looking at trees, ripe with fruit, reaching over the garden wall.

The first floor of the house looked as if it were newly whitewashed, its shutters painted a pleasant blue to match the door facing the street and another door in the wall around the garden. The second story was framed in wood, with a shingle roof and a stone chimney jutting up further back from where we stood.

"We're home, Anna!" Edmund said as we stepped off the carriage. Startling me, he picked me up and carried me in his arms over the threshold of the house. "This is our first home," he said, sounding utterly delighted.

Edmund put me down, and I slipped from his reach to survey the parlor. Behind us, Mr. Lofton chuckled and said something to my husband about folks, keys, trunks, and a landlord named Jesse Fish.

Mr. Lofton was right; the air inside was cooler, although the doors to the back garden were wide open, and a tantalizing scent of cooking wafted in.

The parlor was a square room with a beamed ceiling, wood-framed windows on each side of the front door, and another door leading out to the back porch. There was little furniture, only a bench, a few chairs, and a table, but it would serve us well.

Two small chambers opened up on either side, and a staircase to the second floor tugged on my curiosity, but I couldn't resist the scents coming through the open door. I stepped out to a large back porch, from where I had the view of a sprawling, lush garden. A quaint cottage sat far back on the property, and across a small courtyard was a partially open kitchen, where a young Negro woman chopped vegetables on a large wooden table. Beside her, a pot simmered over the fire, and I sensed that something delicious was baking in the brick oven.

She looked up and smiled when she saw me. Putting her knife down, she wiped her hands on her apron and hurried toward me. "Welcome, Mrs. Ashton. I'm Jane Weston," she said, stopping a distance from me.

"Splendid," my husband said, putting his arm around my waist. "I see you have settled in."

"You knew..." I looked from Edmund to Jane, but her eyes were downcast.

"Of course. We have a houseman too. Malcolm, is it not?" This time, Jane nodded in reply.

"We shall return shortly," Edmund said, pulling me back into the house before I could say another word.

* * *

As we ventured up the narrow stairs to the bedroom, I couldn't refrain from speaking. "Servants, Edmund? Or are they slaves? You wouldn't?" I asked, almost hissing, as I followed him out of Jane's earshot.

"Dear, dear! They are our very own slaves and were purchased at my request before we left England. How else would we have an orderly house to come to?"

"It is hardly kind to own people, Edmund! We will pay them a wage and have them manum—"

Edmund glared at me. "This is the Americas! Everyone has them, and we must adjust to the customs here, or we will find ourselves without a single friend."

I wanted to say, "You have Thomas," but my father's voice rang in my ears: "Bite your tongue and bide your time." I would obey my father, for there would be time to consider this and have Jane and Malcolm manumitted.

The second-floor bedroom was small, but it had a four-poster bed covered with a quilt and a night table on each side. Two armoires framed the door, and a stand with a pitcher and basin stood in the corner with a mirror hanging above it. Doors on the east and west sides of the room opened to small balconies, allowing a welcomed breeze to flow through.

Taking in the view from the balcony over George Street, we watched a cart with our trunks being pulled toward us on a street filled with people rushing about to get newcomers settled, many of them looking up and waving to us in greeting.

"So, these are our new slave-owning friends, Edmund?"

He sighed deeply. "You must stop this. Keeping slaves is legal and necessary."

"But still awful."

"Anna!"

"Very well," I said. "This will keep for another day."

From the balcony overlooking the garden, we discovered two half-barrels of water that Jane was preparing for our wash, modestly shielded by the garden's lush foliage.

By the barrel farthest away, a young black man with an exquisite muscular physique appeared with a brush and clean cloths. Certainly, this was Malcolm.

Edmund seemed unfazed, but the thought that Malcolm could become one of his paramours gave me a sudden chill.

In a town so small, could such a secret go unnoticed? Thankfully, Edmund showed no interest in him.

"Are you ready? Your thoughts appear to have taken flight," Edmund said, nudging my side with his elbow.

Startled, I turned to him. "Ready for what?"

"Good God, you were far off! A wash, of course! I won't be crusted in salt for another moment."

Perhaps my thoughts had been exaggerated. Perhaps Edmund just had a lapse of judgment and his emotions had carried him away. Or was that kiss a sign of true passion? Had he fallen in love with Thomas, and would Thomas visit our marriage over and over again?

I was burning to ask him, but not here, not now.

Jane shielded me with a sheet while I disrobed and stepped into the tepid water. A wash had never felt quite as good as this, and being clean had never felt so exhilarating.

* * *

My husband made love to me that first night in St. Augustine in the same gentle manner as before, never saying a word, nor looking at me. Still, I found pleasure in his nearness and tried to forget I would never be his heart's desire.

"You are remarkably silent," he said later as we lay in each other's arms.

"I know about Thomas," I said. "I saw you kissing."

My husband bolted up, looking both horrified and shocked. "Do I disgust you?"

I sat up and reached for his hand. "No, you don't, and I will keep your secret. We can still live a good life."

He looked so dumbfounded, I had to smile. "I will not shame you. I swear it. Thank you."

He looked more vulnerable than I had ever seen him.

"There is no need," I said, pulling the quilt over me. "Good night, husband."

* * *

The following morning started quietly.

Edmund left early, eager to see the infirmary, while I lingered on the back porch with a cup of strong English tea. Jane and Malcolm had begun to unpack our trunks in the garden, where most of our sea-drenched clothing went into the half-barrels used for our baths last evening, and each trunk was scrubbed as it was emptied. As they worked, I noticed that Jane chattered away, but Malcolm only answered her in hand gestures, a hum, or a wordless melody.

I called Jane to me. "Why does Malcolm not speak like any other man?"

"The slavers cut his tongue out, ma'am. Punishment for talkin' back."

She said it as if it was a normal occurrence, hurting my heart.

CHAPTER SEVEN

———

St. Augustine, August 1763

In the late morning, a clatter of hoofs announced the arrival of a carriage, which delivered a woman to my doorstep. Watching from the balcony, I barely noticed that Jane suddenly stood behind me with a gown, waiting to ready me in haste.

By the time I stepped outside to join my visitor, Malcolm had offered her a seat on the back porch.

"How do you do, Mrs. Ashton!" the woman said, rising to greet me. "I'm Georgina Hornsby. I have come to welcome you to St. Augustine, for everyone is simply delighted that you and your husband have joined us in our little town!"

She was dressed in a low-necked muslin gown, not unlike the gowns I brought from London, but she wore a wide-brimmed hat that hid much of her hair and seemed a wise protection against the sun.

"Thank you," I said. "How kind of you to come."

Jane brought a plate of delectable sweets to our table, and Malcom served us each a glass of Madeira, all gifts from my guest.

"It's thrilling to have a new doctor in town, especially newlyweds such as yourselves. The one we have is so drenched in sin with that Miss Ross that it is just scandalous! It drove his wife right back to Boston, the poor dear." Georgina turned to me. "But, more importantly, I have heard your voyage was quite dreadful."

I took a long sip of the Madeira. "It was grievous," I said, finally. "The saddest was having Mary Blackwood's child die in my arms."

"It must have been terrible for you," Georgina said, patting my hand.

"It was, but how fares Harry Blackwood? Do you know?" I asked, glancing at her. "I should like to give him my condolences."

Georgina sighed. "He is lost in grief. He's hardly been seen since the arrival of the *Penny Rose* and has taken to drink more than usual."

Before I could say a word, I felt Georgina's gaze settling on me again.

"Is it true that you saved Charles Rushmore's leg by using maggots? The Admiral cannot stop speaking of you!"

"It's true."

Georgina's eyes widened. "That sounds like something Abbie Birdsong would do."

"Birdsong? What an unusual name," I said.

Georgina leaned closer and whispered, "She's a strange native who tends to many of the slaves here. They say she is the offspring of a Creek medicine man and an Irish slave he freed after purchasing her with alligator skins."

Georgina broke into a fit of giggles.

"So, she is a healer of sorts?" I asked.

"She uses native plants and brews potions her father taught her. When she is in town, you can easily spot her by her wild hair and the multitude of bright colors she wears," Georgina said. "You should keep your distance. It's said that she is mad."

"I see," I said, instantly intrigued. "I would be curious to meet her."

"Oh," Georgina added, "give her no mind. Once the governor returns, he will certainly want to make the acquaintance of the Angel of the *Penny Rose,* and you and Mr. Ashton will be introduced to Lieutenant Governor Moultrie and his family, Major Peavatt, and Captain Warrick."

Georgina giggled again as an air of conspiracy came over her.

"In spite of being married to the best of husbands, you know, women still have eyes, and you will find that Captain Warrick is the most handsome man in this entire territory. He has the most arctic-blue eyes and the fairest hair, and how fine he looks in those britches!"

While she gushed, my thoughts drifted to Captain Ortega, for never could a pair of blue eyes compare to the mysterious draw of that man's gaze.

* * *

The first time I stepped out into the streets of St. Augustine alone I followed Jane's directions, walking south and west to the outskirts of the city, where I found an elongated thatched house that was larger than I expected and well kept.

Like my guest, I chose to knock on the garden gate rather than the front door. Soon a wide-eyed Negro girl greeted me and led me into a courtyard, where I waited while she slipped into the house.

The woman who finally came through the terrace doors left me dumbstruck, and it seemed that I startled her too.

Abbie Birdsong had an almost regal bearing that immediately pulled me from my slouch. I suspected she was older than me, but her golden skin likely concealed her true age.

I had never seen anyone quite like her. Her slanting eyes were huge and had a dark glimmer to them. Her cheekbones were high, her nose straight, and her lips full, but her hair was a magnificent cascade of wavy black curls, and her close-fitting dress was covered with a mastery of beads in every hue, as beautiful as the ones that hung from her ears.

After a long pause, she broke into a smile. "Welcome. Not a single white woman has ever come this way. I am honored you seek me out, or are you perhaps lost?"

I shook my head. "Not at all. Jane Weston told me where to find you."

Tilting her head, she looked into my eyes. "And why was it me you wanted to find? If you are Jane's mistress, you are Mrs. Anna Ashton. Or perhaps the Angel of the *Penny Rose*?"

I cringed. "That name has followed me. I much prefer you call me Anna."

Abbie's eyes widened in surprise. "If that is your wish, ma'am, and of course, you must call me Abbie, but I understand the name given you on the ship was well earned. Your maggots are on everyone's lips."

At this, I doubled over in laughter, breaking the formality between us.

She laughed too.

"I could not bear it if everyone in this town bore maggots on their lips! It would be awful!"

When we calmed, wiping the tears from our eyes, Abbie gestured for me to sit down on one of the chairs on the porch.

She slipped onto the one next to me as a young woman brought us steaming cups of fragrant tea.

"You must pardon my error. I speak many native tongues, French and Spanish, as well as English, but this error was quite horrid."

"And quite amusing," I said.

Taking a deep breath, I looked around at many unfamiliar plants framing her courtyard and a variety of fruit trees growing farther back in her garden. From the road, her house appeared plain, but this inner enclave of hers was bursting with color, from the painted walls and doors to the chairs we sat on, to everywhere my eyes rested. I felt dull in comparison.

Abbie watched me take in her surroundings. "Why have you come?" she asked when I turned back to her. "People will talk."

"My curiosity was piqued when Georgina Hornsby spoke of your knowledge of plant remedies. I should like to learn from you."

Abbie Birdsong looked at me with her huge dark eyes. "From me?"

"Yes, from you. My father is an apothecary, and he entrusted the laboratory to me since I was quite young."

Abbie smiled. "You are still young."

To my surprise, Abbie lit a pipe I hadn't seen lying at her side. Blowing fragrant rings into the air, she looked pensive, but then she turned to me. "You're not like the rest of them, are you, Anna?"

* * *

When I came home, Edmund had already had his supper. Jane started to fill a plate for me, but I sent her back to the cottage she shared with Malcolm in the back garden and went upstairs. Edmund was usually to be found on the porch at this hour. Was he ailing?

I found him reading by a lantern when I opened the door and entered.

"Why have you retired at this early hour? You haven't taken ill, have you?"

My concern was genuine, but he seemed to glare back at me.

"Only as ill as I will be when it spreads all over St. Augustine that you frequent the lodging of a native medicine woman, and a mad one at that!"

His words stopped me from taking a step further.

"She is not mad! She is actually far more intelligent and knowledgeable than most. You probably also know that Georgina Hornsby came to call, as well."

He put his book down and stood. Crossing his arms, he towered over me. "I have, and she is a far more proper companion for you than a half-slave, half-savage woman living in a hut on the outskirts of town."

"Abbie doesn't live in a hut! Her home is wondrously colorful, and it's well cared for."

He sighed loudly and looked up again, apparently searching for words that would reach me. "Anna, English people befriend English people."

"And healers befriend healers."

His fists clenched, startling me. I had not seen this side of him. "I will not have this behavior from you. People will talk."

I startled, but then I stepped closer and looked into his eyes. "How dare you, Edmund," I whispered, "when your inclinations are far more perilous than mine."

CHAPTER EIGHT

St. Augustine, August 1763

I had dreams of water, rising water, cool and refreshing at first but then forceful, pressing the air out of me, leaving my limbs numb and too weak to pull myself free from the torrent. Suddenly, Muriel clung to me, and for a moment we smiled at each other, her blue eyes sparkling, her lips cool against my cheek, but then she slipped away as quickly as she had come, swirling away through the rushing water. Before I could reach for her, Mary soared up from the depths of the sea, bolting toward her child with a force that would have caused Neptune to kneel at her feet. Her outstretched hands were but inches from her daughter, but then Muriel was carried away with a current that neither of us could brave. *Not again. Not again.*

I awoke with a start, gasping for air.

"Are you all right, ma'am? Was it dreams again?" Jane asked.

"Yes, yes, the one about the child slipping away." I reached for the tray beside me. "Where is my husband?"

"Already at the infirmary."

Jane watched as I drank the juice she had prepared. "Mrs. Neville will be calling on you this afternoon. She is Major Neville's wife. She is always eager to meet newcomers."

"I see," I said, still dazed from my dream. "Is she not the woman you said was visiting in Charles Town and whose husband is a friend of Harry Blackwood?"

"You remember well. The two of you should perhaps pay Mr. Blackwood a visit. The dreams will not stop until you do, and there is no potion that can help you."

I said nothing. She was outspoken for a servant, but she might be right.

* * *

Katherine Neville arrived shortly before noon, dressed in the lightest fabric I have seen, making me feel even hotter in my thicker cotton.

"How good it is to meet you! I've longed for news of London, and another Englishwoman is always welcomed here!" She took my hands in hers.

"Thank you. You are most kind," I said.

We settled in the parlor and quickly found ourselves lost in conversation. After a while, she mentioned Harry Blackwood. The sound of his name reminded me again that I had unfinished business with him. I was meant to see Mary at the Matanzas, but it wouldn't be so.

"He is not faring well after the loss of his wife and child." Katherine looked down and shook her head sadly, bringing back my grief.

"My heart breaks for him," I said. "Mary was so eager to show him how their lovely daughter had grown, and the thought of reuniting with him brought her such happiness."

I paused. "I think I shall visit the inn this afternoon. It is time I pay my respects."

Kathrine seemed to approve. "Allow me to make the introduction. I was going to the inn once I leave you anyway."

Glancing at Jane, who seemed to have overheard, I noticed her subtle smile. Today might be as good a day as any to face Mary's husband.

After I changed to a lighter dress still, Katherine and I walked side by side toward the Matanzas. The heat was almost unbearable, and I started to feel parched and irritable. Jane had brought me a large brimmed hat and advised me to wear long sleeves to protect myself from the sun, which apparently wasn't kind to light English skin.

I felt encumbered compared to Katherine, who strode quietly at my side with her head raised and not a drop of sweat on her brow, despite the heat.

Reaching the Matanzas Inn distracted me. A white wooden building on Bay Street, it had a view of Fort St. Marks and the Matanzas Inlet.

It was the imposing two-story structure with large balconies and sweeping porches I had seen from the *Penny Rose*.

"It is beautiful here, Katherine. So beautiful," I said, feeling a tug of sadness as I took in the sight that Mary would never see.

Katherine shifted impatiently by my side, shielding her face from the sun with the brim of her hat. "Come, Anna, lest your skin burn in this sharp sunlight," she said, interrupting my thoughts.

Following her up the steps to the front door, we were greeted by a servant hardly more than a child.

I learned that many of the guests of the inn were high-ranking friends of the governor. And that he had made sport of bringing them to the region to acquire land grants to expand their holdings. Securing land and slaves to transform raw land into productive plantations was the route to wealth in this region, and Governor James Grant sought to make East Florida prosper beyond expectations during his governance to assure favor with good King George.

I remembered Edmund's excitement over land grants, but I hadn't known the tracts were so large, meant for plantations rather than farms, nor that we would be required to own many slaves to be considered. What I envisioned was a charming orange orchard and my own herb and vegetable garden, nothing so big that we couldn't manage with a hired worker from time to time.

Harry Blackwood looked up when we walked in. He was towering now that I saw him close up, and he had long, curled hair that hung untied about his shoulders. Fine clothing did nothing to improve his unkempt image, for his waistcoat was carelessly unbuttoned and his necktie hung loosely over his chest, as if dressing was a bother to him.

Katherine elbowed my side. "That's Harry Blackwood," she said as if I didn't already know this bear of a man was the husband Mary had longed so desperately for.

I stood up straighter and watched as he approached us with his mournful eyes fixed on me.

"Good afternoon, Harry. Let me introduce—"

"My dear Katherine, I know who this woman is." He reached out and ever so gently locked his hands over mine. "Let me hold the hands of the woman who held my daughter in her final moments and who was my dear Mary's friend," he said, bringing tears to my eyes. "Please allow me this small comfort, Mistress Ashton."

Tears rolled down his cheeks, but he still held my hands, making no effort to dry his face. It felt odd to stand so close to this huge man, odd to still have my hands in his, but I didn't dare move lest I insult him. Lest I insult Mary's memory.

Katherine bit her lip and looked down. After long minutes, he released his grip on me and led us to a table where he sat down next to me.

"I shall leave you to talk while I speak to Mordecai about next week's gathering," Katherine said.

Harry looked up at her and nodded. "Thank you. You'll find him in my office."

As Katherine walked away, he turned to me. "Mordecai is my most loyal servant. I would have collapsed under the weight of this inn had he not been here in this mournful time." He looked painfully sad.

"I'm so sorry for your loss," I said, feeling myself trembling.

"Thank you." Looking away, he swallowed hard before turning to servants waiting to be called upon. "Lads! Bring me ale and sweets for the ladies," he called out to them. "Mrs. Neville will return shortly."

They scurried off. Guests seated at nearby tables watched us curiously, some glancing over their shoulders, others craning their necks, but they blurred as I turned to Harry Blackwood.

The young girl who had opened the door for us placed sweet pies and cider on the table and handed Harry a jug of ale. As I took a bite of the pie, I could feel Harry's eyes fixed on me, but he said nothing.

"Mary was a good friend to me," I said, trying to smile, although the memory brought with it pangs of misery. "We spent long days and weeks together before she died."

Harry shook his head and struggled to find his voice. "I should have been there with her. I shouldn't have left her alone while I had quite an ordinary journey with the Nevilles."

"Katherine and her husband were on board the same ship?"

He nodded. "I should have waited until Muriel was older."

"You couldn't have known, Mr. Blackwood," I said, hoping, but not believing, my words could be of comfort.

"They threw them overboard," he said. "Didn't they?"

It wasn't a question, just a statement. Nodding, I bit my lip, trying to let go of the memories, but the vision of Mary and Muriel both dropping into the sea still haunted me.

"What befell them?" Harry asked. "Were they sickened?"

I hurried to explain. "Mary was sickened, but there was nothing that could save her. Then there was a gale wind, a terrible storm. We thought we would all die."

Harry leaned forward. "And?"

"Muriel died in the floodwaters entering the ship during the storm."

Harry sank back, shaking with sobs. Leaning forward, I put my hand on his shoulder, careful not to appear bold, but just then Katherine returned and sank down across from us.

"Thank you, madam. Thank you for being there with my Mary and my sweet child," Harry said when he finally looked up at me.

"You are welcome, Mr. Blackwood."

I opened my locket and pulled out a strand of bright red hair and handed it to him. "It's Muriel's. I thought you might want it for a mourning ring."

He took it. "So beautiful, like her mother's hair." He sighed. "Mrs. Ashton, I am indebted to you. Thank you for bringing me this dear woman, Katherine, but I must have a moment… Pardon me, ladies…"

"I understand," I said, trying not to cry over the sadness of it all.

He rose and walked away with the lock of hair clasped between his fingertips, leaving Katherine and me alone at the table.

She reached forward and squeezed my forearm. "You did what you could, Anna. You barely survived yourself."

I nodded, too numb to speak, and pushed my plate away.

"We should take our leave," Katherine said.

I nodded and gathered my skirts about me.

Walking down the front stairs, we stopped when a carriage came to a halt in front of us. A man's laughter billowed out as the door opened, and a tall, well-dressed man leapt out, still in conversation with the others inside. His long hair was so fair that it was nearly white, but he was hardly an older man. With his lanky elegance, he still had the exuberance of youth.

Even from a distance, I noticed that his hawklike eyes were a bright blue. Clearly, he knew Katherine, for as soon as he took note of us his face beamed into a wide smile. Just then, a young lady reached for his hand and stepped out of the carriage behind him. She eyed Katherine and me with sudden yet obvious irritation.

"That is Captain Patrick Warrick and his soon-to-be wife, Sofia Moultrie, the lieutenant governor's niece," Katherine whispered.

"And the other two?" I asked when a young couple stepped down from the carriage.

"Sofia's sister, Charlotte, and her fiancé, Thaddeus Edgefield, from the Government Office."

The captain approached us, removed his tricorn, and bowed. "Mrs. Neville, I hope this day finds you well, and you, Mrs. Ashton," he said, nodding in my direction before replacing his hat. "It is an honor to welcome you to St. Augustine. I am Captain Patrick Warrick."

Katherine smiled, tilted her head to the captain, and stepped back.

"Thank you, Captain," I said. "But how do you know me?"

He chuckled. "This is a small town. We knew of you and Mr. Ashton from the moment you arrived, for Admiral Rushmore is a dear friend who sings your praises. May I make known to you my intended, Sofia Moultrie," he said before introducing their companions.

"My pleasure," Sofia said, holding the captain's arm, guarding her claim to him.

She was prettier than most, but I had seen more pleasing expressions.

"I'm delighted," I said, not meaning it any more than she did.

Thaddeus Edgefield and Charlotte Moultrie greeted me with the same weary indifference.

The captain was far more engaging. He seemed more joyful than anyone I had met in a long time, even in London, and he was certainly a handsome man.

"It would be my pleasure to have you and your husbands dine with us one evening," he said. "We should become acquainted, and the Nevilles and I can tell you more about East Florida and its coast than you want to know!"

Sofia Moultrie's lips tightened.

"Thank you, Captain. I am certain that Mr. Ashton would be delighted."

"Thank you. Mr. Neville, as well," Katherine said.

"Splendid! I will send a servant to you with an invitation for dinner next week. Would that suit you both?"

"Indeed," I replied, "very much, Captain. Thank you."

Katherine nodded.

"It will be our pleasure," the captain said, smiling at Sofia. "I am quite interested in hearing news from London, but it also intrigues me to think of the skills you possess to have dealt so well with young Master Charles. There is not a woman in this territory who has impressed old Rushmore more than you, or who has such abilities."

"Have you forgotten the Birdsong woman? Rushmore is said to fancy her skills as well," Charlotte said, leaving no doubt of her mockery.

I noticed Sofia elbow her sister ever so gently, though squelching a smile herself, while the captain chose to ignore them both.

"Now that I think of it, why don't you join our wedding celebration at our home? It will be a fine time for you and your husband to meet those you should know."

"Splendid!" Turning to me, Katherine added, "We can come for you in our carriage and make all the introductions!"

"Thank you, Captain," I said, noticing Sofia roll her eyes at her sister. "And thank you, Katherine. It would be a pleasure to join you."

With their tresses tucked under feathered hats and the soft pastel dresses suggesting a sweetness that neither of the sisters apparently possessed, I couldn't help but wonder why a lovely man such as the captain would bother himself with the likes of them.

To my surprise, the captain leaned in toward me as if we were more than well acquainted. "I must know. How do you find our settlement? Will it be long until you yearn for the sophistication of London?"

I smiled, although his familiarity was unexpected. "If we sought London, we would have stayed there, Captain. But we wanted an adventure, and that brought us here."

My words seemed to have amused him, for he smiled widely. "This coast certainly offers adventure, but I hope you both find our town lives up to your expectations."

"Thank you, sir."

"Until we meet again, ladies." With that, the captain led his companions up the stairs, leaving me to exhale.

"You made quite the impression, Anna," Katherine said when we were beyond earshot.

"Men seem to be drawn to what they shouldn't have," I replied and walked on, ignoring the smile that drifted across Katherine's face while thoughts of Thomas Wingfield taunted me.

CHAPTER NINE

———

St. Augustine, July 1764

Edmund seemed pensive as we lingered at the kitchen table after supper.

"What troubles you?" I asked, impatient with his silence.

"Sometimes I wonder if it would have been better for you to have stayed in England," he said, looking up at me. "This first year you have bravely endured so much that you wouldn't have had to in London."

"What, pray tell, have I endured as of late?" I asked, pushing my plate to the side.

He sighed. "Perhaps the stifling heat, mosquitoes, and horrid storms? But, what of my inclinations and clandestine liaisons? I must admit your acceptance is a gift, but surely, they dismay you."

"You are not suggesting—" My heart skipped a beat.

"That you leave me here, broken hearted?"

"Edmund, no one suspects we are not the happiest of couples. I have no fear of our secret, and I have no regrets."

He smiled, and I could see that any hint of worry had melted away. "You know what I want to hear."

As Edmund took a long sip of his ale, there was a fierce pounding at the courtyard door.

The door flew open before we could reach it, and half a dozen men in tattered clothes, smelling of seafaring and a good splash of rum, stormed in through the gate, dragging three barely conscious youths between them. They looked ominous, these men, unpredictable and lawless, and from the blood draining from the wounded, I feared they were taking their last breaths.

"How dare you enter my house!" Edmund yelled as the men heaved one of the wounded up onto our kitchen table and laid the other two on the porch.

"Edmund! They—" I stopped myself and rushed to the wounded man only feet away from me. He was writhing in pain, and the pressure I applied to his leg did nothing to soothe him, but hopefully it would slow the hemorrhage.

Edmund was still tense with anger. "We will see to these men, but then I bid you leave us unharmed."

"Indeed," a voice said, coming from behind us.

We turned and found Captain Ortega.

"Pray, excuse this interruption," he said, glancing at me but fixing his gaze on Edmund. "I am Captain Sebastian Ortega of the *Nuestra Habana*. We have had a great misfortune, for these young men may have but a short time to live. I trust you will not let them die."

"I promise nothing," Edmund said without hesitation, heading into the house.

One of the men stepped closer to him, wielding a sword, and Edmund stopped.

"My tools?"

The captain gestured to his men to lower their weapons, and they did, clearing the way for Edmund, while I showed one of Ortega's men where to apply pressure to the youth's leg and took in what needed to be done.

"Jane, bring the bench and table outside to lay these men on, and..." I turned to Ortega. "Should you seek to help, please surrender your men's daggers to the fire, for there are many wounds in need of sealing."

It only took the subtlest nod from the captain for his men to do as I asked.

Malcolm was already at the well, bringing up buckets of water, and sang out to me when he caught my eye, making hand gestures like rising steam.

"Yes. Boil it!" I called back. "And tear more rags from sheets!"

Just then, Jane handed me a tin of healing mushrooms.

"Thank you," I said. "Now get Abbie, and make haste."

A look of surprise came over her face, but then she hurried away.

After dropping scant measures of opium elixir into the mouths of the injured youths, they stilled, allowing us to explore the obvious sword injuries they had suffered. From the number of them, the battle must have been fierce.

"Good God," Edmund muttered. "We have not enough skilled hands or time to ensure their lives."

Just as he had spoken, a woman's voice rang out, startling us. "I'm here," Abbie Birdsong said.

Edmund turned, his jaw dropping at the sight of her.

"There is much to do," I replied.

Edmund cleared his throat, but before he could say a word I put a cloth in Abbie's hands and Malcolm put a basin of steaming water at her side.

"Edmund, this is Abbie Birdsong, and Abbie, this is my husband, Mr. Edmund Ashton," I said, but neither of them seemed to acknowledge my introductions.

"We don't need your help, Mistress Birdsong," Edmund said, glaring at me.

"We can't lose a single one of these sailors for not trying our best," I said. "Stay, Abbie."

Abbie stood there, looking from me to my husband.

Edmund glared at me, but then he assented. "I have no time for quarreling," he said. "Begin. Tarry not!"

As we worked, Captain Ortega paced, raking his fingers through his unbound hair as he threw long glances at the injured. I didn't have to look up to know he was near me, for my body sensed him, as if it had a will of its own.

Surely, he was the type of man my father had warned me against, a rogue possibly holding secret loyalties, a proclaimed privateer, practically a pirate, and a man living a life of danger and engaging in an assortment of unacceptable ventures, yet nothing could dissuade my racing heart.

Thankfully, Edmund took no notice, barely spoke, and continued to sear bleeding wounds with the red-hot daggers Ortega's men handed him before they returned them to the fire to heat again.

The youth on the table before Abbie muttered that his name was Alfonso as she moved his shoulder about, but when she put her foot against his torso and tugged at his arm until he groaned, we both looked up.

"Mistress Birdsong—" Edmund started, looking at her in disbelief, just as Abbie released the man's arm into its socket, and Alfonso found that he could move his arm again.

"His shoulder was out of its socket," Abbie said.

"You could have asked for help."

"I thank you, but I didn't need it, Mr. Ashton."

Edmund shook his head, but I saw the half smile he tried to suppress. "I see why my wife favors you," he said, glancing over at me.

Edmund continued to tend to his patient, but I caught him watching her from time to time, apparently without finding anything to question.

When she caught my eye she winked, for she had clearly won him over, in spite of his concerns over wagging tongues.

After several hours, when we had cleaned and closed each wound, Edmund stepped away and washed his hands, while Abbie and I finished securing the young men's bandages.

"We have done what we can, and they have fared better than I expected," he said.

"We thank you," Captain Ortega said, looking at Edmund and me. "These men have been with me since they were ship›s boys. It would have pained me greatly to lose them."

"I had two adept women at my side," Edmund said, surprising me with his generosity. "I must thank you, Mistress Birdsong. It would have been a greater challenge without your help. You are most skilled."

Captain Ortega winked at Abbie, and she smiled back at him.

"It's an honor," Abbie said, with a smile that should have charmed my husband.

Captain Ortega's face softened as he looked at Abbie, revealing a gentleness I hadn't thought likely, but how did he know her?

"My sister-in law is a treasure, like none other," he said.

"Sister-in-law? I did not know," I stammered.

Seeing the tears fill Abbie's eyes made me regret asking.

Hesitating, she glanced at Sebastian before she turned to me. "My sister was Sebastian's wife. She died giving birth to their son. They both died that day."

Sebastian put an arm around her, and she nestled against him. "They live in our memories, Abbie."

Abbie nodded, wiping a tear.

"Our condolences," Edmund said, speaking for us both. "We are sorry for your loss."

"Thank you," Sebastian said. "But think not that your efforts today will be forgotten. We will remain in your debt for this lifetime."

Signaled by a glance, Ortega's men lifted the injured off the tables and headed out the garden door with them.

"But wait!" I said. "They are hardly fit to sail."

Sebastian turned to me. "We will not trouble you further. They can continue their recovery aboard. We shall not leave port for days yet."

"It must have been quite a battle," my husband said.

"Hardly," Captain Ortega replied. "We captured the *Luisa* quite swiftly, now with no loss to us, and we will return the cargo the Archer brothers intended to abscond with."

"The *Luisa*?" Edmund asked. "It was carrying precious medical goods that

I have been waiting for most of this year."

Ortega smiled. "It will be my pleasure to place these goods into your hands, once I find them."

"It would be a relief," Edmund said, but before I could utter a word, Abbie turned to the captain.

"I will watch over those reckless youths of yours, Sebastian," she said, "for they will need much care."

"We have an abundance of bandages now," I said, looking at Malcolm.

"And readied salves and tonics."

"Perhaps we should collect some of your precious maggots, should we come to need them," Abbie said, making us laugh in spite of our weariness.

Edmund rolled his eyes, but Captain Ortega seemed perplexed.

"Have you not heard of the Angel of the *Penny Rose*?" Abbie asked. "That is what she was called after she deftly treated Admiral Rushmore's son with maggots!"

The captain's eyes brightened. "I did hear mention of this name, but I thought it was because of your undeniable beauty, Mrs. Ashton," he said, looking into my eyes.

"A logical conclusion," Edmund said flatly. "She is quite lovely."

Before I could say a word, Captain Ortega tipped his weatherworn tricorn to Edmund and bowed even deeper to me. "We must depart, but again, we thank you. Should you be in need of us, you can rely on us. It is a matter of honor."

* * *

Only days later, Edmund's medical goods were delivered, exciting my husband greatly—in particular, because a case of glass rods had arrived unscathed.

Putting three rods on the table, he reached for his knife and motioned for me to join him. "Look at this. You would have liked to have had this back in London."

"What would I have done with glass rods? Surely, they would easily break if I were to stir with them." I eyed the rods with some suspicion. "Are these the same as those that were destroyed on the *Penny Rose*?"

"Exactly," Edmund said as he carved a line into the glass and then another a little higher on the shaft.

"Pour me wine," he said without looking up. "And bring me an empty goblet as well."

He rarely asked for wine, but I decided not to question him.

Giving him a good pour of claret, I put an empty goblet next to him and sat down.

"Look, now. I asked for the wine because its color will show you what I am doing."

He put the rod into the wine, and I watched as it filled the rod halfway. When he removed it from the goblet, the wine was still inside the rod without slipping out.

"How is that possible?" I tilted my head and squinted to look closer.

He laughed. "Look now."

I hadn't noticed he had been holding his finger over the top of the rod, but when he released it the wine splashed into the empty goblet.

"Oh!" I said, surprised at first but then more curious. "Of what importance is this?"

"Anna, think. By drawing the wine into the rod and releasing it by removing my finger from the top, I can control the amount of wine in the rod."

"And that amuses you in some way?"

Husbands could be so odd at times.

"It amuses me greatly that I can measure the exact amount of liquid so easily by drawing it up to the line I choose."

"So, it's for measuring tonics! Has anyone told you that Anna Ashton's husband is the most brilliant doctor in the Americas?"

"Cheeky little lady, you are, Anna. Be glad I care for you as much as I do."

When he finished carving lines into the rods, I watched as Edmund slipped three rods into three bottles of elixir and tucked them carefully into his medical bag.

They were long enough for him to remove without touching the liquid but short enough for the top to still fit snuggly. He seemed joyous, and I reveled in the pleasure he seemed to find in these new tools.

* * *

After a ceremony at the Shrine of Our Lady, Captain Warrick and Sofia Moultrie's wedding feast took place at the captain's villa.

"We are delighted you could join us," Captain Warrick said when we arrived with James and Katherine Neville. "I trust you will find many friends here, but there are many more to become acquainted with."

Katherine kept her word and introduced us to everyone, pleasing my husband greatly as he and James Neville became absorbed in conversations with landowners from as far away as Virginia and Carolina.

After a while, Katherine mischievously tugged at my sleeve and pulled us away from our husbands' sides when the conversation of acreage became too much to bear.

"You must meet Baptiste," she said. "If we are fortunate, Alexander will be here as well. Baptiste is the governor's personal slave, but he is most unusual, for he is a chef trained in the finest of French cuisine. Alexander is a baker of similar learning who puts every woman, and every bakery, in this territory to shame."

From the exquisite scents wafting toward us, I could tell she was leading me toward the kitchens.

"And... they are preparing this evening's feast?" I asked, wondering as we sped along if she would let go of my sleeve.

"Yes! The governor lent them to Patrick for the wedding, and no cost has been spared."

"You make me hungry just listening to you," I said as Katherine opened the doors to the kitchen and a dozen or more servants turned to us.

A stout but pleasant-looking woman in a crisp white apron, who might be Captain Warrick's cook, stepped away from the group and came toward us. "Ladies, may we be of service? I am Mrs. Oglethorpe. My husband and I are the caretakers of the captain's homes."

I smiled and spoke before Katherine had a chance. "A pleasure, Mrs. Oglethorpe. We could not resist the scent of the Confit de Canard. I never imagined such a delicacy would be offered in St. Augustine."

From the smile on the face of the tallest of the Negroes, I knew who Baptiste was.

Mrs. Oglethorpe followed my gaze. "Yes, we are most fortunate to have such a chef with us today," she said as Katherine moved forward to watch the man, who must be Alexander, assembling over a hundred delicate cakes. "Should you two ladies like to taste something?"

Before I could reply, a voice roared up behind me.

"I thought I saw two of my guests slip into this enclave of delights," Captain Warrick said as Mrs. Oglethorpe offered us a plate of confit. "Is it not a marvel?"

I chuckled. "It is pleasant to see a man with a taste for such nuanced flavors."

"Spoken like a true herbalist. I imagine you might enjoy the spice garden. I have brought back seeds from my travels, and I have species rarely heard of in the Americas." The captain filled his mouth with treats from yet another sampler.

I could see the pride in Baptiste and Alexander's eyes as they snuck peeks at him while he continued to indulge. They were so unlike the many downtrodden slaves owned by people who were thought to be our friends, and it made me happy to see it.

Katherine laughed. "Our Anna is far more joyful grinding herbs than playing a good game of cards. She takes the most unusual pleasure in flavoring egregiously offensive elixirs, so I'm sure she would see your garden as a treasure trove."

"Is it so?" Captain Warrick asked, looking at me with those arctic-blue eyes of his.

I nodded. "Yes, I confess."

"Well, then, please feel free to explore my gardens whenever you wish. But I do ask one thing." He looked serious.

"What would that be, Captain?"

"You must tell me what you create with what you take away from here."

"It will be my pleasure." I smiled up at him. "Thank you."

A door swung open behind me, and I noticed the servants stiffen.

"And precisely what pleasure are you thanking *my husband* for?" Sofia asked.

Before I could say a word, Patrick smiled and pulled her closer. What he saw in her still eluded me, for looks and breeding were hardly enough when it concerned the likes of Sofia.

"Sophie, darling," he said, "I was just chatting with Katherine and the Angel of—"

"Spare me, Patrick. I know who Mistress Ashton is."

She stared at me with surprising disdain, causing both Captain Warrick and Katherine to look from her to me and back.

"This is *our* wedding feast, Patrick. We have guests of considerable rank, and I find my husband in the kitchen, giving this woman admittance to our gardens at her pleasure! It is me you should think to please," she said, gently tugging at his arm and gazing up at him with a smile dripping in honey.

"We should find our husbands," I said to Katherine, smiling back at the servants as we fled through the double doors and out into the gardens, where guests were gathering.

The air was unusually dry for a summer's day, but it was still warm, tempting guests to take to seats in the shade of the great canopy of large oak trees. Looking behind me, I spied a well-tended kitchen garden further back behind blooming azaleas, competing with hibiscus of all colors growing in front of a thicket of trees. A faint whiff of lavender suggested the location of the herb garden, tempting me to explore, but when the music started, Edmund and I joined the Warricks and the other guests on the dance floor.

"Are you enjoying yourself, little wife?" he asked, more cheerfully than usual.

Little wife, indeed. Of course he was joyous. It hadn't escaped me that Thomas Wingfield was among the guests, and I couldn't help the jab of envy that struck me, knowing I would be the one who would sleep alone tonight.

"Of course, darling husband," I said, beaming up at him with practiced perfection. He drew me closer, staring adoringly into my eyes with the same rehearsed deception.

"Please dance Sofia's feet off," I whispered, surprising him as I pretended to murmur something sweet into his ear. "There is something about her that I feel bodes ill."

CHAPTER TEN

St. Augustine, August 1764

A knock on the door stirred me from sleep. My eyes fluttered open to catch a glimpse of Edmund carrying a lantern as he left our bedroom. I heard his footsteps on the staircase and then the creak of the front door opening. As I suspected, it was George Stuart, the night watchman, who had come to fetch Edmund because someone had taken ill in the night. I heard them mention Samuel Smithfield, a fisherman I had met at the market.

I was barely awake when Edmund came back upstairs and kissed me. I reached up and slid my fingers through his hair, pulling him closer and drawing in the scent of him as he laid me back down and tucked the quilt around me. I drifted back to sleep as his footsteps faded in the distance and the door slammed behind him.

* * *

In the early morning, another loud knock startled me. The latch was probably stuck again, I thought as I rambled down the stairs, but why didn't Edmund come in through the garden gate as he usually did?

"Just a moment, Edmund!" I called out as I fumbled to unlatch the door and flung it open.

It wasn't Edmund; little wonder he hadn't answered.

I blinked, taken aback by the couple at our doorstep; that explained the knocking. The woman looked familiar, but I couldn't recall ever seeing the tall, thin man standing next to her.

"I'm sorry. My husband isn't here," I said. "He is either at the infirmary or the Smithfield's house."

They looked worried, but I tried to smile. God only knows what people are going through.

The man cleared his throat. "I'm Joseph Hobart," the tall man said. He gestured toward the woman. "And this is Mary Evans. We've met at the infirmary, if you recall."

I didn't.

"Could we possibly come in?" he asked. "It's important."

I held the door open and let them enter. The sun was about to rise, and Edmund should be home soon. I'd make them some tea and let them sit on the back porch to take in the sunrise while they waited for Edmund.

Before I could make the suggestion, Mr. Hobart stepped in front of me. "I regret to tell you this, Mrs. Ashton." He paused, looking down at his feet, and then he lifted his gaze to meet mine. "It's about your husband." He seemed to struggle to get the words out.

Mary Evans glanced at him and took my hand in hers. "My dear woman, your fine husband has died. It is a loss to us all."

I pulled my hand away and stepped back, looking at them as they stood in my house. Edmund's shoes were by the door, and the half-written letter to his father still lay on the desk. Surely, he couldn't be dead. Why would they say such a thing?

The man seemed to find his voice. "Your husband was stabbed during what seems to have been a brawl, or a possible robbery, at the infirmary."

I gasped and laughed loudly at the absurdity. "None of this is true! You are sorely mistaken. My husband doesn't brawl!"

Mary Evans reached out to embrace me, but I turned away, holding my hands up to ward her off. These two had gone mad; certainly, they had.

"You have to leave," I said, opening the door behind me. "You have mistaken Edmund for someone else. Don't waste your time here with me."

Mary reached into her purse and pulled something out of a kerchief. I recognized Edmund's pocket watch in an instant. It had been my grandfather's, and I gave it to Edmund after we married. Snatching it from her, I felt my hands get suddenly sticky with blood. Edmund's blood? How did this woman have his pocket watch in her possession?

I searched her face for an inkling of understanding, but she just stood there, as somber as the man by her side.

"This can't be!" I whispered, clutching the bloodied watch to my chest. But if nothing had happened to Edmund, why was his watch blood-drenched, and why did this grim woman have it?

I started to tremble, realizing that nothing would be the same after this moment. Edmund wouldn't come home, not today, not ever.

The room started to pull away, and I had a sudden urge to be sick.

Mr. Hobart and Mary Evans caught me as my knees buckled. Together they steadied me into Edmund's chair, pushing away the letter he had left there. I squinted at the words on the page, but tears filled my eyes, and I felt unsettled. The surface of my skin felt eerie cold and moist in the early morning heat, and I wished the shrill screams would stop since they bothered my head even more than the cold sweats and nausea that had taken hold of me. My mouth felt dry, and as I swallowed I realized the spine-chilling screams were my own.

My teeth chattered as I tried to pull myself together, but the trembling wouldn't stop, and cries that I couldn't control filled the air.

Mary Evans put her arms around me and held me. She smelled of lavender and fresh linens. It felt strange to be held so tightly by a stranger, but if she let go, surely, I would fall apart, sink into the floor planks, drown in my own tears, and, hopefully, die, putting an end to this madness.

I mustered the strength to look up at Mr. Hobart, who stood there with his hands behind his back, watching me.

"Edmund was stabbed?"

He nodded. "Yes. He must have died quickly, ma'am."

"Is this an absurd attempt at kindness to tell me that my dead husband didn't suffer long?" I asked. "It is not kind!"

Mr. Hobart opened his mouth but shut it again.

Turning toward the garden door, I did not recall when Jane and Malcom had come in, but from their tear wet faces I knew they had heard it all.

"Get Abbie for me. I need her," I told them in a whisper but not soft enough for Mr. Hobart not to hear.

"That won't be necessary," he said. "She has been arrested. Mistress Birdsong was found with her hand on the knife she stabbed your husband with. I was going to ask if you knew he entertained other women."

I rose, staring at the two of them. *They believe this.*

"This is madness!" I cried out before doubling over, shrieking with laughter. "The world has gone mad!"

I sank back down to the floor and sobbed, not caring that they were probably watching me.

"Edmund can't be dead," I said when I caught my breath, "and Abbie would never hurt him. I have lost my mind! Far better than losing Edmund."

I took a long look at Joseph Hobart and Mary Evans. Still holding Edmund's bloodied pocket watch in my hand, I fled out the front door and ran toward the infirmary, not realizing I had forgotten my shoes until gravel cut into my feet.

The guard at the infirmary didn't try to stop me as I ran past him. I probably looked like a madwoman, and I was close to feeling like one, so he could hardly be blamed.

Once inside, I turned down the hall to Edmund's consultation room. A ray of flickering light escaped through the crack of the door, which had been left slightly ajar. Without thought, I pushed it open. Agonizing wails escaped me as I stared at the blood-splattered walls. Edmund's desk was overturned, and his chair had been reduced to mere sticks. Shards of glass from shattered cabinets and broken bottles covered the floor, and nothing at all was left whole.

Squelching the urge to be ill, I crossed the courtyard into the main building. Nurse Newsome came out to meet me. I could see that her eyes were red-rimmed.

"It's a tragedy," she whispered, as if she couldn't find the strength to raise her voice.

I nodded, unable to speak at all, and let her grab my arm and steady me as we walked inside.

The air felt suddenly cool on my damp skin, and the hallway that took us toward the morgue seemed painfully long.

As I opened the door, the smell of blood hurled toward me, and just as I caught a glimpse of a sheet-covered body, the room seemed to overflow with the eerie silence of death.

"Are you prepared?" Dr. Catherwood asked. I hadn't noticed him in the room until now. I shook my head, but I stepped closer to the body on the table, growing more certain it wasn't Edmund. It couldn't be Edmund.

For a moment, I stood there, plucking up my courage. Finally, I reached out with a quivering hand and drew back the sheet. I gasped, and my footing threatened to falter, but Nurse Newsome and Dr. Catherwood kept me standing while the moment locked itself into my memory.

It was Edmund.

My Edmund. My husband. A man of flesh and blood, of strength and weakness, compassion and convictions, and dreams, many dreams. Now there would be none to pursue. There would be no more laughter, no more words of wisdom. At last, my husband was safe from his hidden passion for Thomas, and for a moment, my worry shifted to the man my husband loved.

Edmund's face was dreadfully pale, his lips barely visible save for their raised contours. I reached out and stroked his forehead, startled by the cool I knew to expect before I bent down and kissed his cheek for the last time.

Stepping back, almost blinded by tears, I took one last look at him, and then I let myself be led out past the courtyard and through the massive doors I no longer recalled entering. I refused offers of ale, sustenance, or bandages for my feet, but I let them put me in a carriage that took me home.

* * *

On Sunday I walked with Katherine to the church, where a service was to be held for my husband before his burial in the small St. Augustine cemetery. Everyone I had met from the infirmary had come, along with town officials and many of St. Augustine's residents.

I saw Harry Blackwood when I entered the church. He weaved through the crowd of people until he stood directly in front of me, looking down at me with those mournful eyes of his. Now I understood his suffering, and he knew the abyss I found myself in. There was an odd inkling of comfort in our shared agony, the only comfort I had felt as of late, despite so many kind people trying to console me.

"This is a travesty, Anna," he said. "I am so sorry, so very sorry."

"Thank you, Harry," I whispered.

Katherine stood by my side. "We had better take our seats," she said.

Lost in my thoughts, I barely noticed that she took my arm. Glancing over my shoulder, I saw Harry Blackwood following us with his gaze, still standing where we had left him.

We sat in the front pew, only feet away from Edmund's plank casket. I imagined him inside it and felt dazed by the madness of it. Edmund should be with me, not lying cold and lifeless in a wooden box.

My husband's burial. The words echoed oddly in my mind as I struggled to suppress the hysteria that was building inside me. I don't know how I can bear this. I'm a widow, Edmund Ashton's widow.

I sat through the service with my eyes glazed over with tears, barely listening to the drone of Father Greyson's voice, wishing I could flee yet uncertain of where I would go.

Who could kill Edmund, the kindest man there ever was? Had anyone discovered where his true affections lay? I let my mind wander, indulging in secret thoughts of finding Edmund's murderer and inflicting a slow death upon the wretched person for robbing us of our future.

When Father Greyson raised his voice and startled me out of my unchristian thoughts, I rose with the rest of the congregation and followed along to the graveyard in back of the church.

CHAPTER ELEVEN

———

St. Augustine, August 1764

In a sweltering jail cell, Abbie awaited her fate. The Governor was away, as were several members of the Royal Council, but it was expected she would be hung when they returned. Having been found with her hand on the knife that killed Edmund, there was little chance of a fair trial.

Walking through the familiar streets in a daze, I barely noticed the sweltering heat or the putrid smell that enveloped me when the guard brought me into the jailhouse and down the hallway to the cell where Abbie was held.

My thoughts twisted in my mind as I passed each cell, not looking in on the pitiful beings confined behind the iron bars. How would anyone find the real murderer if they already thought they had the killer locked up?

It would be easy to accuse Abbie Birdsong and forget her. Once they executed her, they would go about their lives, and I will be the only one left to care. They would go home to their wives, sit down at their dinner tables, and not think of her, ever again. I couldn't let this happen, but those who held the power in St. Augustine would hardly be swayed by the pleading of a grieving widow.

The guard left me by a cell at the end of the hallway. Carefully, I approached the barred door and peeked in, horrified to see her sitting there, leaning against the stone wall, lost in thought.

"Abbie!" It was more a gasp than a call out to her, for my voice cracked, and I feared the expression on my face was just as brittle.

Abbie turned when she heard me, her eyes softening at the sight of me.

"I know you didn't do it; you couldn't have," I blurted out, bringing us both to tears as our hands entwined through coarse iron bars.

"No, but I am going to die for it." Abbie's voice was grim and oddly flat.

"You are not! You can't!" I said, surprised by my own outburst.

Abbie's eyes widened. "The kitten roars." She attempted a smile, reaching out to wipe a tear from my cheek.

"This is wrong, Abbie. Wrong..."

"How are you faring?"

She barely had to ask.

The hysteria I had felt over the last few days had drained out of me, leaving me empty. It surprised me I was standing at all.

I leaned in toward Abbie and lowered my voice. "What happened, Abbie? Why were you in the infirmary? Do you know who killed Edmund?"

Abbie shook her head. "No, I don't. Mistress Littleton is the only other white woman who has dared to befriend me since you came to town. She has been in the infirmary with a dreadful cough, which didn't improve until Dr. Catherwood gave in to her pleas of bringing me to the infirmary with my tribal elixirs, so I've been at her side for the last two days. What I heard was voices and a shuffle, but I couldn't even say with certainty that Edmund's voice was one of them."

"There has to be something to prove you didn't kill Edmund."

Abbie hesitated. "Are you certain you want to hear this?"

I nodded, bracing myself.

"No one was anywhere to be seen, so I rushed toward the sound, hoping I could help, and I realized that the noise came from Edmund's treatment room."

As Abbie started to describe the details of finding Edmund, tears rolled down my cheeks, and my insides clenched. As I listened, I searched for a detail in that dreadful story that held a clue, but there was none. Had I not known better, I would have accused Abbie myself.

"Someone must have heard or seen something, Abbie. Think!"

She sighed, looking at me hesitantly.

"What, Abbie? Tell me!"

"The only person who can say I didn't kill Edmund is Thaddeus Edgefield, and I am not going to jeopardize his engagement."

"Thaddeus Edgefield? The Admiral's nephew who is engaged to the Lieutenant Governor's niece? How would he know?"

"Yes..." Abbie hesitated, before lowering her voice. "He is also Mrs. Littleton's nephew, and Thaddeus usually passes by to speak to her nurse after his nights at the tavern. So, when he found me sitting with his aunt, Thaddeus and I withdrew into a storage room where we could be alone."

"What? I don't understand."

Abbie sighed, looking at my bewildered face. "We are lovers… and have been for some time."

She paused, waiting for me to make sense of it, but this just added to my confusion.

"Lovers? You and Thaddeus Edgefield?" I knew my face reflected every nuance of my surprise. "Really?"

Abbie nodded. "Yes, it is of no importance. He is just a past-time, but we were together when we heard the noise coming from Edmund's consultation."

"So, he knows, yet you are here?"

Abbie nodded.

I was already turning to leave.

"I will find Thaddeus and bring him here. He might not know what has happened to you."

Abbie reached out through the bars and held me back. "No, don't!" she said, causing me even more concern.

"Why not? He can have you released with his word alone! He works for Governor Grant, and there is no formal court in this town as of yet."

"No, I won't have it. He has to marry Charlotte, and she won't have him if she learns about me and our liaison."

"Why is that your concern?" I struggled to understand, for the look in Abbie's eyes was surprisingly unyielding.

"It is important, Anna. Let it be."

"Is she with child? What care is that of yours? This is a matter of your life, Abbie."

Abbie scoffed. "No, she is not with child! The virgin has no fire. It's important that they marry, and I am not going to stand in the way."

"Do you love him?"

Abbie looked at me as if I were a complete fool. "No, it's not about love! I enjoy this man, and he is so eager for our forbidden lust that he is mine for the keeping, married or not. A marriage between us would be a scandal he would not bring upon himself, and I will be no man's wife."

I felt my jaw drop, as the oddity of her thoughts sifted through my mind. Surely, I had never met a woman such as Abbie, and I had never known a woman so bold.

"You are brave, Abbie, but this time you are wrong. You can't die so Charlotte Moultrie can be happy."

"I wouldn't lift a finger for Charlotte, but she holds deeds to Creek land. Land that belonged to my father's people. Much of it is sacred tribal burial grounds that were stolen from our people when the Spanish as well as the English divided the land they came upon between themselves, as if it were theirs for the taking. Thaddeus has sworn to me that when he marries Charlotte, he will return this land to the Creek Tribe, my tribe. For that, I will willingly die."

My gut clenched. "If he doesn't speak up for you now, why would he later? How can you trust he will keep his word?"

"It is a matter of honor. He understands this." Abbie looked at me, as if she could will me to understand. "This is important, Anna."

I sighed. Doubt nagged at me, and I was more certain than ever that the world had shifted on to a maddening course, and even Abbie had fallen prey to an uncharacteristic naivety.

"There is a way," I said. "I know there is. I'm just not certain of what that way is."

I looked at Abbie, feeling tears fill my eyes. Thaddeus Edgefield was not worthy of even the silk of his cravat if he sent his lover to the gallows to save his good name.

"You leave me no choice. You don't deserve to die, and I can't lose you too."

I gave Abbie's hands a squeeze before I turned away from her and walked back down the hallway.

"Anna, don't!" Abbie called after me, but I was already on my way to see Thaddeus Edgefield.

* * *

I walked across the Town Square, heading toward the sprawling government building on the opposite side. It was likely that I would be dismissed as a grief-stricken widow without a single sensible thought in my head. I would have to prove them wrong, although the thought of challenging an official turned my stomach and made my fingers numb. The prickle of fear made me want to turn away, but that was no more possible than flinging myself into Edmund's arms.

It was likely that I would be told the matter was closed and not to worry myself further, for justice would be served and I needn't bother myself with the workings of men. Their smiles would be placating, if they even smiled. They could send me on my way, a woman without a husband to speak up for me, a widow with no great family behind me.

Lifting my head, I put my shoulders back and took a deep breath before I pulled open the massive door, trying not to look as if my insides trembled.

A clerk with a heavy mustache reluctantly walked me toward Thaddeus Edgefield's chambers, in spite of my refusal to state my concerns. He had glared at me over his spectacles and expected me to cower, but the thought of what Edmund would have wanted, and Abbie in that wretched cell, steeled my resolve, and he was only my first hurdle.

"Mrs. Ashton is here for you, sir," he muttered when we reached the open door to Thaddeus Edgefield's office.

"Bring her in!"

The sound of his voice reminded me of how young he was, but he still wielded influence. I noticed my heartbeat hasten and tried to slow my breath so I wouldn't seem frightened. Suddenly, it occurred to me that I could be making matters worse, if they could be worse.

Thaddeus Edgefield stood up from his desk and walked toward me with his hands outstretched when I approached him. He was a tall, handsome man, at least a decade younger than Abbie. He was dressed well in a fitted gray jacket and white breeches, with his long auburn hair gathered at the nape of his neck with a silk cord.

When he took my hands in his, the smile disappeared.

I looked up at him, struggling to conceal the disdain I felt for him for allowing Abbie to spend even a moment in that wretched cell.

"Your tragic loss grieves me, Mrs. Ashton. It is an abomination that such a thing should happen here. If there is anything at all I can do to be of help to you, please come to me at once."

Those were the words I wanted to hear, sincere or not. I took a deep breath and readied myself as if I were to step off a cliff.

"Actually, there is something you can do for me, Mr. Edgefield," I said, hoping my smile would be coy enough to gain his confidence.

As I pulled my hands from his grip, he looked at me inquisitively.

"Anything at all, Mrs. Ashton. You have only to ask."

I swallowed hard and raised my eyes to his, but I couldn't stop the tear that rolled down my cheek.

"Thank you, I am grateful," I said as calmly as I could. "Then you will see to it that Abbie Birdsong is free before nightfall."

Thaddeus Edgefield's smile stiffened. "That is not within my power, Mrs. Ashton."

Somehow I found the courage to step closer. "Certainly, you will find a way, Mr. Edgefield."

He looked at me, still too composed to have understood how much I knew about him. "It is for the Governor and the Royal Council to determine Miss Birdsong's fate. I cannot let a woman accused of murder go free. It is most unfortunate."

I took another step forward, noticing that my closeness caused him unease, and resisted the urge to further narrow the space between us.

"You know she is innocent," I whispered, watching his face for a flicker of surprise. "You were there the night it happened; the nurses caring for your aunt can attest to that."

There it was. The color drained from his face, and his lips tightened.

"So, perhaps you killed my husband? It is as likely as Abbie Birdsong committing such a heinous act, wouldn't you say?"

I couldn't believe my own daring and drew a breath, bracing myself for his reaction.

His eyes widened, and he looked as if he had reached some level of discomfort, with his brow glistening ever so slightly. "Mrs. Ashton, I assure you, I didn't! I wouldn't!"

"But you were there," I continued, holding his gaze.

"Yes, I was." He cleared his throat, his eyes suddenly shifting. "I was checking in with my aunt's nurses on my way from the tavern."

"I know about you and Abbie," I spoke softly, wanting my words to sting more than the sound of my outrage. "She won't speak up because you promised to return a section of Charlotte's land holdings to the Creek."

He sighed, rubbing his chin with his hand as he pondered. "Without Abbie, there is no reason for that land to leave Charlotte's hands. It was a statement, whispered in the throes of passion. I have regretted it."

My fists clenched. I was right about this man.

"Without Charlotte, you will never count that land as your own, for I have no qualms about telling her."

He laughed. "Grieving widows often go mad for a spell. Who would believe you?"

I hesitated but gave in to an urge to push further. "I have only to mention markings on your person that Charlotte will not admit to have seen before her wedding night," I said, praying that there were such markings. Surely, this man's person must have some physical flaw to match his questionable character.

"Ha! She would believe you were my lover before she would believe I would take up with Abbie. Widows tend to be lonely creatures." He moved toward me. Suddenly there was a gleam in his eyes. "Maybe we can strike a bargain."

My insides twisted. "Dismiss the thought. I won't fall prey to you!" Heat rose in my cheeks. "All the same, Charlotte would not look well upon any of your dalliances, whether with me or Abbie."

Thaddeus Edgefield looked at me with unconcealed wonder and growing concern. "How I have misjudged you. You have the face of an angel—"

I took a deep breath, struggling to control my nerves. "Don't flatter me. Just see to it that Abbie is free by nightfall, and all that has been said between us will be forgotten."

"I have your word?"

I looked up at him. "You have my word, but if you betray me in any way, you will not fare well."

I didn't expect him to look at me as thunderstruck, as if he were suddenly in awe of me, for I could barely understand my own daring.

"I will see to this immediately," he said, attempting a smile that was neither warm nor reassuring.

I looked up at him one more time. "Then we understand each other."

He bowed. "We do."

I nodded and turned, letting the door slam behind me, and went home.

When the garden gate creaked open before nightfall, my relief was immeasurable, for there, in the light of the setting sun, Abbie stood smiling at me.

CHAPTER TWELVE

———

St. Augustine, Late August 1764

"What do you mean?"

I looked at the plump little man on my doorstep. I'd heard him correctly, but the chill that started to creep up my spine an inch at the time made me doubt myself. This couldn't be. A mistake had been made, surely it had. I steadied myself against the doorframe, gripping it so tight that my fingers hurt.

"I'm Mr. Blumford from the Government Office," the man said, his gaze barely settling on me.

"Yes, sir. I heard that, but what do you mean, I have sixty days?"

"Mrs. Ashton, you have sixty days to vacate this residence and marry, or you will be put back on the *Penny Rose* on her return and shipped back to England. Those are the rules."

"Whose rules? Why?" I asked. "The journey here nearly killed us. I would not attempt it as a widow."

"Then you must find a new husband. This town has no funds to provide for widows without means, and a new doctor will be arriving to occupy this house as soon as one can be found," he said without meeting my gaze. "It's all here in this document."

He reached forward and handed me a large envelope. "I don't know how well you read, but you have been told. Sixty days, ma'am."

I felt him watching me as I broke the thick government seal and ripped the envelope open, pulling out the document within it.

"I can read as well as any man, Mr. Blumford," I said, studying the document as he waited. "It's the content that's lacking."

Mr. Blumford looked up at me for a moment. I met his gaze, unwavering, although I felt myself tremble. I wondered if my impertinence would cost me, but the man looked away.

"Very well, then. I'll be off," he stammered. "Not a thing I can do about it."

Mr. Blumford lifted his hat to me and turned down the street in a hurry, quickly putting distance between us.

I shut the door and sank into Edmund's chair, letting the document slide across the table in front of me. For a long time I just stared at it, wishing for a way to make it vanish. Embarking on the voyage back to London without Edmund would be impossible. I could not bear another storm without him, nor could I be confined to a hammock below deck, and the thought of marriage to anyone but Edmund made me feel ill.

* * *

The following morning came with thunderclouds, rain, and lightning bolts. The house, that was no longer to be mine, trembled under the fury of the sudden storm. I lay in bed with the doors to the balconies open, watching the rain fall, still numb from a night of tormented dreams. Waking was no better.

I slipped out of bed and stepped on to the balcony. Rain drenched me in an instant, cool enough to give me a shiver. My wet hair hung heavy down my back, and my night shift already clung to me. Holding out my hands, I felt the flow of water run through my fingers and down my arms, fresh and cleansing, as if it could wash away my sudden misfortune. Water could be the death of me after all, but this time, I wouldn't fight it if it came for me. I would encourage it.

Lightning tore through the sky, followed by deafening bursts of thunder in rapid succession. Still, turning my face to the sky, I felt oddly calm as I drew in the fresh earthy scent of the rain.

"Let it be over," I whispered. "God, I beg you."

I could feel Edmund's disapproval as the thought swirled in my head, and certainly God would give me more penance than I could bear.

* * *

"Stop pacing, Anna," Katherine said. "You have walked the length of the porch a hundred times, as surely as one."

Abbie nodded in agreement. "Katherine is right."

I dropped the letter from the government office on the table in front of them. It was already crumpled from hours of scrutiny. Odd how one sheet of paper could bring with it such turmoil, as if my life was not burdened enough.

Abbie read it, her face expressionless, before she handed it to Katherine.

"I don't know what to do!" I said, not sure of what was possible here in the Americas.

"You marry," Abbie said, slipping a wedge of an orange into her mouth. "You just marry."

Katherine handed the document back to me and nodded. "She's right."

I felt my chest tighten. "That sounds absurd to me. I don't want to. Edmund and I were good together. God knows I might not find that again."

"You don't have a choice, Anna." Katherine hesitated before she added, "You can't sell enough elixirs to keep a roof over your head."

"I'd die," I whispered, certain of it.

"That might be what it comes to, if you don't," Abbie said.

"You don't understand; you're being cruel."

Abbie looked at me the way someone looks at a small child to coax it into some unacceptable task. "In time, grief will pass, but for now, you marry. There is no choice."

"I can't!" I said, looking at the two of them. They'd gone mad. I wished desperately that Edmund would appear and rescue me from the impossible demands that were being made of me.

Abbie stood and wrapped her arms around me. "You will. You are not the first woman to be married off like chattel. It has to be."

I nodded, reluctantly. "I know. I just never thought it would happen to me."

I sighed, but my mind was still fighting the urge to rebel mightily.

Abbie and Katherine glanced at each other.

Katherine took a deep breath before she looked up at me. "The tides have turned, Anna. The only thing you can hope for is that Edmund's killer is found and hung for what he did."

"As if that would bring him back." I sank down on the bench next to her. She had mentioned Edmund's killer. It didn't seem real, even now. In what world did Edmund have a killer? It didn't make sense.

"There is the Widow's Walk,'" Abbie said, after a long pause. "You might see that there are possibilities better than you imagine."

I looked up. "The Widow's Walk?"

"It's the stretch of land between Harry Blackwood's inn and the fortress. Soldiers and unwed townsmen know that women who walk there are looking for husbands."

I stopped, my jaw dropping. "I have seen people strolling there, but I didn't know it was for that reason. I couldn't bear it. I would feel as if I were selling myself to the highest bidder."

Katherine sighed. "It's not like that."

"You could wear the blue dress," Abbie said, standing up. "It makes your eyes even more beautiful, and we'll pinch some color into your cheeks."

She started to walk toward the door, gesturing for Katherine and me to follow her, but I stood as if locked in place.

"Now? You don't mean now?" I looked at Katherine, hoping for a glimmer of understanding, but Katherine shook her head.

"There isn't much time. Might as well begin. I imagine you would like some time to consider which man would suit you the best," Katherine said, following Abbie inside.

"The world has gone mad, and you two along with it."

Reluctantly, I went inside and up to the bedroom where Abbie triumphantly pulled the blue dress from my armoire.

As I let Abbie and Katherine prepare me for the spectacle I would have to face, my thoughts drifted.

"Try not to look so dour," Abbie said, startling me.

"Dour? This is hardly a joyous moment."

I should probably be grateful, but Abbie seemed not to care that I was less than enthusiastic.

"Remember why you are doing this," Abbie said.

I nodded, exhaling as Katherine tightened my corset. What would it matter if I were an inch thicker? I was already thin for my height.

"Edmund would not have wanted this for me, to be paraded out like an object for anyone to take," I gasped as Katherine pulled tighter.

"But nor would he want you to be sent from St. Augustine to brave the voyage on your own," Katherine said. Finally tying my laces, she stood back and looked at me with the scrutiny of a tailor.

"I feel like a lamb being brought to slaughter," I said.

Katherine sighed, but Abbie stood back and said nothing.

I looked at myself in the mirror. My cheeks were flushed, and sleepless nights had left a darkness about my eyes.

How have I become the prize that would drive men to pursuit? Strange men, biding for attention, men who could make demands of my body, my time, and my life, and expect me to bear their children.

"Are you ready?" Abbie asked.

"I never will be." I pinched my lips together, giving them a long look before I picked up my purse and headed for the door.

"It won't take long. There is hardly an unmarried woman in St. Augustine, so the selection will be yours."

We walked in silence to the Matanzas where Harry greeted us. His eyes rested on me for a long moment.

"So, this is what it has come to," he said when Abbie told him why we were there. "Life never goes as we expect."

I nodded, willing myself not to cry.

Harry lifted his arms as if to reach out for me, but he lowered them, and looked away. "Good luck to you, Mrs. Ashton."

I nodded. I wasn't going to thank anyone for wishing me well in this most humiliating display. Instead, I looked out toward the bay, reluctant to move.

"So, go," Abbie said, giving me a nudge. "We'll be here when you return."

I took a deep breath and stepped forward, straightening my back and lifting my head. Glancing back at her, I knew my expression was far from pleasing. From the way I felt, there might as well be a scaffold around the bend.

On my first days in St. Augustine, I had noticed women strolling idly on this path, not knowing their struggle. Now I was one of them—me, Mrs. Anna Ashton.

* * *

Before I had walked a third of the length to the fort, I noticed I was being watched. A young soldier looked at me with a grin, gleaming as brightly as the brass in his blue uniform, but I turned away. Tears of anger, more than grief, started to flow down my cheeks, but I forced myself to walk on.

"What's wrong, Mrs. Ashton? A soldier not good enough for you?"

I turned and glared at him, but he laughed. He was tall and red haired, undaunted by my glare, a mere boy who wouldn't have dared to shout at me a few weeks ago when Edmund was alive. Bounding forward, he boldly stepped in stride with me.

"There's no need for you to be alone, ma'am. I make enough to support a wife now, should I find the right one, and I think I have," he said, grabbing my arm and swinging me toward him.

I gasped, struggling to free myself. His mouth was so close to mine that I could smell the ale on his breath.

"Unhand me!" I shouted at him, but my words had little effect, for the boy just grinned and held tighter, drawing me to him, and laughed as I resisted with all my might.

"Now, now, I thought you'd be missing a man by now," he said, pinning his leg between my thighs as he drew me closer. "We would have a good go at it, we two."

Revolted, I struggled harder, but my most valiant efforts did nothing to deter him.

"Be gone!" a voice shouted from behind me.

I recognized Captain Sebastian Ortega's voice in an instant.

The boy's eyes widened when he turned to see who had yelled out to him. He released his grip on me and fled, leaving me there, face to face with the captain.

I lowered my eyes until I realized I was staring at the gold chains lying against the taut muscles of his bare chest showing through his open shirt. Quickly, I drew my gaze back up to his face, but he had been watching me and smiled as I cringed.

"He didn't harm you, did he?"

"No, he didn't. Thank you, Captain," I whispered.

"Think nothing of it." He stepped closer. "I am sorry for your loss, Mrs. Ashton. Your husband was a good man."

Unhindered by his absurd magnetism for once, I noticed there was a softness in his eyes that had previously escaped me.

"He didn't deserve such a death."

Ortega nodded. "Certainly not. And you, dear woman, do not deserve what has been put upon you. Grief does not make wise decisions."

I shrugged. "You don't know what it is like to be a woman. It appears we are destined to be handed from one man's keeping to the next."

The captain nodded again. "Insightful, indeed... and you are quite right. I don't know what it is like to be a woman," he added, lightening the moment. "But although I would always offer my protection, I know the Angel of the *Penny Rose* should never have her wings clipped."

I stepped back, suddenly calmer. "Shall I never be rid of that name?"

His expression became questioning and suddenly serious as he reached out and tenderly lifted my chin, studying me as if I were a newfound treasure. "You would always be an angel to me."

For a moment my eyes closed, and I remembered how good it felt to be touched. My mind escaped to Edmund, and I remembered how he sometimes cupped my face in his hands and kissed me so tenderly. I relaxed and felt the corners of my lips curl up until my eyes fluttered open. Looking into the Captain's dark eyes, I startled and pulled away as the heat rose in my cheeks. He must think me a fool.

Was I so tired and horribly alone that I let a man of such a questionable reputation lay a hand on me? That I would let this man, whose eyes could so easily pull me into a snarl, captivate me? What had I become?

"Please don't touch me," I whispered.

"Pardon me, Mrs. Ashton. I meant no disrespect. I was just taken by your beauty, so please, forgive my indiscretion." He bowed, smiling ever so slightly.

The tenderness in his eyes as he looked at me drew me in, but my mind yanked me back. However kind, brave, and incredibly attractive he was, respectable women should not be seen with a rogue like him. He was no more than a privateer, practically a pirate, or at least as lawless!

"This is no concern of yours," I said, taking a step back. "Please don't touch me!"

He bowed, and I noticed a flicker of a smile reaching his eyes.

"You are forgiven, Captain," I said, hoping that would end our conversation. "I have to go back to the inn. I can bear no more of this pitiful parade."

The captain offered me his arm. "May I escort you?"

"No! No, don't touch me again. I can manage on my own." I held my hands up in front of me and, taking a few steps backward, increased the distance between us.

He didn't move. He just stood there, watching me, but somehow that unsettled me too, and my heart leapt in my chest.

"Mrs. Ashton, you have nothing to fear," he said. "I can be quite pleasant. At least, I would try to be. I would make a great effort for a woman like you."

His grin was disarming, and for a moment I wanted to laugh at his attempt at seeming forlorn, but our surroundings brought me back to my reason for being here.

"Just let me go," I said, trying to be convincing, but we were still looking into each other's eyes as if our souls were speaking some secret language that I wanted no part of.

He bowed. "As you wish."

I gave him a curt nod back. After watching him for a second, I turned and walked toward the inn. I tried to clear my mind of him, but it seemed futile. He had been so kind, even amusing, leaving me to consider that he might be a far less perilous man than I thought.

* * *

In the distance I could see Katherine and Abbie on the porch with the towering figure of Harry Blackwood standing between them. I still felt a surge of guilt every time I saw him. *Sweet Muriel, you would be there with him, if it weren't for me.*

When I approached the porch, Harry stepped down and offered me a hand to steady me as I ascended the steps. "You didn't fare well, I gather," he said, offering me a seat.

I shook my head and sank down next to Katherine.

"You won't find a man stomping around with that haughty look on your face," Abbie said, rolling her eyes.

I stared at her, too numb to care.

"That's rude, Abbie," Katherine said.

Abbie looked up. "It's true."

"Whatever did that privateer have to say?" Katherine asked.

"Nothing at all," I said, lifting the glass of wine Harry put in front of me. Taking a sip, I looked up and noticed Abbie watching me, but she said nothing.

Harry rested his hand on my shoulder and stroked it gently. "The right man will find you. Have faith."

CHAPTER THIRTEEN

St. Augustine, September 1764

After relentless coaxing by both Abbie and Katherine, I reluctantly agreed to return to the Matanzas a week later to take that dreadful walk again. The thought of the barren stretches of land leading up to the fort brought back the humiliation of my last attempt. I thought of each step I would have to take and the madness of snaring a man that I desperately needed but truly didn't want.

"Try harder this time," Abbie murmured. "I couldn't bear it to see you sent back to England."

I shrugged. The men who approached me ignited nothing in me other than despair.

The thought of leaving St. Augustine tormented me too. The *Penny Rose* would have left Liverpool by now and was on her way back across the Atlantic. I envisioned the vessel blazing through the waves in full sail, determined to bring me to my doom. I wouldn't be given a tiny cabin like the one I shared with Edmund. Instead, I would be given a cot or a hammock below, like the one Mary died in. There would be rough seas, crude men, dirt and endless days, all without the safety of having my husband with me.

"Stop fretting. I can see it on your face, and you haven't even gotten to the Matanzas yet," Abbie said.

"I couldn't bear to marry and lie next to a groping young soldier every night," I said, standing still for her to place flowers in my hair. Anywhere else, a widow would be allowed to drape herself in black and grieve in peace. Here I was prettied up like a harlot to sell myself off to the highest bidder.

"You might come to love him."

"I will endure, if I must."

"Oh, you are grim!" Abbie stood back and looked at me, as if admiring her masterpiece. "It's time to go."

* * *

Harry Blackstone made a habit of watching me from the back porch of the inn as I took to the Widow's Walk. Every step I took irritated me, every face I looked into reminded me of my predicament, but as the days progressed I was reminded that the *Penny Rose* would soon be sailing into the Matanzas Bay.

Reluctantly, I learned to converse with the men who approached me, although with feigned politeness, since most of them bored me with their boasting and clumsy advances. Since Harry had started watching me, I was less fearful of being grabbed or taunted, but there was no remedy for the bitterness of having to put myself on parade each day.

When I was too weary to continue, I went back to the Matanzas where Harry waited for me, ready to talk over a steaming cup of tea or sometimes a glass of his best wine.

"I envy you, Harry," I told him one evening.

"How so?"

I seemed to have surprised him, for he turned to me, suddenly curious.

"No one would dare to take your home from you, or force you to marry when your heart is broken, or threaten to send you away."

He sighed. "A woman should not have to be troubled with such, Anna. A woman like you should be protected and tenderly cared for."

His face softened into a smile, and it was during moments like this that I understood how Mary could have loved him so deeply.

To my surprise, Harry took my hands in his. "Look, lass. You need a man to take care of you, and from what I see you are giving everyone the cold shoulder." He paused. "I can be your man."

"What?"

I sank back into my seat. I wasn't sure I heard him correctly, but when I looked into his dark eyes, they were lit with hope, but visions of Edmund and Mary flooded my mind, making it difficult to think.

"I see that I have startled you," Harry said. "Am I not worthy of your affections? I believe I need you, as much as I think you need me. I have not done well with my grief. Together we can live again."

I gasped. "You are as worthy as any gentleman," I said, resorting to courtesy, barely able to avoid spilling my confusion.

"I can be patient with you," he continued. "I know what your lot has become, and I know what it is to be lonely."

My heart skipped. Perhaps he understood me even more than Abbie did, for we shared so much, Harry and I, although I was hardly lonely.

Harry was brash and brusque, and often drunk, but he had always been kind to me, even if it was just for Mary's sake. With a wife at his side, there probably wouldn't be a need for the excess of drink to fill the loneliness. But could that wife be me?

"Let me be your husband, Anna." He lifted my hand to his lips, kissing it gently, his eyes drawing me to him, making me feel oddly cherished.

"You are kind," I said, hesitating, trying to take in what my life could become.

"I owe you at least that." He looked out across the bay, his eyes suddenly darkening.

I followed his gaze out to the depths where I thought he must be imagining his two red-haired loves lay. Mary's face flashed in front of me, and the memory of holding Muriel in my arms made me ache.

"So, what will it be, Anna Ashton? Will you be my wife?"

I hesitated. "I... I don't know, Harry. I didn't expect this."

I looked up at him. He looked as tired and as worn as I felt, yet there was a kindness to him. I could feel it. He wanted to take care of me, and I could stop struggling against everything that had come at me since Edmund's death and just bask in this man's good will toward me.

"Go home and think about it. I will tenderly care for you, and you will be the mistress of the Matanzas Inn. It's not so little I am offering you."

* * *

I told Abbie about Harry's proposal the following morning when we were sitting in the shade of her porch.

"The man is a beast," Abbie said, not bothering to subdue her opinion. "It's only a matter of time until you will see it. Certainly, you can find better."

I sighed. "Perhaps, but hardly one who understands my plight as Harry does."

"He is only kind because you are beautiful and widowed. He is circling like a vulture. Do you not see? He is no better than the lads you scoff at on your walks."

I stood, crossing my arms. "Harry and I have grieved together. There is an understanding between us, and I think he would be good to me."

Abbie rolled her eyes. "Don't sacrifice yourself for the sake of Muriel. She did not die by your hand, and marrying her father with not lessen his grief."

"Mary loved him, Abbie. She yearned for him. That means something."

Abbie sighed. "Yes, that she was a dim-wit."

"Now you are being grim," I said. "He may be garish at times, but to me, he is nothing but gentle and kind."

"Mercy," Abbie whispered.

* * *

The following morning, I went to see Harry.

"Have you considered my offer?" he asked as we took seats in the tavern.

There was an urgency about him that made me smile.

"I have."

He seemed breathless for a moment. "And?"

"And I accept your offer. I will be your wife," I said, trying not to make it sound like a statement of surrender, although marrying him was choosing the lesser of unbearable choices.

His eyes shot open, and he grinned. I wished I shared his enthusiasm, as he wrapped me in his arms, and we swayed, as if to music only he could hear.

"You will not regret this. I will be a good husband to you."

Seeing the smile fade from my face, he bent down and looked at me, his eyes tender. "It will be all right, Anna. We will be all right."

* * *

A week later, Harry sent his servants to collect my belongings from the doctor's residence, while I sat on the back porch with Abbie, watching as the remnants of my life with Edmund were carried off to the Matanzas Inn.

"We have faced so much, Abbie." I looked at the servants carrying out a trunk that had been in our bedroom. "I wish you could be happy for me now."

Before Abbie could answer, Mordecai stepped up on to the porch with his hat in hand.

"It's done, ma'am. The cart is full, and there's nothing left in the house. We're heading back to the inn."

I nodded. "Thank you, Mordecai. You have made this difficult task less of a burden," I said, noting the sparkle in his eyes as I praised him.

When he left, Abbie and I lingered on the porch for a while before we walked through the house one last time. I looked at the chair were Edmund used to sit by the table and locked the memory of him sitting there into my mind. At least no one could take that from me.

Just as I was about to leave, Harry came to walk me back to the inn.

"I said goodbye to the house," I said, as we walked along Bay Street.

"And in time, you'll say goodbye to Edmund." He looked down at me, and gave my hand a squeeze, as if he believed it was possible.

At the Matanzas, we dined together under the stars, feasting on lobsters brought in from the bay. We sat so close, I could feel Harry next to me, but I was unable to stop thinking about the oddity that he would become my husband. I would learn his ways, I would know his body as he would come to know mine, and together we would create our own rhythm and our own world. It doesn't seem real, but one day, it would be so.

"You seem pensive, Anna. You're not having doubts, are you?" he asked when he caught me staring out across the bay.

Seeing the concern in his eyes, I tried to smile at him. "Certainly not," I said, "certainly not."

I watched as the light reappeared in his eyes and wished I could feel something other than the sinking feeling in my stomach.

CHAPTER FOURTEEN

St. Augustine, September 1764

The day I was to marry Harry Blackwood, I woke up feeling ill.

It could have been regret, but it mattered not. The day would unfold according to plan, despite any misgivings I might have, for I had no choice but to squelch them for the sake of safety.

When the sun was low in the sky, I met Harry on the shore of the Matanzas Bay. He held my gaze as our friends parted, clearing a path for me, and I walked slowly toward my new husband in a dress of pale blue silk, but my hands clenched around a bouquet of fragrant white lilies.

I tried to return his smile while attempting to hide my sadness over the irony that the woman who had loved this man lay dead in the sea behind us, and the woman who was to stand here with him wished for a husband so recently buried nearby.

As the sun was about to set, we were pronounced man and wife. Harry took me into his arms and kissed me, bringing forth cheers and yelps from our guests, but all I could think of was that no one could put me on a ship and force me to leave East Florida.

To the delight of our guests, we danced, and the ebullient singing and drinking continued for hours. I had never seen such drunkenness as in St. Augustine. It seemed to be something prideful here, and it was apparently legendary, for compared to towns far greater and grander it was known to be the town of many taverns to indulge in.

Close to midnight, I reached for a candle and carried it upstairs with me.

Looking at myself in the mirror as I undressed, I tried on the sound of my new name. *Mrs. Blackwood, I am Mrs. Anna Blackwood*, but the gratitude I should have felt seemed beyond reach.

I loosened my hair, imagining Harry running his hands through it and pulling me to him, as I wondered how many women before me and how many after me would have to endure the trials of marriage of necessity.

Harry sat at the end of the bed when I came into the bedroom. His shirt was open, and he unbuckled his trousers as he watched me standing there in my thin night shift. His dark hair fell to his shoulders, and the intensity of his eyes made him look more looming than usual. He smirked as he stood and walked across the wood floor in bare feet. The drunken sway in his gate alarmed me, but there was something tender about the way he kissed me, surprising me with his gentleness.

"What a fine wife I've got me," he murmure as he lifted my night shift over my head, leaving me naked and exposed. "What a fine one indeed."

I blushed, no longer comforted.

He stood back and looked at me, his palm grazing my buttock as he circled around me, scrutinizing me.

Just as I was to speak up, he lifted me into his arms and carried me to bed. Willing myself to accept that being nude against Harry's unfamiliar body would be my plight, I knew that surrendering to him was necessary.

The music from downstairs wafted up to us, but it seemed like the moment stood still.

Hovering over me, he took my hand, guiding it to him, moaning as he coaxed me to stroke him.

"Don't act like it's your first time, woman," he said, squeezing my hand, moving it faster, bringing an urgency to his voice. "You're gonna be beggin' for this one, wife. Just wait."

I blushed, banishing the thought.

Suddenly, separating my legs and drawing my hips toward him, he plunged into me, releasing a groan. I braced myself as he pushed harder with each thrust.

Pinned beneath him, I tried to release the resistance in my body, as each muscle tensed in protest.

"It won't take me long, but I want some fight in you, Mrs. Blackwood!"

When his teeth dug into my skin, I cried out and grabbed his shoulders, desperate to push him away, but it only excited him further.

"Feels good to have a man again, doesn't it, Mary?" he said and collapsed, smothering me with the weight of him.

When he rolled to the side and propped himself on his elbow, I caught my breath and decided that telling him he called me Mary wouldn't be worth the words that would follow.

"You will like it someday, Anna. Mary did. Someday, you will even love me," he said, and thankfully, he turned away.

* * *

I awoke at first light and watched it sift through the half-open shutters. I was alone, unsure of when Harry had left our bedchamber, but I welcomed the reprieve.

The thought of him touching me again wasn't inviting. Shifting in bed, I pulled the quilt around me, noticing the ache in my body, surely caused by the haste of my new husband's passions. By the grace of God, it would subside by nightfall, for surely he would seek to have me again, and I would have to abide.

Mary should have been laying here in this large iron bed, not me. Mary had wanted to be here with this man, she had loved him, and from what Harry had uttered, there was something between them I could never aspire to.

Sounds from the kitchen below reminded me that the day had begun. I should perhaps make a show of myself downstairs and look the part of a contented wife. It would please Harry, and it would be what he expected of me.

I slipped out of bed, washed with soap scented with citrus and sage, and put on one of the new silk dresses Harry had ordered for me. Oddly, his taste in clothing was impeccable.

The servants looked up when I walked down the stairs and greeted me with smiles and nods. Harry's staff was a group of sixteen, all of whom I had met and knew by name. Ten of the servants who were subjected to Harry's demands any time of day lived at the Inn, while a fortunate six escaped to their families by the end of their shifts.

I smiled back at them, acknowledging their welcome, feeling more like an actress than the mistress of the Matanzas.

"Mornin', ma'am," Mordecai said.

He was as polished this morning as he had been through the festivities last night. I doubted he slept much, and he appeared to have little interest in anything beyond the Matanzas. His dark hair was neatly pulled back and his clothing freshly starched.

"Come to me if you desire anything at all, or if the staff displeases you in any manner," he continued, bowing slightly. "Harry says you should want for nothing."

"Thank you, Mordecai."

Before I could utter another word, Harry's deep voice bellowed behind me.

"My bride has awoken from her slumber!"

There was nothing subtle about my new husband. I gathered myself before I turned to see him approach me with outstretched arms, as if he had waited all morning to see me. He smiled and embraced me tenderly. "How beautiful you look this morning!"

"Thank you," I whispered, looking into his eyes, searching for something, anything to help me understand the smiling stranger whose impatient passion had overwhelmed me last night.

"Come, sweet wife of mine. There is a meal prepared for us."

Harry led me to a small table outside where hibiscus plants grew tall and the fronds from massive palms sheltered us from the early morning sun.

Jane brought us a steaming pot of tea, while Mordecai followed with boiled eggs, freshly baked bread, newly churned butter, and mango jam. I doubted that he often took upon himself to serve at a table, but I had the feeling he wanted me to be aware of the span of his reach, for he was everywhere at the Matanzas, and he was not to be displaced by me.

Our eyes met, and he smiled. *Worry yourself not, Mordecai. I am not at all certain I want to vie for any place in this establishment that I am now bound to, other than that of being a wife, sworn to obey its master.*

"What are your plans for the day?" I asked Harry when Mordecai was out of earshot.

I wasn't certain he heard me, for he busied himself buttering a wedge of bread before adding a heaping dollop of jam on it and steering it toward my mouth. Reaching an arm around me, he grinned. "Only to pleasure my new wife, Mrs. Anna Blackwood."

Taking the wedge from him, I took a small bite, hoping that pleasuring didn't mean a midday thrust, for I would barely be fit by evening.

"That does have quite the sound to it... Anna Blackwood," I said, hoping to divert his thoughts. "It will take some time to become accustomed to."

"Indeed, my wife. But we have time, God willing."

A few days later, there was a surprise.

"Captain Warrick and Thaddeus Edgefield, with their women, will be dining with us this evening," Harry said as we took our tea in the parlor. "The cooks will take care of everything; you have only to entertain our guests."

"I thought Warrick was away in the Carolinas."

"He returned this morning," Harry said. "No need to worry yourself about the captain's whereabouts from now on, Mrs. Blackwood."

"Should I not see to the menu?" I asked, pretending not to be taken aback by the warning in my husband's words.

"No, I have tended to that already. This place has been without a woman's touch for a long while. There is not much for you to do, other than see to your husband's needs." Harry took my hand and kissed it, teasing me, as he looked into my eyes.

"I shall do my best."

"That you will." He smiled, looking genuinely happy. "And soon there will be young Blackwood children for you to take care of, and soon your life with Edmund will be a faint memory. You will see."

"And, Mary, will she too be a faint memory?"

"A man's got to have a wife. I have one now. Mary is dead and gone. No use thinking about her anymore."

Stunned by his answer, I couldn't keep myself from wondering if he didn't wish I were her. I was hardly the robust woman he desired in his bed, but in his nightly drunkenness, I sometimes wondered if he even noticed who he put beneath him.

"There hasn't been any more talk about finding Edmund's killer," Harry said, startling me. "The bastard is probably long gone, a vagrant probably. A despicable human."

Avoiding his gaze, I nodded, wishing he wouldn't talk about Edmund.

"You are going to get over him," he said. "You will. I am your husband. You will know your place." It was a command that he tried to soften by giving my hand a squeeze, but I wasn't fooled.

* * *

Captain Warrick and his wife arrived with Thaddeus Edgefield and the elegant Charlotte Moultrie in the late afternoon, sending Harry's staff into a flurry to provide them with the best the inn could offer. From cider to cognac, beverages were readied, venison with squashes, gourds, and corn roasted in the ovens, and apple pies awaited their turn.

I greeted Charlotte and Sofia with a dutiful smile and accepted their demonstrative pecks on my cheeks as they swooshed by me, already bracing myself for an evening of their mindless chatter.

Thaddeus Edgefield greeted Harry and bowed to me, avoiding my gaze. I watched as he made an effort to put as much distance between us as possible, without drawing attention to it. A wise move, for the tension between us strung us together like an invisible cord I longed to snip. Hopefully, Harry wouldn't notice, but I wondered what excuse would make any sense at all, if I needed one.

Harry seemed pleased to see the captain and greeted him with a handshake and a pat on the arm.

"So, Harry, you've got a lady to keep you in line now, old scoundrel!" the captain chided.

Harry laughed heartily. "That's too much to ask of any woman,"

They both chuckled, as if they were privy to some knowledge only men were handed.

When the captain turned to me, he reached for my hand and held it for a moment before he brought it to his lips and kissed it. Little wonder that anyone in his presence felt as if they were the only person of interest to him.

"It is a pleasure to see you again, Mrs. Blackwood," he said. "The thought of your suffering since we last met grieves me, but I trust old Harry will be a good husband to you."

"Thank you, Captain," I said. "I believe we will be very happy."

I sat down on the chair Harry pulled out for me, watching in wonder as the two sisters unleashed their charms on their men.

Mordecai brought us the finest wine, and the servants hurried after with trays of canapés, fashioned after those made by the governor's own French chefs.

"Your selections are exquisite, Anna," Charlotte gushed, filling her mouth with a hearty chunk of spiced salmon.

Harry answered before I could find the words. "My bride has had other matters to tend to," he said, beaming with unconcealed pride. "Her talents would be wasted in the kitchen."

I felt my cheeks turn crimson, and I noticed Charlotte raise a brow while a quick glance passed between the sisters.

"From what I have heard, our Mrs. Blackwood has the skill of an apothecary," the captain said, turning to me. "Most unusual for a woman." The praise in his tone was surprisingly comforting.

"My father is an apothecary," I said, grateful for the turn of the conversation. "It seems his tutelage prepared me well."

"Indeed, a most advantageous skill," Harry said. "The woman knows what soothes my sorry soul! Let us drink to my beautiful bride, for I am a contented man on this day."

Harry's voice slurred, and I wondered how much he had already had to drink, but as the glasses clinked around me and emptied, they were quickly refilled.

After a meal intended to impress, I sat back and glanced out across the sea, pretending not to notice the captain's eyes darting back to me, nor Thaddeus Edgefield's carefully concealed contempt, nor the sisters' insincere fawning over the bride of Harry Blackwood. This was my life now, and I had been dealt a role to play, along with a name that rung odd in my ears. Harry, to whom I would be a companion in life, sat at my side, towering, like a wall I had shackled myself to.

* * *

"I would go mad without the two of you," I said, sinking down on the bench next to Katherine and Abbie on Katherine's back porch. "It's been a month since we married, and Harry has been drinking every day, claiming he's still celebrating our joyous event. I don't know what to do!"

Abbie scoffed, and Katherine hardly looked surprised.

"Let him drink. He will do away with himself faster," Abbie said. "Or, offer him a swig of Nightshade or Devil's Snare." She grinned, but Katherine rolled her eyes.

"So that is his latest excuse. Thank God for Mordecai, or the inn would be in ruins," Katherine said. "It takes more than a drunkard to run an establishment as prosperous as the inn."

"I don't think he has always been this prone to drink," I said. It seemed to me that it was grief that drove him to ease his pain by whatever means he could.

"Wrong, wrong, wrong, Anna Blackwood. Your husband has been drinking from the day he came to St. Augustine, don't be fooled." Abbie turned to Katherine, suddenly serious. "And you are wrong about Mordecai. There is a troublesome current running through that man."

"Mordecai seems harmless," I said. "And Harry has a firm hand on the workings of the inn, drunken or not."

Abbie looked far from convinced. "Just watch him, Anna. You will see what I mean."

"Yet another man to be vigilant of? I don't know if I could bear it," I said, trying to make light of it, not quite able to expel the doubt that crept into my mind. Abbie had a way about her, and what she said was not to be scoffed at.

I threw my head back and raked my hands through my hair, leaving my forearms exposed as my sleeves slipped upward, immediately regretting my carelessness.

"Anna, what is this?" Katherine pushed my sleeve further up, revealing bruises on my arms.

"Harry has urgent desires, with little thought to his own strength."

I blushed, wishing I had worn longer sleeves.

"If you don't shy away from him, maybe he won't hurt you so," Katherine said. "Have you asked him to be gentler with you?"

Abbie snuffed and looked out the window, taking a long puff from her pipe.

"There's no taming that beast, Katherine," I said. "I do stand up to him, although by nightfall he is too drunk to reason with."

CHAPTER FIFTEEN

St. Augustine, October 1764

On the third Thursday in October, St. Augustine suffered such oppressive heat that it was the talk of every visitor who came to the Inn.

Guests retired to their rooms early, leaving Harry and Mordecai to drink undisturbed. I escaped to my balcony, my husband's drunkenness heavy on my mind. It was something I had to prepare myself for every night, never knowing what state he would be in or how I would fare.

I took a deep breath, savoring the salt sea air, and my body relaxed against my cushioned rocking chair. I had almost drifted off into my dreams when I heard Harry's heavy feet on the creaking staircase.

I had barely a chance to turn before he reached out for me, pulling me to him by a lock of my hair. There was nothing in his eyes but the wildness that could come about him when he was like this.

Pulling his thumb, I yanked my hair from his grasp. It startled him, and for a moment he staggered, but then his mouth was on mine, wet and putrid from drink.

I pressed into the wall behind me, awaiting a chance to flee, but he grabbed my chin and forced me to look at him.

"Fight, woman. Let me see fire in you," he said. "I don't want you quivering under me like a dying fish."

Flinging me on to the bed, he hurled himself over me, but before I could stop myself, I kicked with all my might.

Harry groaned and doubled over. Clutching his groin, his face turned crimson and the veins on his forehead bulged ominously.

"Not like that!" he sneered, glaring at me.

"I didn't mean to, Harry. Forgive me," I said, hating my words, but they were all that could save me.

Harry got up, shooting me a hateful look, but then he rambled into the adjacent room where he often sat with his papers at day's end.

I heard him move something, and then there was a creaking sound, as if a cabinet was being opened. Seizing my chance, I ran to the door. Harry had locked it! He often did, but this time he must have stuffed the key into his pocket. Despondent, I tiptoed back to the bed, pulled the quilt around me, and listened.

"Damned woman, that damned woman!" he muttered, as he moved something about, but I couldn't tell what.

It sounded as if he was stacking a pile of books, but how many books did he have? He wasn't one to read.

I was unable to make sense of it, until I heard a crisp clang of glass. I tensed and listened for the sound as it rung out again, followed by the thud of a bottle slamming down on the table.

I heard the sound of the cabinet door shutting, a chair moved with a scrape against the floor, and suddenly his footsteps drew nearer. Quickly I lay down, cursing how well I knew the charade of pretending to be asleep. I tried to steady my breath as I felt him sit down next to me. There was no means to calm my pounding heart, echoing through my ears. I startled as Harry gently put a hand on my head and ran his fingers through my hair.

"My angel," he whispered. "Why do I treat you so badly? You have been nothing but kind to me."

I opened my eyes, looking into his face before I pulled myself up. I was cautious not to disrupt his sudden change in mood, but it seemed that the evil had left him, for now.

"Harry—" I started to speak, but he put a finger over my lips.

"Hush," he said. "Go back to sleep. I will leave you alone."

I slid down under the quilt, watching as he walked away, closing the door behind him. I waited until I could hear he was outside, and his footsteps trailed off in the distance.

When the house was still, I tiptoed out of bed and into Harry's sitting room. The small cabinet against the wall creaked when I opened it. There was no bottle in sight, only a book of verse, a few blue ledgers, and a Bible. I doubted that Harry ever read the Bible, but still, I lifted it out and found a stash of half-empty bottles.

Astounded, I stared at them for a moment. There was something familiar about them, but then there is not much variation to bottles. With trembling fingers, I lifted out the largest one. When I heard the clear clunk of glass within it, I startled. I knew the Elixir of Opium as soon as I opened the bottle and the vapors tickled my nostrils. I had blended this tonic back in England, adding a pinch of cinnamon and cloves to flavor the ghastly brew. No one else did that.

Willing myself to peek into the bottle, I already dreaded what I would find.

My heart sank, and I felt as if every drop of blood drained out of me. There. Edmund's glass rod.

My fingers shook as I pulled it out. The etchings Edmund had made on it were there. I choked a sob as I put the rod back into the bottle and tucked it back into the cabinet, shielding it behind the Bible, before closing the door tightly. Shaking, I sank into Harry's chair, struggling to think clearly.

The bottles Edmund had taken to the infirmary must have been stolen the night he was killed. There were only two other rods unaccounted for, and I had them. They were in Edmund's medical bag, which I kept in my trunk. Had Harry taken one of them? Was this one of the bottles from Edmund's bag, or was this from the infirmary?

I scrambled to my feet and rushed back into the bedroom, where I tore the trunk open. Under layers of blankets and clothing, Edmund's medical bag looked untouched. I opened it and pulled out two bottles, Tincture of Opium and Tincture of Infinitium, both almost full.

My fingers felt cold as they closed around the Tincture of Opium. I could hear the sound of glass hitting the bottle as my shaking hands rattled it. The rod was safely lodged in the other bottle as well.

If I had the only rods that weren't at the infirmary, why did Harry have the other? Was Harry the one who robbed the infirmary, or did he know something about it? He couldn't have killed Edmund, could he? I felt the chill of every hair on my body rising, and my stomach suddenly squeezed into knots.

Could Harry have killed Edmund and then married his widow? *Am I married to Edmund's murderer? Am I?*

Suddenly shaking, I steeled myself to remain calm as the answers to my questions became clear. The elixirs, carelessly ingested with rum, could have brought out the madness in him. He must have been in that unpredictable state when Edmund came across him in the infirmary, and certainly Edmund would have tried to stop him, but had Harry ended Edmund's life for the wretched lure of opium?

I froze, trembling in the heat of the balmy night. *Edmund, forgive me.* I stood up and walked out to the balcony in a daze, sinking down into my rocking chair, and let the tears come, sobbing until I was limp with exhaustion and fell into a dreamless sleep, covered only by the night sky.

* * *

When I awoke, I was in Harry's arms. I felt him lay me down on the soft coverings of our bed, and for a moment I indulged in its comfort, until my eyes flew open and the sight of him brought me back to the night before.

I bolted up.

"Whoa, wife of mine!" he said. "I'd think you were glad I took a spin out, considering the foul mood I was in."

He reached for me, smiling his disarming day-time smile, but I pushed back with both hands and leapt out of bed. I would not be lured, not this time, not ever again.

"You have to tell me the truth, Harry! You have to!" I hissed at him.

"Anna, a man has the right to go out as he pleases," he said, looking at me with a bit of amusement. "I will not be hen-whipped by a wife of mine."

I glared up at him, not caring what he would think. "It's not that. I don't care where you go. And I don't care if you come back!"

I ran into the sitting room, hearing his footsteps behind me.

Tearing open the cabinet, I pulled out the Bible. Holding it over me like a shield as our eyes met for a brief second, I could see that he was starting to grasp the reason for my fury.

"Wait," Harry said. "Don't!"

My hand and his reached for the bottle at the same time, but mine was faster. I dropped the bible and ripped off the top, glaring at him with the bottle in one hand and pulling out the rod with the other. He looked dumbfounded.

I took a step toward him, certain that my face reflected every bit of my rage. "Explain this to me, Harry. Explain it!"

The color in Harry's face darkened to a feverish hue, and his thick brows came together over eyes that showed no mercy. His jaw tightened and his fists clenched, but I didn't care. It didn't matter. It wouldn't matter if he tore me to shreds.

"What is this, Harry? Tell me!"

The challenge in my voice irritated him. I could see it in the way he looked at me. He lunged forward and pulled the rod from my hand, grasping my wrist so hard that the bottle dropped and shattered. With his hand still locked around my wrist, he flung the rod against the fireplace. I watched it shatter.

I gasped.

My proof was gone, lying in shards on the floor, and it was my fault. I had let my emotions erupt without restraint. I had practically destroyed the rod myself.

He let go, and I stumbled. My wrist throbbed, and his grip had rubbed my skin raw.

Too angry to cry, I flung myself at him, pounding my fists against Harry's torso, not caring that my wrists burned with every stroke. Fighting with the strength I had left, I punched wildly, wanting to hurt him as badly as he had hurt me.

Unscathed, he flicked me off him and flung me against the wall, striking me across the face so hard that my neck snapped backward, sending an agonizing jolt of pain trough me.

"No woman raises a hand to me!" he said in a voice that thundered over me.

Unable to fight back, I covered my face with my hands as he lifted me up and flung me onto the broken glass on the floor.

The shards cut into my skin, but I refused to move.

"The rod is gone," he said, hovering over me. "One word about this and I will kill you, like I killed him."

I froze. Hearing him say the words I had barely dared to think felt like a punch to my gut. My teeth chattered as Harry came toward me and pulled me to my feet. Pushing me against the wall, he grabbed my chin, forcing it upward.

"Look at me, woman!"

I stared up through a veil of tears, wanting to spit at him. Wanting to kill him.

"Do you understand?" His voice was barely a hiss.

I nodded. I understood everything. He stood back, looking at me, as if he didn't know what to do with me. I watched him pace for long agonizing moments.

Finally, he stopped, suddenly calmer. "So, we understand each other."

I suppressed a laugh, quickly reining in what could have been a descent into hysteria, but I nodded, knowing he misread my silence.

He looked almost relieved. "I will take care of you. You are my wife. I owe you that. I owe you something..." His words trailed off, and I saw he was searching my face for a trace of acceptance, but I stood defiant, blank, and vacant, not caring that it frustrated him.

"I'm sorry about Edmund. It couldn't be helped," he said. "He stood in the way of the potions; the only thing that made my sorry life livable. He got in my way!"

My brows rose as I met his gaze, but I bit my lips together and said nothing.

He let out a deep sigh. "There is nothing either of us can do about it now."

I stood silent in front my husband, Edmund's killer, who was free to continue living while Edmund lay dead in his grave, and the only evidence had been shattered. Harry was free to take another breath, and another after that.

I felt as if my mind would burst through my skull, but I stood silent, biding my time, gathering my wits.

"Forgive me, Anna," Harry said, searching my face. "So, perhaps not quite yet. But you will silence your tongue, and remember that you are my wife, Anna Blackwood. I will have no trouble from you. Understand?"

I nodded and watched as he turned and left the room, leaving me there, still trembling. I carefully pulled the fabric of my gown from my back, prying loose the glass fragments I could reach, and undressed.

"God, have mercy," I whispered, seeing my reflection in the mirror. Droplets of blood sprung from wounds scattered across patches of skin, still discolored from Harry's hard-handed handling of me the week before. There was still glass in some of the wounds, but I couldn't reach it.

Glass was a minor grievance, considering that I was married to Edmund's murderer.

Yet, if I weren't, would I ever have known that Harry was the killer? But now that I knew, I was doomed to carry his secret, for no court would take a wife's word against her husband, and he would surely kill me if I tried.

Resolutely, I dressed and tiptoed downstairs. Slipping out the back door unseen, I was glad not to run into Harry, Mordecai, or any of the staff. It could be a while before anyone would seek me out.

* * *

Abbie's smile faded as soon as she looked into my eyes. "Something is wrong." She sprung to her feet as soon as I came through her garden gate. "What is it?"

I had been so ready to tell her my horrible story, but now the words were stuck in my throat.

Abbie waited, her huge dark eyes fixed on me as she stroked my hair. "Let it out," she said, seeing my struggle. "What has he done?"

"I know who killed Edmund." I said.

For once, Abbie was at a loss for words too, and we spent most of the afternoon in shared outrage, during which Abbie spent what seemed like hours picking glass out of the wounds across my back. When she was satisfied that every shard of glass was out, she washed my back with boiled water and vinegar and covered my wounds with honey and soft cloth.

"The wounds will heal," Abbie said, holding up my gown to help me into it. "I'm not so sure about what remains of you."

I stood and let her drape it over me. "I wish I had listened to you, Abbie. I shouldn't have married Harry," I said as she tied my laces. "I am in a trap now."

Abbie's eyes were as dark as tar pits when she turned to me. "You need time to think. If you leave him, you could be back on the *Penny Rose* within the week, and from the looks of you, you wouldn't survive the month. But if you let this destroy you, he wins. So, keep standing, my friend. Keep standing, until you see your path clearly."

"How would I fare without you, Abbie?" I whispered, "You are a true sister to me."

"And you to me, sweet woman, but we are an unlikely pair in this dismal town, you with your fair looks and English ways, and me!"

* * *

I left Abbie's cottage, lost in my own rambling thoughts.

As I turned the corner toward the bay, my attention shifted to a commotion in front of the Inn. I was still at quite a distance, but I could clearly see Dr. Catherwood step out of a carriage and rush into the Matanzas with Jane running in behind him. Several of the locals had gathered outside too, something that wasn't particularly unusual, but with Dr. Catherwood making a house call, it piqued my curiosity.

When Ernest Brooks, one of Harry's young houseboys, saw me in the distance, he ran toward me, stumbling to a halt on the sandy street.

"Mrs. Blackwood, make haste! Mr. Blackwood has fallen down the front staircase, and he is not faring well!" His dark curls were matted against his forehead, and his face was flushed as he heaved for breath. The boy had a wheeze and knew not to run unless there was a matter of great urgency.

For a moment, I stood dumbstruck.

"How did this happen?" I asked. "Is he speaking?"

Ernest tried to catch his breath. "Ma'am, he looks dead to me. But I'm a boy, how am I to know? He certainly hasn't said anything." He paused, his lip trembling. "Doctor Catherwood has just arrived."

I felt myself frozen in place.

Harry could be dead. I squelched the unchristian burst of relief, for his demise could unleash another avalanche of problems. I could be given another sixty-day notice and be thrust back out on the Widow's Walk in a race for time where the prize was another hasty wedding before I could be hauled back aboard the *Penny Rose.*

"Are you certain, Ernest?" I asked.

The boy looked as shaken as I felt. "His eyes were starin' up like saucers, and he wasn't breathing, ma'am."

Ernest looked away, and I noticed he had become pale, looking like he was about to spew up his last meal.

"Good God," I whispered.

We were both breathless by the time we reached the inn. As I hesitated by the door, Ernest slipped away, and I braced myself for what lay ahead.

The foyer was crowded with Harry's staff and curious guests, but they parted when they saw me and allowed me a path to the foot of the staircase where Harry lay. I sank to my knees next to him just as Dr. Catherwood placed two fingers over Harry's eyelids, closing his brown eyes for the last time.

My jaw must have dropped, for I realized my mouth was open as I looked from Harry to the doctor, then to the sea of faces hovering over us. My hands lay limp in my lap, as if I couldn't move them, and a profound weariness came over me, draining me of the strength to pull myself up or to speak.

"I am sorry for your loss, Mrs. Blackwood," Doctor Catherwood said, looking at me with practiced empathy. "May it comfort you to know that Harry is in the arms of the good Lord as we speak."

I stared at him blankly. He must have thought I was stunned into silence, but oddly, I felt nothing at all. Harry was dead. I knew that the moment I saw him. I didn't feel anything, not sadness, not fear, not joy, not relief. I felt nothing.

CHAPTER SIXTEEN

St. Augustine, October 1764

A knock on the door roused me from a dreamless sleep.

"Mrs. Blackwood?" Jane's voice filtered in from the hallway. "Mistress Birdsong is here for you."

I sat up and rubbed my eyes. "Let her in," I said, waiting for the door to open.

Abbie entered, and Jane followed with a tray with steaming hot tea and biscuits, instantly filling me with gratitude.

"The widow awakens," Abbie said, handing me a cup. "It's midday. Rise, woman!"

"You are without mercy!" I moaned. "I've slept poorly."

She sank down on the bed next to me as Jane discretely slipped out the door, closing it behind her.

"I think your staff was relieved to see me," Abbie whispered. "They are so distraught they don't know what to do, and they have been wary of awakening you."

"Surely Mordecai is downstairs, isn't he?" I couldn't imagine Mordecai wouldn't grab the reins as quickly as he could get his hands on them.

She rolled her eyes and toyed with the layers of beads around her neck. "Yes, there's him."

Apparently, her dislike for Mordecai hadn't changed as of late, but there were other things of greater importance this morning. There was the burial to plan, unless Mordecai had already seen to that too.

"What do I do now, Abbie?" I asked.

Abbie took a sip of tea and looked at me over the rim of her cup. "You bury him. That's what you do." She put the cup down and turned toward me, studying me. "How do you feel?"

"Stunned, but that's not what I meant. I can't marry again. I'd rather die than to suffer at the hands of another man I barely know."

A subtle smile crossed Abbie's face. "There will be no such thing, Mistress Inn-Keeper. You're woman of means, so you are free!"

I felt a jolt in my chest as my heart must have leapt over several beats.

"That hadn't crossed my mind," I said, gasping. "If you are right about being free, it will be the first time in my life that I can choose my own path."

A wave of excitement started to stir inside me, but I suppressed it. I had to make certain, for I could bear no more surprises of the kind I had been given as of late.

"So, would you know how to run an inn?" Abbie asked.

"No, but how different can it be from an apothecary shop? I will do it, if I must."

"You must,» she said. "But there will be those who expect you to fail and will be ready to steal it away from you, so beware."

"If running the inn will keep me off the Widow's Walk, I won't fail," I said and hoped that God himself heard me.

Slipping out of bed, I went to the balcony to draw in the sea air and calm my nerves, which for once were piqued by anticipation and not dread. Somehow, I would have to find a way to master the task at hand.

I looked down to the street below where merchants brought their wares in from the docks and delivery boys scurried down Bay Street with packages tucked under their arms. From my balcony, the world seemed as it was every day, but from now on my life would be my own.

Three men making their way toward the docks caught my eye as I looked out toward the bay. I recognized Captain Ortega in an instant by his swagger, while the other two who scrambled along trying to keep up with him were sorely un-noteworthy.

Before they could take note of me, I stepped back inside and noticed Edmund's medicine bag on top of my trunk next to the armoire.

"What's this?" I asked, pointing at the bag. I was certain I'd put it back in my trunk last night. "Did you take it out, Abbie?"

"No, why would I?" Abbie stretched luxuriously on my duvet and barely glanced at the bag. "There is little to entice me out of this bed at the moment."

I ignored her and leaned over, reaching into Edmund's bag. My jaw dropped. "Abbie…"

She sat up, suddenly attentive. "What is it?"

My hand shook as I lifted the bottle of Elixir of Infinitium. It had been full the day before and now it was half empty. *Oh, God.* Harry must have taken a hearty swig of the elixir and that had caused him to fall. He could have been dead even before hitting the floor of the lobby. I uncorked the bottle and looked inside.

"What are you doing?" There was alarm in Abbie's voice. "You are not—"

"This was full yesterday. I think Harry—"

Abbie's eyes widened. "If he did, he had it coming to him."

"Should I tell someone? The doctor?" I asked, putting the bottle back into the bag and slipping the bag back into the trunk.

"No," Abbie said, without hesitating. "It wouldn't make any difference. He's already dead, and by his own hand. Let it be."

* * *

Harry Blackwood's funeral was attended by most of the townsfolk. He had been a colorful and towering presence in St. Augustine, and as brash and bold as he often was, he was also seen as a gentle soul who had not hesitated to lend a hand when needed.

Sitting there, I wondered what they would think if they knew the truly dark side of this man they mourned, the man who killed Edmund and lured me into his lair. Whether it was due to guilt or an odd sense of compassion, I'll never know, but regardless, nothing could redeem him..

When the sermon had droned to an end, I walked behind the casket in a daze. The heat was sweltering, and I was thirsty. Gentle eyes greeted me as I walked toward the gravesite where Father Martin led the procession that had gathered to bid Harry farewell.

There were many graves in the little churchyard. Too many for a town of only three hundred counted inhabitants, although there were many more, considering the free Negroes living at Fort Mose and Natives who camped nearby. They spent most of their time at the market or near the harbor, trading wares and sharing stories. No one ever counted them, but they were surely part of the town.

I walked on, looking down at the hem of my dress, avoiding the sympathetic glances of those who genuinely mourned.

They think I am numb with grief, not sick to my stomach and secretly relieved that I am free of him. I trusted Harry. We grieved together, and I put my life in his hands by marrying him, the same hands that killed Edmund. I felt suddenly faint, but strong arms reached for me as I started to sink.

"Let me steady you, Mrs. Blackwood."

That voice. I knew that voice. It was unmistakable. I hadn't seen Sebastian Ortega in the crowd of townspeople, and I hadn't thought to look.

"Thank you, Captain," I whispered. "You are most kind."

I took a deep breath and tried to steady myself, as his grip on my waist tightened. I caught a glimpse of Abbie looking at us, concealing a hint of a smile as she walked on next to Katherine and the schoolmaster.

By the time we reached Harry's grave, I was grateful for an arm to lean on, although even a funeral couldn't dim my attraction to this man.

My husband's final resting place was a gaping hole in the ground that gave me chills to see. Edmund's grave was only feet away, and the sudden thought of standing between my two husbands' graves, the murderer and the victim, made my knees falter.

Sebastian unknowingly followed my gaze and held me as I regained my stance.

"Lean on me," he said. "If you fall, my arms will catch you."

* * *

After the funeral, Abbie waited for me in my bedroom with lemonade and a basin of lavender water. She had laid the most modest of my dresses across the bed.

"One more hurdle awaiting," she said, handing me a glass. "How are you feeling?"

"It matters not," I whispered. "This chapter is over, and another is about to begin."

"Not yet. Rest for a moment, then let me help you into the gray dress so you can go downstairs. Tomorrow will be another day."

Mordecai had a banquette waiting for the mourners. I would have to greet the friends and neighbors who had loved Harry. I would mingle among them for one hour, for more I could not bear.

* * *

Early the next morning, I slipped out unnoticed and walked to the imposing Government Building on the south west corner of the square. I found what I was searching for on the first floor. Looking at the small sign dangling above the door to the clerk's office, I prepared myself for what was to come before I entered and tapped on the counter.

"Mr. Blumford?"

The startled man nearly toppled his chair at the sight of me.

"You saved me a trip to the inn," he said, looking up at me. "How are you faring, Mrs. Blackwood? It is a shame we have lost our Harry. He was a fine man."

I winced. "I came to ensure that I am not in danger of being hauled back to England, as I was when Mr. Ashton died."

Mr. Blumford rubbed his eyes with meaty little fists and scratched the bald spot on top of his head. "No, I would think not. You have adequate support with the inn, I imagine, and even if you sell the place, you would be a woman of independent means."

I stifled a sigh of relief. "Very well, then. That is all I needed to know. Thank you, Mr. Blumford."

I bade my farewell and stepped out into the morning sun. A woman of means. I am a woman alone in a restless town with fierce storms and an inn frequented by fine people with plans of settling the area, but also by many unsavory, women-hungry characters. For a moment, I felt frozen with doubt. *I am truly alone, but at least I am free.*

When I came to the inn, I looked at it as if it were for the first time. Harry had recently had it painted. The roof was sound and the garden lush. There was little that needed repair at the moment.

I went straight to my room and slipped out of my gray gown, choosing the lightest and the least confining of my gowns and tied an apron around my waist. I might as well get to work. My new life was waiting for me, and I should not allow the staff to make new habits without their mistress in the house.

CHAPTER SEVENTEEN

———

St. Augustine, November 1764

I spotted the two soldiers when they entered the Inn. Dressed in their red jackets and white breeches, they stood out among the other guests. As they looked across the room, I noticed that one nudged the other when he caught sight of me.

"Good morning, gentlemen," I said, walking toward them. "Could we get you a cup of tea?"

"Afraid not, ma'am." The taller one shifted, looking uncomfortable as he spoke. "Lieutenant Governor Moultrie has sent us to escort you to the Government Building. It is urgent that he speak with you."

I cocked my head. "Whatever for?"

The formality of being summoned sent a jolt through me. Paul Moultrie had stopped by the inn many times and could have spoken to me over a cool drink at any time.

"We have merely been told to fetch you, ma'am."

* * *

The Lieutenant Governor's office was sweltering compared to the inn with the breeze coming in from the bay. I wondered how he could bear the heat in his tightfitting topcoat and silk cravat.

"Sit down, Mrs. Blackwood. Do you know why you are here?"

I took a seat as Paul Moultrie sauntered toward me, hovering too close for my liking.

"I don't, sir. Certainly, I have not witnessed anything to report."

Moultrie cleared his throat. "Your late husband, Edmund Ashton… We believe we have found his killer."

So, it was that.

"What does it matter now?" I asked.

"What does it matter?" Moultrie seemed stunned by my response. "A man is dead, viciously murdered by a despicable person with an evil heart, and his loving wife says ‹what does it matter?›"

"Harry Blackwood has already died," I said.

Moultrie stood back. "Indeed, I was getting to that. You have suffered the loss of two fine husbands in a short time, Mrs. Blackwood, and now you have been left the Mantanzas."

"Yes, I understand I will not be sent back to England now that I can provide for myself. Is that what this is about?"

He appeared to have little interest in my question. "Mrs. Blackwood, we believe we know who killed Mr. Ashton."

"I know who killed him," I said.

He threw his head back and chuckled. "I know you do."

When he turned to me, he was no longer laughing.

"When he found that I had discovered that he was the one who killed Edmund, he destroyed the only proof I had," I said. "I knew that no one would believe me, and as his wife, I wouldn't be allowed to testify."

Paul Moultrie's brows rose. "Whatever do you mean, Mrs. Blackwood?"

"Harry Blackwood killed Edmund Ashton," I said, hoping to end this horrid exchange.

Paul Moultrie looked down at me. "It has come to me that you are the one who had them both killed."

I shot up. "No, that is false! You have gone mad, Paul!"

He took no notice. "Or, you killed Edmund Ashton in the heat of passion and married Blackwood to inherit a means of support. Quite simple."

I gasped. "Not so!"

Moultrie scratched his head. "So, how do you claim to know that Mr. Blackwood killed Mr. Ashton?"

Moultrie paced while I spoke, glancing at me from time to time as I told him about the rods and how I had found the missing one in the cabinet, and how Harry had destroyed it and later caused his own death.

When I finished, he gestured to someone behind me. Two guards strode into the room and stopped in unison, their fists clenched as they waited.

Paul Moultrie looked at me for a long time. "Seize her and lock her up. She is to be charged with the violent murder of her husband Mr. Edmund Ashton, and then the intentional poisoning of her husband, Mr. Harry Blackwood, causing him to falter and fall to his death in order for her to take charge of all his worldly possessions. An evil woman with an angel's face! The worst kind!"

I gasped, as the two men grabbed me by the arms. "No!" I screamed, with all my might. "Paul! I am innocent! I beg you, let me go! What has befallen you?"

Paul Moultrie leaned against his desk with his arms crossed over his chest, smirking as the two guards pulled me away.

Seeing the jail filled me with dread. A place where thieves awaited their trials and brawling men were brought to come to their senses, it was no place for a woman.

Bearded faces peered out at me from between the bars on the windows as I was brought through the gates and in through the large wooden door. The stench of human misery permeated the hallways. The air was heavy, and the heat even more oppressive as they led me farther down the hall.

When they stopped in front of an open cell, my knees threatened to buckle, but the two stone-faced guards held me up.

The cell walls were of coquina, with only a narrow wooden bench along one wall and a tiny window so high up that I would have to stand on my toes to look outside. The cell Abbie had been in was nearby.

The taller of the guards pushed me into the cell, and the other shut the iron-barred door behind me. Walking away, neither looked back.

As their footsteps faded, fear spread through my body inch by inch, but it brought me a surge of clarity.

"Guards!" I shouted, grabbing the bars. "I must see Abbie Birdsong! Guards!"

"No visitors today, ma'am," a voice shouted back.

I heard a chuckle from a cell nearby, and a man's voice came through to me.

"Ya might as well settle in, Mrs. Blackwood. This's nothin' you've seen the likes of."

I tried to peer over to the cell beside me but was unable to see anyone at all.

"Who are you? How do you know me?" I asked.

"Everyone knows ya, Mrs. Blackwood. I saw ya walk past me. The name is Charlie McGuire. I worked for Harry a while back. Got myself in a brawl and ended up here for a fortnight. They tend to forget about ya, once you're here."

I sighed and sank back down on the wooden bench, looking out on the sky through the small window. I lay like that until the stars came out and the sun rose the next day.

* * *

Awakening to my first morning in the jailhouse, I heard Abbie's voice in the hallway as the sound of her footsteps came closer. The oddity of our reversed fates struck me for a moment, the madness in it, jarring. Still, I was grateful to hear her approach, for surely this had been another one of those nights that I could add to the growing list of the worst nights of my life. Knowing I was innocent of the charges against me gave me little comfort. Those who had put me here were hardly rule keepers, nor could I rely on a kindness they were not known to possess.

"This is unjust, Anna. What wretched mind would think to place you here?" Abbie said, reaching for me through the iron bars.

"I'm being accused of the murder of both my husbands," I whispered, trying to elude my neighboring jail mates."I don't understand why anyone would think to blame me."

My lips quivered as I clasped my fingers around Abbie's forearms, feeling for a moment that she alone could keep me standing.

"As long as Moultrie is left in charge, anything can happen," Abbie said.

"Does Mordecai know you are here?"

"He does," Mordecai said, joining Abbie in the doorway. "I hear it is a mess you have gotten yourself into, ma'am."

"Whatever the mess. I have to get out!" I looked from one to the other. "I don't want to die like this. I can't bear to think of a noose about my neck."

Abbie and Mordecai glanced at each other, heightening my worry.

"Thaddeus left with Warrick last night, so neither knows anything of this. They would speak up on your behalf," Abbie said, "but since they are not here, I will speak to Moultrie myself and remind him that Thaddeus released me when I was accused of Edmund's murder, and there was no woman in the brawl we heard."

"Moultrie has left for New Smyrna with the Admiral this morning," Mordecai said. "They won't be back until the governor returns in a fortnight. No one can free you without the consent of a Royal Council member."

I felt the color drain from my face, feeling suddenly nauseated. "I can't breathe here. I'll die before they decide my fate. There won't be any need to hang me."

Abbie shifted as if my words had jarred her. "Gather your wits, Anna. I will bring you all that I can to lessen your discomfort, and as soon as Thaddeus returns I will have him plead your case."

Mordecai glanced at Abbie, his brow rising, before he turned to me. "And I will take hand of the inn, so worry yourself not over that." Mordecai attempted a smile.

Certainly, you will, and glad to be free of me.

"Thank you," I said, in spite of myself.

* * *

Days passed a minute at the time, but I struggled to stay hopeful. I refused to listen to the crude bantering of the other prisoners, who saw no need to curb their speech in front of a woman, now that I was one of them.

Abbie brought me clean clothing, my journal, ink well and quill, and an abundance of food I could barely look at, much less eat. I pushed most of it out through the bars of my cell toward the other prisoners who lassoed it in using the empty sleeves of their shirts as loops. At least it kept the rodents from feasting near me during the night, and by filling their bellies, the men tormented me less with their obscenities.

"Is there any news of my trial?" I asked after long weeks had passed. "The governor and Moultrie must be back by now."

The guard's name was Casper, and I knew him from the inn. Now he barely looked at me. "Not a word, ma'am.."

"But it's been three weeks, at least," I said.

Had it been? Oh, God, I barely knew what day it was. If it weren't for Abbie, I would go mad. Katherine hadn't the nerve to set foot in the jail, but she sent greetings and trinkets to comfort me.

"It's gonna be a lot longer, Mrs. Blackwood. Settle yourself down."

His words stung, but I had to hope.

"And Captain Warrick? Have you news of his whereabouts?"

Casper sorted through his keys on a massive iron ring and shook his head. "Last I heard, he was headed to Virginia on request of the Governor. There is unrest after the Stamp Act was enforced, and there's mutterings of rebellion."

I sighed and sank down on the bench as he made his way down the corridor to the clunking of his keys.

By late afternoon, the heat was oppressive. With the sun glaring in through my window, my only shelter was the stone corner already heated by the relentless rays of the sun.

"Storm's a comin'," one of the prisoners said.

"Yep, I feel it too," another answered. "Lord, have mercy on our souls."

I reached up on the tip of my toes and peered out through the window. The sky had not darkened with the thick gray clouds heralding the afternoon thunderstorms I had grown accustomed to.

"There's not a cloud in the sky," I shouted out to the men.

"Don't matter." The voice came from the cell next to me. Zachary Mulligan. I recognized his voice from the inn and cringed.

I stretched up to the window and peeked out again, puzzled. There was an odd calm, not a bird in the sky and not even a rustle in the palm trees.

As the day faded into night, the heat made me feel limp and listless. I lay down and fanned myself until I realized that the wind was picking up and a thunderstorm was rolling in, faster than usual.

"Here it comes!" a prisoner nearby shouted. "Hold on to your arses and pray for your sorry souls."

"Ain't nothin' else to do," someone answered him.

I trembled as I braced myself. Flashes of lightning followed by immediate blasts of thunder seemed to be all around us, and I shook with every burst.

The storm worsened and rain started to gush into my cell through the open window, drenching me regardless of where I stood. The building creaked as the wind tore at it, and the roof shifted ominously above us, taking me back to the *Penny Rose*, and the horror of it flooded through me.

"We're going to hell!" Zachary Mulligan screamed, frightening me further.

Drenched to the skin, I huddled in my corner as the wind pounded against the walls of the prison. The skies had darkened, leaving only flashes of lightning to illuminate my surroundings in sudden bursts.

Seized by fear, I wasn't sure I was of right mind, but with the last flash of light I thought I saw a figure at the door. With the next bolt of lightning, I was sure. There was a man, hovering over the lock, and behind him several others. I squinted to see better, pressing back into the corner as the door broke open.

A towering man lunged at me, lifting me up with one swift movement. I tried to scream, but he clutched me so tightly against his chest that I gasped for air. As the man sped through the hallway, my fear diminished as I realized that, miraculously, I was being rescued.

"Hold tight, Anna," he said as he swung me around to his back, and I wrapped my legs around his waist.

"Sebastian?"

For a moment, fear gave way to astonishment. In the darkness and with his hair tied, I hadn't recognized him.

"Did you expect someone else?"

"I expected to die," I shouted back at him. "You risk much for me."

As we burst out through the open door into darkness and pouring rain, I saw one of the men running at our side hurl a ring of keys at Casper, who caught them and headed back down the hallway.

"This is not a time for talking," Sebastian shouted over his shoulder as I felt his chest heave.

I smiled, tightening my hold on him and tucking my cheek against his neck.

Debris and hail, whipped by the wind, pummeled against us, and Sebastian cursed loudly as fallen trees blocked our path.

"Where are we going?" I yelled out to him.

"You are talking!"

"Sorry! I'm sorry!"

After a while, I felt his chest heave again, and he groaned, taking on an incline, with his men behind us pressing upward against the wind. Squinting open my eyes, I realized we were on the gangway of a ship. Hopefully, his feet would not falter.

Above us hands reached for us, while behind us the men banded together against the gusts of wind.

Once aboard, we skidded across the wet deck toward doors that opened before us. As his disheveled companions scrambled down the passageway, Sebastian put me down and pulled me in a different direction.

"Where are we going?"

"Must you talk so much?" he asked, sounding exasperated.

Holding his hand in a near death grip, I shook my head.

He led me to a cabin where a cot was covered with dry blankets.

"You will have what you need here. Dry off and try to sleep. We can talk in the morning."

As I steadied myself against a sea chest, he moved toward the door.

"What if someone searches for me?"

He looked down at me, but his expression was difficult to read.

"We will be gone the moment the storm stills," he said, slipping out the door and closing it behind him.

* * *

Awakening to the commotion of sailors shouting to each other from one end of the ship to the other while we seemed to move forward in full sail gave me a modicum of relief.

But there were still so many unanswered questions. *Where are we going? How will I be safe? How will I survive?* But for now, looking at my drenched clothes, *What do I wear?*

To my surprise, there was a woman's dress among the items in the sea trunk. It was large, but at least I could cinch it at the waist. There were no dry shoes, but I stepped into mine, lest the leather shrink as they dried.

Walking out on deck brought back memories of the *Penny Rose*, but Sebastian's ship was not crowded, and it was cleaner than the *Penny Rose*. Looking up, riggers were leaping across the ratlines, and the look-outs in the crow's nest looked at ease, giving me hope that no ship was in pursuit.

Sebastian was on the far end of the deck, but just as I was about to call out to him, a woman climbed down from the forecastle, and Sebastian's eyes were fixed on her.

I held my breath, watching her saunter toward him until they were only inches apart. Her black hair, like his, draped freely over her shoulders. Sebastian lowered his face and spoke to her as she laughed softly, intimately. They were both so beautiful, in an oddly enchanting way. She must be Sebastian's woman, and from the sight of her, they were two of a kind. I wasn't prepared for a surge of disappointment, but suddenly their eyes were on me, and I straightened up, hoping they hadn't seen me gawking.

I stepped forward, and Sebastian's eyes lit as I approached them. Moving away from the woman, he reached out to me, taking my hand in his, and kissing it.

"You look better," he said, surprising me.

The woman came closer and stopped by his side. "Meet my sister, Isabella. She is a ferocious seafaring captain herself."

"A pleasure," I said, hoping I could hide my relief.

It was probably her dress I was wearing. She was taller than me and had the sundrenched complexion of many Spaniards, with large dark eyes that sized me up in an instant. There was something bold about her. She wore men's clothing, with tall boots and a dagger swung from a wide leather belt above her curving hips when she walked. I had no doubts the woman knew how to use it.

I startled when she broke into laughter. "They thought you are a killer! Ha! The British are more foolish than I thought!" she said, studying me. "You couldn't kill a cat! But it delights me to meet the woman Sebastian speaks so highly of."

I blushed. He had spoken of me.

Later, when Sebastian sought me out, I had to ask. "Why did you rescue me?"

"Would you rather be dead?" Sebastian looked at me as if I were an ungrateful child.

I shook my head.

With a glimmer of a smile on his face, he said, "Women like you don't last long in a cell. You were fortunate that the storm shielded your rescue."

"I never thought I would have to flee for my life."

He nodded, slightly, while looking at me with those eyes that still held me captive.

"Moultrie must have lost his wits, imprisoning you."

The boat suddenly dipped, and I reached out for his sleeve to steady myself.

"What if I am discovered here?" I asked.

"You won't be."

"I don't even know where we are going."

A faint smile curved the corners of his lips, and I could see a twinkle in his eyes.

"There is much to be said, but for now, just know I will keep you safe."

"Thank you, Sebastian," I said. "I will forever be indebted, but what of my imprisonment? I can't go back to St. Augustine, and I can't return to England, and what will become of the inn?"

He rolled his eyes, throwing his head back. "Aye, woman! I will take you to Cuba, or I can keep you at my side, or we can sail together until death claims us."

My jaw dropped, but Sebastian laughed. "All in time. I'm chiding. For now, have no worries. Cuba it will be, and I will provide for you. It is I who am indebted to you, and Abbie would never let me forget it if you were harmed in my keeping." He paused. "You are safe."

I looked up at him, trying to believe him. As I opened my mouth to ask another question, he cocked his head, and to my surprise he reached for me, planting a gentle kiss on my forehead before he smiled at me and walked away.

CHAPTER EIGHTEEN

———

Nuestra Habana, November 1764

After weeks aboard, there was still no land on the horizon. I was so far from St. Augustine and even farther from England. Never would I have imagined this fate to be mine, but my only choice was to wait.

Nuestra Habana was swifter and lighter than the *Penny Rose,* and I was surprised to find that life on board was far more regimented under Sebastian Ortega's command than I imagined.

Manuel Alvarez, the quartermaster, swiftly put an end to any strife between the crew, though without using any of the seafarer's punishments I had heard of. Tasks were diligently tended to by riggers, gunners, sailing masters, a cooper, a cook, a carpenter, two sailmakers, and a boatswain while Sebastian pored over maps, checking every peg on the traverse board, navigating our course, and keeping a watchful eye on every sail.

We exchanged a few pleasantries during the days, but I often felt his gaze sweep over me from a distance. Somehow,

I always knew where he was, as if my eyes couldn't help but search for him, although I tried to look away.

As the weeks passed and I found my respect for him growing, I couldn't help but look forward to our evening meals together, where talk about my predicament often led to rousing conversations about so many other things. Despite the late hours and generous pours of rum, he always showed me the utmost courtesy and kindness.

"Music, madam?"

Startled from my thoughts, I turned and looked into the inquiring eyes of Rodrigo Chavez, a charming rascal who often danced about the ship, adding merriment to the days at sea and, from what I had heard, utter confusion to any battle, but such were the duties of a ship's musician.

Now he had made it his mission to amuse me.

Before I could utter a word, Isabella slid down on the bench next to me.

"A ballad, Rodrigo. You know the one," she said.

"My pleasure, Captain Isabella," Rodrigo said, bowing deeply before he started to serenade us.

I spent much of my time with her, finding her to be quite intriguing, considering that she had no qualms speaking her mind.

"It is odd for an Englishwoman to befriend a medicine woman like Abbie Birdsong, is it not? Women in St. Augustine seem to think she could cast a spell on them." She laughed at the thought, but I knew her words to be true.

"I'm trained as an apothecary, so my interests are far more similar to Abbie's than that of most Englishwomen," I said. "I am quite fond of her."

"As are we. She never forgave herself for not being there with her sister the day she died, but no one knows if she could have saved her. My brother was distraught, as were we all, but in her grief Abbie consoled us, and we've never stopped considering her kin."

I smiled, thinking of Abbie. "She is loved by so many, but perhaps not the English wives of St. Augustine. Admiral Rushmore had great respect for her."

Isabella pulled her hair back from her face and looked at me. "No surprise, but Rushmore died, did he not?"

I nodded. "Yes, in Savannah, before my troubles began."

When I heard the sound of heavy footsteps behind us I turned to see Sebastian coming toward us with a pair of kittens in his hands.

"What is this? The ship cat was not just fat, the whore!" Isabella said.

Sebastian laughed and handed one to each of us. "I find it insulting that you call my cat a whore, sister!"

The kitten I held stretched lazily in my hands and dazzled me with its vivid green eyes.

"How beautiful they are!" I said, reaching out to stroke the black and white kitten resting against Isabella's shoulder, while mine rolled into a tiny ball on my lap.

"They are good to have on a ship," Sebastian said, but turning to Isabella he pulled another from his pocket and handed it to her.

She grinned, shaking her head knowingly. "You will ask that I take at least one with me when I leave, won't you?" She looked up at him. "My brother makes his enemies tremble, but a kitten can have its way with him."

"You're leaving?" I asked before Sebastian could answer.

Sebastian looked at his sister, slightly deflated. "She is, and perhaps before these young things are weaned."

Isabella looked around. "Have you caught sight of the *Incognita*?"

Sebastian nodded. "She is coming toward us. We saw her clearly only moments ago. We will pull into the next bay and meet her there."

Isabella's smile was jubilant, leaving me perplexed, but Sebastian explained,

"The *Incognita* was in need of repair, but tonight she will be reunited with her captain."

When the *Incognita* came up beside us, I saw she was flying the same colors as *Nuestra Habana* and was only slightly smaller in size, but another difference was that there were several women on board, including one at the helm.

Once tethered, crew climbed from one boat to the other, cheerfully bantering among themselves and indulging in the feasts that were prepared in each galley.

At day's end, the crew drifted up to the torchlit decks of *Nuestra Habana*. Surrendering themselves to the sound of their weeping guitars and the eerie echo of Rodrigo's flute, they danced as if offering their souls to a higher deity.

Sitting back on the steps to the forecastle, I sipped rum and watched, spellbound by the music, the calm of the sea, and the sensual beauty of their movement, a far cry from Englishmen stomping along to a jig.

The moment Sebastian set foot on deck the crew gave way to him. As he stood alone in the flickering light of the lanterns, his body seemed overtaken by the music, and he proved to be the most magnificent of them all. He looked like an ethereal being, and as the light of the moon shone down on him I noticed how close to my secluded spot he had ventured.

"Come to me," he said, reaching for me and bringing me within inches of him. I don't remember rising from the step of the stairs, for all I felt was his hand at my waist, leading me, coaxing me to move with him until my body surrendered to the magical tug of the music and of him. Steadying myself with my palms against his chest, I felt the heat rise between us as he pulled me closer and closer still, until all I could see were his eyes sparkling in the moonlight.

Our lips came so close that he could have kissed me, but he inched away as if taunting me. Finally, the draw became unbearable, and our lips met.

I've lost my mind, I thought, not caring that in kissing him back my passion for him could no longer be hidden.

* * *

When we had danced until I could take no more, I slipped away to my cabin. What I had felt would make Edmund turn in his grave, but I was no longer Anna Ashton, and life was more fragile than I had ever imagined.

After a while the music stopped, and the men's voices faded as all but the sailors on night watch took to their quarters, leaving others to crawl drunken into hammocks or collapse onto the heap of drunken men sleeping off their stupor on deck.

Listening for Sebastian's footsteps in the passageway, I wasn't certain what I hoped for.

I held my breath as he hesitated at my door. I imagined his hand slowly opening it, and as its hinges creaked, I could see his face illuminated by the flicker of my lantern as he appeared in the doorway. Looking into his eyes, I would see that his unmasked desire was as urgent as the torrent tearing through me, and in an instant there would be nothing at all between us but the rising desire of our bodies.

When his door creaked on its hinges, my heart dropped, and when it slammed shut I realized I had been standing there like a fool, a complete loon, staring at my own door, barely breathing, while he probably had not thought of me at all.

I huffed, dismayed at the longing that had ensnared me, willing my body to come to its senses and my mind to put Captain Sebastian Ortega out of my thoughts.

Neither his disturbing eyes, the inviting curve of his lips, nor the swagger with which he moved would affect me. Gratitude is not love, but perhaps this was greater than that. Perhaps it was destiny…

I sighed. "Go to sleep, Anna," I said out loud, "and pray there is still a modicum of reason somewhere inside you."

* * *

By first light, the ships were untethered, and Isabella turned the *Incognita* toward the colonies while Sebastian set sail for Cuba.

I stood by his side as the distance between the two ships grew. Finally, all we could see of Isabella was her silhouette and her red scarf blowing in the wind.

Sebastian looked wistful as he watched the distance between the two ships become greater, reminding me of the ache of being parted from someone you love. I felt a sudden urge to reach out to comfort him somehow, but I held back lest he think me too intrusive.

"When will you see her again?" I asked.

"One never knows," he said without taking his eyes off his sister's ship. "In these waters, nothing is ever certain."

There was a deep love between these two, and anyone in their presence could feel it. When he turned to me, I could see the sadness in his eyes.

"Dear lady, life promises us nothing, but what you can be certain of is that I will protect you."

He reached for my hand and put it to his lips. "I must take my leave, for a captain must tend to his ship. You are the only woman on board now, but my men have been instructed to provide for you. You have only to ask."

* * *

With time, I started to understand much of what was spoken around me, and when I ventured to formulate sentences on my own, it seemed to please Sebastian.

"The Spanish language is even more beautiful coming from your lips," he said. "But understanding it will allow Cuba to teach you all there is to know about her."

I cocked my head, feeling mischievous. "Are you certain that Cuba is a 'she,' then?"

Sebastian looked astounded. "What else could she be? She is beautiful and proud, strong but yielding, wise but compassionate, bold but cautious..." He started to circle me, taking my hand and kissing it when he stood before me.

"Are you speaking of Cuba?" I asked.

"I am not certain. You are a distraction that carries me like the wind to places unknown. My dear island is a beauty to behold, but having you here blinds me to anything else."

I sighed, loosing myself in his eyes. "You are a charmer. A man very difficult to resist."

I expected to see him grin, but instead he was quite serious.

"There is no reason to resist, Anna. Our souls have joined together, and no frivolity can deny it. I know it, and if you allow yourself to be free and unbound by the sadly confining English ways, you know it is true."

I gasped. "Sebastian! You can't mean this."

His grin appeared. "There is no cause to doubt me."

I didn't comment. I just watched him with my mouth agape, wondering how a few silly words about Cuba's possible gender could bring about all this.

"Have no fear, Anna. I am a very patient man."

With that, he winked at me and went back to the helm.

* * *

That evening, the moon was full in the sky. I wandered out of my cabin to take in the stillness of the night, not thinking I could be sent back inside by the night watch should I be discovered. It wasn't the night watch who found me.

It was Sebastian.

Feeling him come closer, I didn't resist his arms pulling me to him and his mouth finding mine, kissing me with a hunger that left me dazed and all too willing in his arms.

"You want me," he said when I freed myself and tried to restore some dignity.

"What—"

"You want me. I know this, for when I look into your eyes, all I see is desire. It has always been there. You can't deny it."

Without a word, and without protest from me, he lifted me into his arms and carried me the few steps to his cabin. Once inside, he put me down and locked the door behind us, causing me unmentionable unrest.

There was no smile on his face and no question to be asked as he pulled me down onto his bed. All I could feel was heat rising from my most private parts as my body arched toward him; with or without my approval, there was nothing I could do to stop it. My hand was the one that opened my bodice, freeing my breasts from their confines and into the warm, wet sensation of his mouth, stirring unnamed feelings I could barely contain.

I moaned as his hand slipped under my skirts, and my legs willingly parted, inviting him in. As we found the rhythm of our bodies coming together, our ecstasy mounted until neither could hold back, and for the first time I felt I could die of pleasure as the world around us vanished and all that mattered was us.

Both spent, he held me close for a long time as my body calmed, leaving me languid and satiated in his arms. My face rested on his chest and the medallions that so often drew my eyes toward them lay peacefully in the palm of my open hand.

Edmund had never brought me to such a place within my own body on the few times we had come together. Never had he given me as much as Sebastian, and never, ever had I dreamt such delicious feelings could exist and that we could lay in each other's arms as if there was nowhere else on earth to be.

After a while, I inched myself away and started to tug at my bodice, suddenly self-conscious, and sat up.

"I've never felt this way," I said. "You do not think ill of me for so easily opening myself to my protector?"

He chuckled. "No. When I look at you, I see my woman. I knew you would be mine the moment I saw you stepping off the *Penny Rose*. I didn't know how long it would take or how it would happen, but every time I looked into your magnificent eyes, they told me that it could be no other way."

CHAPTER NINETEEN

———

Havana, Cuba, January 1765

Sebastian's home in Havana was a three-story building the color of parchment, with deep brown accenting the elaborate ornamentation of the structure with its columned archways and sweeping balconies along the length of the upper floors. A massive double entry door could only be approached from the Cathedral Plaza, but on the opposite side the view of the bay was unobstructed.

Once inside, we crossed a courtyard with a central fountain, and I noticed a door leading into square tower, where I could imagine Sebastian on the very top, taking in the city and looking out over the sea.

We walked through stunning parlors, Sebastian's map room, and the kitchens on the ground floor, and above we perused exquisite bedrooms that opened to a wide gallery with a view of the fountain below.

Each room was exquisitely furnished, and most chairs and benches held cushions bursting with color. I looked at beautiful lanterns, stained glass and artful stone floors, and the great palms that were placed on each side of ornate doors.

Finally, I stopped. "I hadn't expected such…"

"Riches?" he said.

"Well, yes."

He smiled. "This, I expected. And why do I not command my men from this place of beauty and comfort? Why am I a privateer, sometimes assumed to be a pirate, too clever to be caught in any wrongdoing?"

"But…" I said. "It's hardly a mystery why some believe you are a pirate."

"The *Luisa*, you mean?"

I nodded.

"The *Luisa* was never sunk, but I took legal command of her and brought her cargo of slaves a short way from here to the city of Regla, where they were accepted as free men and women. The crew were set ashore as we passed the Cayo Caracol, and the *Luisa*, after some repairs, is sailing under Ortega flags and is called *El Cuervo*, which means 'Raven.'"

My pride in him swelled. "I never thought—"

"And you never thought you would love me," he said. "Come."

I followed Sebastian up the spiral staircase to the tower, to a room where the walls were covered with ancestral portraits.

"My sanctuary," he said, gesturing for me to enter. "Very few are allowed here."

"I'm honored," I said, studying the faces he bore resemblance to.

"My parents," he said, stopping in front of two portraits near his desk. "My mother, Carmen Maria Ortega de Santiago, and this is my father, Captain Diosdado Luis Ortega. He is a stern man but a loving one. You will see, the Ortega clan will welcome you with open hearts, and you will melt his."

"That would please me greatly," I said, smiling up at him.

"Before Isabella took her place, my father wanted a son to command each Ortega vessel, so it is my hope that our children will continue to expand the fleet."

My eyes widened. "Our children? Should we not speak of children before you make plans for them?"

"A child can come, spoken of or not." He seemed almost hopeful when he looked into my eyes. "Could you not already be with child?"

I blushed, thinking of our nights aboard the *Nuestra Habana*, where he had indulged my desires. In a world of uncertainty, my heart had become my compass, and it hadn't failed me. I had finally come home, for wherever Sebastian was, that was home to me now.

Sebastian was watching me. "What?"

Then I remembered his question: *Could I not already be with child?*

"No, I'm not," I said, seeing the light in his eyes dim. "I was just a little seasick that last morning on board."

I thought he would chuckle, but he didn't.

"You need not think of the Americas. I want you here with me, every day, every night, to be my woman in every way."

I gasped. "This is hardly proper, Sebastian," I said, knowing my protest was futile, for I would do anything this man asked, anything at all.

"It has been a long time since I first laid eyes on you, and all you've been through has led you to me. Do you not know? We are destined. You know it, and you feel it. Do not lie to yourself."

I sighed. Every word he had spoken was true. I adored this man. I had dreamt of him, longed for him, and now that I stood here, I was his.

"I want to make you my wife," he said, "for you are the lover I will desire to the day I die, the person with whom I will share my thoughts, the minx who makes me laugh, and the mother of the children who will carry our legacy."

Looking up at him, I hesitated. "My husbands have not fared well, Sebastian." I meant it quite seriously, but he threw his head back and laughed.

"There is no curse on your husbands, and I have no fear of being one."

"We are promised nothing, Sebastian."

"But I do. I pledge that I will love you like no other until I die."

I looked up into the eyes that always captured me, grateful for where that first glance had taken me.

"I pledge the same, but I don't have to be claimed, and you don't have to give me your name to keep me at your side. I will be yours, not because I am bound to you by law, but because I love you with all of my heart, and I will forever," I said with sudden gravity.

Releasing his hold on me, he stood back. "Those are unusual words spoken by a woman, Anna *mia*, but I will honor your wishes. Ours will be a bond of love that will never be broken."

I nodded, beaming up at him. "Never. It will endure anything and everything."

"And, someday we will marry," he said. "Before our children discover that their parents are living in sin."

"You know how to lure me."

I laughed, but as he looked at me the expression in his eyes became determined.

"I will love you and honor you until the day I die," he said.

"And I will love and honor you all the days of my life," I replied, "and I might try to obey…"

He laughed at the unlikeliness of the latter. "Then this will be our pledge, Anna *mia*. I will never betray you."

"*Te quiero*, Sebastian," I replied.

* * *

Casa Ortega became home as much as the apothecary had been, and Sebastian and I spent our days in peaceful domesticity, interspersed with sudden interruptions of heated quarrels and passionate compromise, as we took upon ourselves to add color and splendor to parts of the mansion seldom used.

"Perhaps we should commission a new Ortega ship, once we finish what we have begun here," I said one morning as Sebastian and I took our coffee in the courtyard.

He chuckled. "Enhancing the inner sanctums of a home has brought on remarkable ambition in you, but we hardly need another ship."

I took a sip of the bitter brew. "Did you not say there should be an Ortega for every vessel, or was it a vessel for every Ortega?"

He turned to me, as his brows furrowed in wonder. "What say you?"

"Only that our child should grow up to know a ship is being readied for him."

Sebastian's eyes widened as he bolted from his chair and grabbed me, lifting me high and spinning me in the air. "At last, Anna *mia*, at last!"

"Put me down, or I will be ill!"

He did so immediately and pulled out the chair for me to sit back down.

Smiling, Sebastian pensively drummed his fingers on the table before turning to me. "I shall make my journey to St. Augustine brief, for I must be here before the birth of our child." He thought for a moment. "Perhaps I can add to our joy should I be able to bring you word that Moultrie has seen his error or that your name has been cleared."

I nodded. "Our son would be pleased to know his mother is not an escaped prisoner. But I shall miss you."

"It saddens me to leave, but I will never leave you for long."

* * *

In early August, a storm ravaged Havana, destroying buildings, felling trees, and taking lives. The wind and noise that tore through the streets, battering the city for endless hours, was worse than the most intense thunder, and it rattled my nerves.

Isabella opened the Ortega home to anyone in need of shelter, but while we were safe within its confines, my worry for Sebastian tormented me, for he had been at sea for months, and word from him was infrequent during the best of times.

"You forget that my brother knows the weather better than anyone," she said, "and I would feel it in my soul if he were harmed. It's like that between us."

I nodded, not wanting to disagree, but I worried still. The kicks to my ribs from the child within me were a constant reminder of my desire to present Sebastian with a son, but Sebastian would have to be alive for that. Ships would be forced to the bottom of the sea by this storm, and shore-bound women would be waiting for men who were never to return, but I couldn't be one of them.

There were a great many doctors in Havana, and thankfully I had harvested all I could from the herb garden Sebastian had surprised me with, and every remedy I could supply came to good use.

Gradually, over weeks, Havana started to recover, but the only thing that could give me a moment of reprieve from my fear for Sebastian was to put everything I had into helping those who couldn't come out from their damaged homes, some too sick or injured to even consider it, or caring for children who were brought to us after they had been found wandering, disoriented and lost, until their parents could retrieve them.

Toward the end of August, there still was no word from Sebastian, but our child became restless.

The pain started in the evening of a full moon, and it came in waves. Subtle at first, it quickly worsened, gripping me for long, agonizing moments before subsiding and allowing me time to recover until the next contraction set in.

Everything had been made ready for our little one, from the nursery across from our bedroom to the swaddling cloth and a christening gown fit for a prince.

When a crib arrived, it looked like one of Sebastian's ships, fitted with the Ortega crest, flying its ribbons, and resting on legs draped with indigo velvet as if it were riding the waves. I was brought to tears, thinking of how long this had been in the making and how carefully Sebastian had planned it. The craftsman's servants had brought it this morning, and somehow they had made it up to the nursery without Isabella or me seeing it.

My Ortega baby would sleep well in this crib.

"Sebastian has spared no cost for his son," Isabella said when she saw it.

"If it is a son," I reply. "If not, I pray our daughter will find a way to charm herself into her father's heart."

Isabella seemed not to be listening. She pulled a lever on the crib's side, and the crib rocked like a ship riding the waves, throwing her into a fit of laughter. "He will delight in this, our boy!"

"I'm glad you are amused."

I stood up and massaged my lower back with both hands. The pain returned, spreading through my back and then pressing down into my pelvis, the intensity building until the pain became unbearable.

"Isabella," I said, gasping. "It may be happening now."

Doubling over, I felt my legs tremble.

Isabella caught me before I dropped to the floor, and she supported me as we made our way into the birthing room, which had been set up near the nursery. Before I reached the bed, I felt a gush of fluid spilling from me, warm and wet against my legs as it splashed to the floor.

"My water broke! God help me!"

Horrified, I looked down at the large wet spots on my dress, but Isabella pulled me forward.

"Ha! It won't be long now, Anna. Just breathe!"

She whistled. It was a loud, shrill sound that could have rivaled a foghorn, and it brought her maid to the doorway within moments with Heronimo, our houseboy, in tow.

Isabella turned to the boy, whose eyes were wide as saucers as he looked from me, writhing in pain, to the liquid mess on the floor.

"Get the midwife!" Isabella yelled at him.

Heronimo nodded and ran off without a word. To her maid she said, "Bring me boiling water and fresh cloths. This child could come at any moment."

The flurry of activity made me feel agitated and oddly trapped, while thoughts of what lay ahead suddenly seemed terrifying.

"I'm frightened," I said. "This could be the end of me."

"Nonsense, Anna. You will survive this birth and many more," Isabella said, but I was not reassured.

"I'd rather not think of the others right now. What if I die?" I whispered as new contractions started deep inside me.

"You won't die, Anna."

My labor lasted for two days, and I grew weaker with the contractions, which tormented me, robbing me of sleep. Nausea made taking in anything other than small amounts of juice a prompt to vomit.

Rosa, the midwife, patiently sat by my side, waiting for the child to progress, while I began to plan what words I would leave for Sebastian and my baby if I felt my time was nearing, for I could soon bear no more.

After a while, I closed my eyes and slept until pressure surged through my pelvis again, jolting me awake.

"Push, Anna," Rosa said, instantly alert. "Push with all your might."

I pushed, and as my pelvis pressed open, the pain felt like a bolt of fire surging through me when the child descended. I screamed, unable to bear it for another second, but then the contraction stopped.

Isabella burst through the doors, her eyes widening as she approached. "Good God!" she whispered.

I noticed the sudden stillness in the room.

"What happened?" I asked. The midwife's silence and the shock in Isabella's eyes frightened me. "What is wrong?"

"A footling," Rosa said. "I should have known. The child was not progressing, and I haven't been able to dislodge him."

I closed my eyes, feeling tears roll down across my temples, wetting my hair.

"What can be done?" Isabella asked.

I froze when Rosa answered her in Spanish and Isabella stormed out of the room.

"Rest, Anna," Rosa said as I started to sob. "Save your strength for the next push."

The next contraction tore through me just as Sebastian and Abbie bolted into the room with Isabella, who slipped down behind me. As she lifted my shoulders, I groaned in pain.

"Sebastian, Abbie," I moaned, certain that in my exhaustion I was hallucinating, but their touch was real, as was the shock in their eyes.

Sebastian's eyes were on Rosa.

"It's a boy, sir," she said, looking up at him. "But get yourself out of here. This is no place for a man."

The tone in her voice wasn't reassuring, but as another contraction ripped through me, all that mattered was that Sebastian was standing by my side, although he looked paler than I had ever seen him.

"What is to be done? I can call for a doctor! Gonzales is nearby."

"It's too late for a doctor," Rosa said.

Sebastian raked his hand through his hair as I looked at him through squinting eyes, still unsure he was truly here as another wave of pain tore through me.

Suddenly he bent down, and I felt him grab hold of the child.

"Sebastian," I moaned. Abbie took my hand and held it, but Sebastian didn't hear me.

"Move!" he said, pushing Rosa aside.

"Sir, don't!" Rosa cried out. "You will send them both to their graves!"

"Never!" Sebastian snapped back.

As another wave of pain came, so close they seemed continuous, Abbie put her hands on my belly and pushed as if she would free the child from my body with her bare hands. In a blur of tears, I saw Sebastian tear off his headband and felt him wrap it around our child's body as he pulled, gently coaxing him loose.

I felt the release of the child's arms and shoulders as they were being freed, and then, at last, his head.

Triumphantly, Sebastian rose. Holding our son in his hands, he rubbed him vigorously until he cried out and his color changed from a translucent blue to a furious red.

For a moment, I closed my eyes as our son's first cries etched themselves into my soul, becoming a memory that would never leave me.

Isabella's sigh brought me back to the moment, and my heart melted as Sebastian lowered our child into my arms.

"Anna *mia*," he said, smiling at me, "let me present our son, Diego Federico Ortega de Bouvion."

CHAPTER TWENTY

Havana, April 1769

When the first of Sebastian's ships returned to Havana in April of 1769, Captain Marquez brought the fear of the pox with him.

"It's been raging through the colonies! People are dying, and there's no end in sight," he said, making the conditions sound ominous. "I've seen ships set ablaze to keep the pestilence from coming to port."

Sebastian rubbed his chin while he listened, his gaze locked on his old friend who paced before him and gestured with his hands as he spoke.

"Best keep the ships at sea so we burn only what we must," Sebastian finally said.

"Aye." Captain Marquez nodded. "It would be a cryin' shame to lose any
Ortega vessel."

"But worse to lose our men." Sebastian's voice was like velvet, but there was an undertone not to take lightly.

Abbie looked up from the beading she had been working on. "I am no stranger to variolation, but without the illness in Cuba, I have no source to take from." The room became silent as we all turned to her.

"Of what are you speaking?" Sebastian looked at her as if she had gone mad.

Abbie smiled wistfully. "It is known because an enslaved man in the colonies told his master that the slaves were inoculating themselves to stay well while others were dying."

"Inoculating?" Sebastian looked puzzled, but it pleased me that he didn't dismiss the thought of a new remedy.

The captain's wife, Teresa, slid to the edge of her seat. "I have heard of such a thing! There is a doctor in Charlestown who has embraced this, but so far most have only offered their slaves."

Sebastian shook his head, suddenly weary. "The cowards. I should take it myself before I demand it be tried on another."

"Oh, Sebastian. You were born a saint. Not everyone is like you," Teresa said, bringing a smile to our faces for a brief moment before we sobered at the thought of the pox.

"So, what is needed for this variolation and inoculation you speak of?" I asked. I noticed Captain Marquez was watching me and hoped he would not scorn the possibility of something other than burning ships and maintaining distance could be of help.

"What is needed is a person suffering the pox," Abbie said, causing the four of us to gasp out loud.

Captain Marquez slapped his thigh and chuckled, but Teresa's lips tightened.

"That is the talk of loons," he said. "Why would we bring close what we seek to avoid?"

Sebastian stood, but his gaze was still on Abbie.

"Because that is the way, except perhaps that doctor in Charlestown has found a different source, perhaps as good as the pox itself."

"Cowpox," I said, trusting my guess. "Once sickened with cowpox, no other pox can take hold of you."

"Are you certain?" Sebastian asked.

I nodded.

Sebastian paced slowly. I could see his brows furrow as he contemplated the possibilities. I already felt a quiver inside me, for knowing Sebastian, we would be heading for Charlestown within days.

* * *

Charlestown was beautifully nestled between two sparkling rivers, and unlike St. Augustine, its streets were wide and treelined. Although small, there was a bustle of activity, reminding me of Havana, even parts of London, making me hope we could take some time ashore.

Sebastian was the first to hold out his arm for the small cuts the doctor would make before swabbing the wound with a wand that would yield the protection we sought.

When it was Diego's turn, he was as brave as his father until the first cut was made, and his lower lip quivered. He looked up at the doctor with his tear-filled Ortega eyes, stunned by the painful betrayal of the jolly man he didn't think would hurt him.

"You might want to stay for a few days," the doctor said when he had inoculated Abbie and me, along with the entire crew. "To see that all goes well."

"I think you seek to worry me," Sebastian said. "But we will stay until the tide is high on Sunday."

* * *

Before we returned to *Nuestra Habana,* we dined at a tavern near the pier, astounding Diego with dishes so unlike the Cuban fare he was accustomed to.

As we were about to leave, a man bumped into Sebastian. "I beg your pardon, sir," the man said. "Clumsy, I am."

Sebastian's eyes narrowed. "Might I know you?" He paused. "I am Captain Sebastian Ortega."

The man shook his head. "Don't believe we've met, Captain," he said, tipping his hat to us as he left.

Sebastian still pondered. "I've seen that face, but I cannot recall where," he said, taking Diego by the hand as we headed for the door.

"You can ask the coachman about him, for it appears they know each other," Abbie said.

I followed her gaze to where the coach waited, but upon seeing us, the conversation between the two came to an end, and the man hurried away.

The coachman had little to say, just that the fellow was a local who frequented the tavern and was of the friendly sort.

Lulled by the rhythmic clatter of hooves, Diego fell asleep between Sebastian and me as soon as we reached the harbor.

"This is Gadsden Warf," Sebastian said as we passed a large pier. "This dock receives more enslaved people than anywhere in the Americas."

The look in his eyes startled me.

"These ships are the devil's chariots," he said. "Slavers, every one of them."

"Are you certain? These ships are quite large."

Abbie and I looked up at the towering masts of six large ships tied up at the dock. Bathing in the golden glow of the setting sun, they hardly looked like vessels of horror and grief.

Sebastian snuffed. "For a reason, dear woman. They are large to fit their unwitting captives shackled side by side in the hull and on every deck of these despicable vessels, many in spaces smaller than you would offer a goat."

"This evil will carry through generations," Abbie said, staring at the ships with unconcealed disdain.

"I fear you are right," Sebastian said as a young boy standing in the road brought the coach to a halt.

"Away with you, child!" the coachman yelled, but the boy only came closer.

"A word, sir? Are you not Captain Sebastian Ortega?"

The boy stepped back, and I could see he held a sealed letter in his hand.

"Who asks?" Sebastian replied. "And how do you know me?"

"Captain Archer, sir. Captain Angus Archer. I am to give you this." The boy held up the letter, but he stepped no closer. "You were at the tavern, were you not?"

Sebastian sighed. "He was Archer's man! Bumping into me was hardly an act of clumsiness."

Sebastian leapt from the carriage and tore the letter from the boy's hand.

At that same moment, I felt Diego ripped from my side, and strong hands pulled at my waist, bringing me down from the carriage as the horses reared and bolted.

Diego cried out as Abbie cast curses on our three abductors. Glancing behind me, I saw Sebastian lay lifeless on the pier, and as a hood came down over my face I heard an ominous splash that sent shivers through me. My heart started to pound as jubilant cries rose, but a meaty hand over my mouth silenced my screams.

My head was snapped back as my abductor's lips came close to my ear. "Be still, unless you want that boy dead too," he said. "You'd be a fool to fight me."

Struggling to breathe, I was too enraged to cry.

When we entered a building, the brute who held me dropped me to the stone floor. As I tore off the hood, my son leapt into my arms, and Abbie gave me a nearly unperceivable nod from a few feet away. We were unharmed so far, but the pallor of my son's face and the angst in his eyes forced me to stay calm.

We were in a small, wood-paneled room with only one window, and before me a narrow-faced, bearded man sat at a large desk while a few others stood around.

He rose slowly, came around the desk, and looked us over as if we were chattel.

"Madam Ortega, we meet at last. Do you know who I am?"

I shook my head, not correcting him for assuming I was married to Sebastian, for it mattered little. "Whoever you are, I gather you are not a good man."

He laughed. "I am Captain Emanuel Archer. Surely, you have heard of me."

"I have," I said, not offering more. Emanuel was Angus's brother, and both were slave traders who had once owned the *Luisa,* the ship Sebastian had taken from them in the light of day.

"What do you want with us?" I asked, glancing at Abbie, whose brow furrowed at my question. Surely, she wondered about Sebastian too.

He crossed his arms and leaned back on his desk. "I thought to put the mighty Ortega on a ship headed for the coast of Africa, where he would be obliged to fill the ship for her return. After that, I hadn't quite decided, but plans don't always come to fruition. Ortega is—" He hesitated. "But I do have you, and I'm pleasantly surprised to see that you have an accomplice certainly worth a bounty."

Bristling, I was barely able to contain myself. "If anyone here has guilt, Emanuel Archer, that would be you!"

He looked at me, astounded at first, but then he smiled. "Feisty. I like that. A lot. I see how you were able to snare a man such as Ortega. The Angel of the *Penny Rose,* a beauty and an accomplished woman, but surely, he must have enjoyed that spark, that fight in you. Most women are quite lackluster, but I can only imagine you and he—"

"What is your intention with us?" I asked, cutting off Emanuel's rambling before he could vent his distorted fantasies.

Emanuel sat up a little taller. "I could have many intentions with the two of you," he said, his gaze drifting to my bosom before shifting to Abbie. "But there is a good price on your head, so I will give you safe passage to deliver you in good condition. But should you cause me to regret my kindness, I have many thoughts of what could be bestowed upon the young Ortega."

I gasped. "Touch him and I will kill you," I said, not able to stop myself.

Emanuel Archer was no longer amused. "Don't give me a reason. I can make what's left of your life much worse."

* * *

Weeks later, when we arrived in St. Augustine, Emanuel walked us across the town square, past the slave markets, past the infirmary, to the government building where our fate would be sealed. He kept his hand on Diego's shoulder as we walked, and I could see it tighten when Diego failed to keep up.

It didn't take long before townspeople gathered to gawk. Among them were familiar faces, but they said nothing.

Forbidden to speak, Abbie walked silently next to me, holding her head proudly. She looked neither left nor right, and certainly not down like someone already condemned.

The only member of the Royal Council available to accept us was Patrick Warrick, but my stomach twisted at the thought of being brought before him, for I didn't dare assume we would have his mercy.

Emanuel had cared only that we showed no sign of injury, but he had given us no chance to put ourselves together, muttering that considering where we were going, it wouldn't matter.

After walking through a long hallway, a page opened the door to Patrick Warrick's office. Patrick barely glanced at us, but as we came closer his blue eagle eyes caught sight of me, and his jaw dropped in recognition.

I knew that I looked nothing like he remembered. With my hair wild about my sun-darkened face, my blouse slipping immodestly off my shoulders, and my skirt cinched at the waist with a band of crimson silk, there was little to remind him of the Englishwoman he had thought so genteel in St. Augustine.

Still, his face broke into a stunned smile when Emanuel brought us to a halt before him.

"I never thought I would see you again," he said, looking at me as if I were the only person in the room.

"I beg your pardon, sir," Emanuel said. "I am delivering these criminals into your keeping. I suspect there will be a reward. This one is known to be a danger to the best of men." He gestured toward me, but it was Abbie who glared back at him.

Patrick's eyes revealed nothing as he scribbled a quick note. He stood and handed it to one of the guards, who quickly made away with it.

"So, Archer," Captain Warrick said. "Pray tell where you came upon these two, for surely they would have been plucked out from hiding had they been here."

Emanuel straightened up, gaining an inch from pride alone. "We picked them right off Gadsden's. And like any good Englishman, I brought them straight here for the hanging and the bounty."

Before the captain could reply, and despite Abbie's grip on my arm, I spun toward Emanuel. "We are innocent! It is you who abducted us! And your despicable men threw Sebastian into the sea!"

Emanuel held up his hands as if to ward me off, and he raised a brow to the captain. "See, Captain? She's wilder than that half-breed!"

Abbie didn't stir, but the captain's eyes shot up. "Say you Sebastian Ortega?"

"The very one," Emanuel replied, beaming.

"My father," Diego said, surprising us all.

Looking at Diego, the captain rubbed his chin and looked back at me.

"The child… is yours?"

I nodded.

"What is your name, young man?" The captain bent down and looked Diego in the eyes, but my son didn't flinch.

"My name is Diego Federico Ortega de Bouvion," my son said with an assurance that would have made his father proud.

Captain Warrick paced and turned to Emanuel. "So, Captain Ortega was killed in the capture of these three, but surely, he is not known to be guilty of anything."

"He is guilty of much, but the trouble he caused me was relieving my ships of their bounty, and now he sails the *Luisa* under his flags with no claim to her at all."

Captain Warrick leaned against the desk and crossed his arms. "Captain Ortega was commissioned to seize the *Luisa* when you absconded with the Governor's property, and after he stopped you, he took legal claim to her and the slaves she carried, but now say you that he is dead?"

Emanuel nodded.

"I see." Captain Warrick gestured to someone who had come in behind me, but I did not dare to look.

Emanuel grinned, and I reluctantly turned to see two guards approaching us.

"Captain Emanuel Archer. I shall have you placed under arrest for the suspected murder and abduction of a man not known to have committed any crime, as well as for the abduction of two women and a child, none having been found guilty of anything. Be it known that Mrs. Blackwood's name was cleared more than a year ago, although her whereabouts has eluded us, and Mistress Birdsong was never proven to be an accomplice."

Captain Warrick and I looked into each other's eyes for a long moment before Emanuel grasped that his fortune was being reversed.

"No! I took part in no such thing; I only brought these ladies to safety. I am guilty of naught!" he said, moving toward the door.

"Seize him," Captain Warrick said, looking back at Emanuel. "And lock him away."

Emanuel's ranting faded as he was dragged down the hall, but the captain took no note of it.

"Thank God you have been found," he said.

"My name has been cleared? It is certain?" I asked, needing to hear the words again.

Captain Warrick returned to his desk and gestured for us to take seats before him. "Someday I shall like to hear your story, but not today. You are indeed free."

Abbie and I looked at each other, bewildered.

"How did my name come to be cleared, Patrick?

Captain Warrick leaned an elbow on his armrest. "I carry guilt for this, although I knew nothing of it until my wife made her deathbed confession about having lied. Having something to hold over her uncle's head, it was she who claimed you likely killed your husbands, while Paul omitted the word 'likely.' It pains me to say that deception came easy to her. With that said, Abbie, neither can you be accused of harboring a criminal if the person in question isn't a criminal."

Abbie smiled, reaching out to take my hand. "You are free," she said, although I was certain that without Sebastian, I would be a captive of grief forever.

"What killed your wife, Captain? I assume it is not too bold to ask, as she would have sent us to the gallows if she could have." Abbie looked at him with steely eyes devoid of the compassion I had become accustomed to.

"She died in childbirth. My daughter, Emma, is four."

"I'm four," Diego said.

The captain smiled wistfully. "And I thought you were at least seven."

From the smile on my son's face, I feared he had paid much attention to our conversation.

"I'm sorry for your loss," I said.

"I as well," Abbie added. "Have you a new mother for your daughter?"

I thought her bold to ask, but the captain shook his head, seemingly unfazed, while Abbie's gaze darted toward me.

I rose. "Thank you, Captain. I fear we must take our leave before we succumb to exhaustion. This is much to take in."

"There is one more thing," he said. "The Matanzas Inn."

"The Matanzas?" I asked.

"Mordecai Bennington has kept the inn running since the day you disappeared, but it was put up for auction by the council a few years back. In my sorry state, I bid and won, thinking to keep it for you should you ever return, and now that you have—"

I was too numb to grasp the vastness of his words, as fatigue heightened.

"Thank you, Captain. Your kindness overwhelms me, truly, but I can bear no more tonight. We are sorely in need of sustenance and rest."

"I understand," Captain Warrick said. "Then I shall take you there now and ensure that all you need is provided for you. And, Abbie, I will send word to your household that you have returned and that you are to be found at the Matanzas."

Abbie nodded. "Thank you. You have been kind, sir."

The captain sighed. "I'm afraid my Christian spirit will not absolve my guilty association anytime soon. Should either of you need anything, I am the one you should seek out. I vow I will never turn either of you away."

Captain Warrick stood with his hands behind his back, looking suddenly much older than I remembered, but then I had never seen such sadness in his eyes.

CHAPTER
TWENTY-ONE

St. Augustine, East Florida, August 1769

Shattered by the realization that Sebastian was gone, it took weeks before I could do anything more than have my son cared for. I spent days in bed, but after a while, I felt as if Sebastian willed me to rise.

"It's time we get down to business, ma'am," Mordecai said when I walked into the office and slipped into the chair across from the oak desk where he sat.

"I agree completely, Mordecai," I said. "I am ready, and, of course, I hope you continue in the position you had when Harry was in charge."

A smile flashed across his face as he sat back and tapped his fingers against the armrests of his chair. "Much changed while you were gone. Although Captain Warrick purchased the place, I built it into the solid endeavor it is today, far better than in Harry's days."

"I imagine you would have liked to own the Matanzas yourself," I said, wondering how loyal he would be to me.

He scoffed. "The inn is my life, and I put my heart into making the Matanzas as magnificent as she is today. There is only one way you could compensate me."

"I feel you have something to propose." I braced myself for one of Mordecai's longwinded explanations.

"An excellent choice of words." He smiled, and his eyes gleamed as he looked at me. "No reason to mince words, ma'am. I propose a marriage between us."

At a loss for words, my jaw dropped.

"We will run the inn together as husband and wife. I will be a father to your son and to the children we will have together. We—"

I drew a sharp breath.

"Stop, Mordecai," I said, rising from my seat. "There will be no such marriage. This is my inn, and what became of it in my absence does not concern me. You will be well compensated for your labors. Call yourself head butler, manager, my right hand, or all of that, but you will never call yourself my husband."

We glared at each other, but I stood firm.

"You are an ungrateful and spoiled woman, Anna Blackwood. Someday your looks will be gone and no man will come to your aid."

"For that, I should dismiss you this very moment!"

He stood. "Anna... Mistress Blackwood... eh... Mistress Ortega, let me stay, and this conversation will be forgotten." He looked down with practiced humility. "The Matanzas means everything to me."

I sighed, too weary to argue or to start a search for the numerous servants it would take to replace him. He was valuable to the inn, and if he understood his place, he would be valuable to me.

Mordecai backed away from the desk and pulled out his chair for me. Settling into it, he took the chair opposite me and studied me intently.

"Very well, you may stay, but never propose to me again or assume there ever could be anything between us."

"Thank you, ma'am, but that is most unfortunate. We could have been happy, we two."

"Mordecai!"

"Very well, ma'am. It will be my pleasure to serve you, nothing more."

I could see the relief on his face, but there was something contemptuous about his manner that I hoped would pass in time.

"You are welcome. Now, return to your duties, please."

I spent the next few hours going through Mordecai's ledgers, studying his carefully written entries. His accounting was meticulous and accurate, better than what Harry had accomplished in the past. Everything was accounted for, and Mordecai had created an atmosphere of luxury not expected in this little town.

By late afternoon, I had had my fill of being confined to my office.

Gathering my things, I retrieved Diego from his nursemaid and started to walk toward the cemetery.

"Where are we going?" Diego asked when I pushed on the iron cemetery gate and it creaked open, bringing back unwelcome memories.

"We are going to pay our respects to people who lived long before you were born," I said.

"I have no money. How much do they require?"

He looked genuinely worried, and my heart just broke into pieces at the thought of his endearing childhood innocence Sebastian hadn't lived to see.

"They don't require money," I said. "They just ask that we remember them. Like your father, we must remember him."

My son seemed content with my answer, and we continued to walk along the grassy path, shaded by large oak trees draped in Spanish moss, which Diego reached his hands up to grab for no reason at all.

There were more graves than I remembered.

Admiral Rushmore's was the first I encountered, then Katherine's. She had died in childbirth while I was away. Seeing my dear friend's name on a tombstone cut through me. She would have loved to be a mother, but instead she was buried with her infant in her arms, or so I'd been told.

"We are not promised anything in this life, Katherine," I said. "Still, this isn't fair."

When we came to Harry's grave and I looked down at it, I felt oddly indifferent.

We had been like wounded birds for a very short time, lost in grief, until he had let rum and heroin rule him. God willing, he would be with Mary and Muriel somewhere in the hereafter, for maybe Mary could forgive him.

I moved on to Edmund's grave a bit farther away in the clearing. Sinking to my knees at its foot, I felt suddenly close to him.

Edmund, my husband, who had changed my world and brought me to this exotic land where life had taken me on an unimaginable journey.

"Thank you, Edmund," I whispered.

As I stood, I felt Diego behind me.

"Mama?"

I turned, surprised to see my son, with his raven-black hair and sparkling dark eyes, approach me with a little girl at his side, as opposite of him as she could be. Her eyes were equally luminous but of the brightest blue, and her skin was like porcelain, as if it had never seen the Florida sun. Her blond hair was gathered on top of her head in a pink bow to match the pink muslin of her gown. She reminded me of someone, but surely I had never seen her before.

Sofia Warrick's image came to my mind just as I looked up to see Captain Warrick approach us.

"This is Emma!" Diego said, introducing me to his new-found friend. "Can we take her home?"

"Diego," I said, "she's hardly a puppy!"

Turning to the girl, who looked up at me with unmasked wonder, I bent down and took her little hand in mine.

"How do you do, Emma?" I said. I could see she had inherited her mother's smile and that persuasive honey-dripping sweetness that could have cost Abbie and me our lives.

Before the child had a chance to speak, her father came up behind her.

"Quite a peculiar place to meet, wouldn't you say?"

I shrugged. "I've given up on the word 'peculiar,' Captain, for I think nothing can surprise me any longer."

"Still, you have given a difficult day a ray of sunshine. I try to keep Sofia's memory alive for Emma, but her memories of her mother are fading."

I glanced at Diego and Emma, who had wandered a distance away from us. Their cheeks had become rosy from the heat, and their little faces glistened with sweat.

"Perhaps a cemetery is not the best place to keep her mother's image alive," I said.

Looking toward the ocean beyond the bay in the quiet dawn hours of the day, I often envisioned *Nuestra Havana* blazing toward me, with Sebastian standing there as alive and vibrant as I remembered him. The ship would come to port, and he would be the first ashore, sweeping me up into his arms. I always had the same thought, always the same dream, but then I would come in from my balcony and go downstairs to meet the day.

Della, one of the kitchen maids, was the first to see me.

"Captain Warrick is waiting for you, ma'am," she whispered. I noticed a slight blush rise in her cheeks. "He's been here quite long," she said, blushing more.

"Do you know what he wants?"

"He asked for you, ma'am," she said, looking at me as if I had lost my wits.

"Where is he?"

"Outside by his carriage, speaking to Diego."

Turning away from her, I hastened my step and hurried through the lobby and down the stairs to the spot where, indeed, his carriage stood

"What have we here?" I asked, less cheerful than the captain seemed to expect.

He beamed up at me as I descended the stairs. "Good morning to you! Emma had the presence of mind to ask that we come and offer Diego a ride to the schoolhouse, if you permit?" He hesitated. "Should you join us, it would be my pleasure to show you my plantation. It's quite lovely seen from horseback."

I felt my jaw drop. "That is an odd invitation, Captain. You give me no time to consider."

He glanced at the children, who were both grinning up at me. "Master Clarkson will not be pleased if the children are tardy, and my cook is expecting me to take my breakfast at the plantation on Tuesdays, so how long must we delay to ensure your presence?"

The children giggled outright at my stern look, but there was something conspiratorial about them.

Before I could open my mouth, Della dashed down the stairs and handed me a shawl and my purse.

"Thought you might need 'em, ma'am," she said.

Gaping, I took the items from her. "Della!" I said, but she had swiftly retreated, and I was left looking down at my son.

"Please, Mum," he said.

"Mum" had already replaced "Mama," which used to have the most beautiful ring to it. What else would replace his memories of Cuba, of his father?

"Mistress Ortega," the captain said, startling me. "Step down to us here, and then take one step up into the carriage, and we'll be off."

Surprising myself more than the three conspirators, I did as he said.

Despite the rumored wealth Warrick was said to have, the plantation was not large. It looked more like the little farm I thought Edmund and I would have had someday.

Near the stables a longhouse surrounded by old oaks covered in Spanish moss piqued my curiosity.

"Surely, that building is not where you keep your slaves?" I asked. "It seems not like others I have seen."

He glanced at me. "I have no slaves; I have paid workers."

I could feel my eyes widen. "That is unheard of in these times."

He hesitated. "Anna, I have more wealth than Emma's grandchildren could spend in their lifetime, and I won't make myself richer on the backs of tormented people."

"You take my breath away," I said. "I'm quite impressed."

He grinned. "That pleases me," he said, making my cheeks flush.

* * *

"You're back," Mordecai said, looking up from the Matanzas's ledgers when I came through the door to my office. "I'm checking to see what we can spare to repair the roof."

I sank into the chair opposite him, not bothering to have him relinquish my desk chair. "We?" I asked. "And what repairs do 'we' need on the roof? This is the first I have heard of it."

"Be glad you have a man to oversee this structure, for I have come across a leak that must be repaired before it causes damage to the wood below."

I rolled my eyes. "Have you, now? I mean, thank you, Mordecai. It is your job, is it not? It should have nothing to do with having a man, or my widowed state."

Mordecai lifted a brow. "Which widowed state, ma'am? Is it twice? Or is it thrice?"

I gasped, leaped from my chair, and took hold of him as soon as I rounded the corner of my desk. "Get out of my chair!" I said as he bolted up. "How dare you! See to the roof and make yourself scarce, for I have no wish to see you!"

He seemed far calmer than I would have liked.

＊ ＊ ＊

Somehow, the roof was repaired without distressing me further, but blistering arguments between Mordecai and me became commonplace and sent the staff scrambling as soon as they sensed them coming.

I had barely regained my concentration when there was another knock, but it was harder this time.

"Yes," I called out.

The door opened, and Della stuck her head in.

"You have a visitor, ma'am. A lady."

From the way she looked over her shoulder, I gathered the woman was within earshot, so I stood.

"Well, please show my guest in," I said, not caring who it might be.

To my surprise, Emma Warrick came through the door, clutching a small basket with both hands. There was a sweet bow in her hair, and again she was dressed in a gown fit for a fine lady.

"Good day, Mum Ortega," she said, startling me. I'd never been called that, certainly never by a blue-eyed child.

I bent down to face her. "Welcome, Emma. What brings you here?"

Reaching into her basket, she pulled out a piece of crumpled parchment and handed it to me.

"What have you?" I asked, unfolding it.

"Please, Mum Ortega, you must read it."

"Mum Ortega" again.

I looked at the scrawling child's script covering most of the page, inviting Master Diego and Mistress Anna to supper at the Warrick home this evening.

I smiled, wondering how much my son had had a hand in this.

"Does your father know of this?" I asked, folding the parchment and holding it in front of her.

Her lips tightened and she nodded, but a tear trailed down her cheek.

"Oh, dear," I said. "I didn't say no, and I didn't mean to be cross."

Suddenly, she plunged into my arms, weeping softly. Compared to my boy, who, at times, could smell like a wet pup, a scent of rosewater wafted from this little girl, and the softness of her little body in such a voluminous gown felt unfamiliar to my arms.

Footsteps approached us, and soon Patrick stood at the door. The sight of him sent her into his arms, her lower lip still quivering pitifully as he lifted her.

"What have we here?" he asked his daughter.

"She didn't say yes," she said, looking at me with large, moist eyes.

I stepped closer and took her hand. "I didn't say no."

Patrick chuckled. "So, what did she say?"

Emma looked from her father to me, and then back to him, squirming in his arms.

"I don't know, Papa. You try! You ask her!"

Patrick smiled, and I fought to stay serious. "Should I?"

Emma nodded quite seriously.

Putting her down, he turned to me. "Mistress Anna, will you and Master Diego give us the great honor of sharing our supper with you this evening?"

I pretended to contemplate the offer, putting a finger to my chin and looking up at the ceiling beams. Finally, I said,

"Yes… we would be delighted. It would be our pleasure to join you, and I thank you for the lovely invitation."

Emma smiled; her tears already forgotten.

Taking his daughter by the hand, he winked at me. "Then we'll be off to pluck the chickens!" he said, as if he really knew how to do it. "I shall send my carriage for you."

* * *

Late-afternoon games and a sumptuous meal left our children tired and easily coaxed indoors to hear a story from one of Emma's books while Patrick and I lingered on the porch, sipping brandy.

"There is something I have meant to ask you," he said, putting his glass down. "If you don't mind a rather personal question."

"You can ask," I said. "But I might not answer."

That seemed to amuse him, but then he became serious. "I have wondered why you haven't left for Cuba."

I shot up in my seat. "Why, Captain Warrick! You seek to be rid of me?" I laughed, but he didn't.

"Not at all," he said. "But I've heard you say you wished to return to Havana. Why haven't you?"

I clasped my hands, blinking away tears that started to fill my eyes. "I long for it, but I can't bear it. Havana is the most beautiful city I have ever seen, and the Ortegas became my people, but I can't go back and not find Sebastian there. I can't live at Casa Ortega, dine at our table, linger on the terraces without being enveloped in his arms, and I couldn't lie in that bed…"

As Patrick exhaled, his brows furrowed.

"You should think twice before you question me again, Captain."

I could hear the bitterness in my voice, but I couldn't help it.

"Anna," he said. "You are the most free-spoken woman I have ever met, but truly, I did not mean to bring back this pain."

My lips curled into the faintest smile. "It wasn't brought back, for it has never left."

Patrick reached for my hand. "I understand."

For a while, we sat in silence, but then he turned to me again.

"So, you hide your heart and battle on at the Matanzas, braving inevitable challenges, unsuitable suitors, and much more."

I smiled. "Many women would vie to be one of only a few unmarried women in a town brimming with men, but there is only proposal that has me concerned."

Patrick's interest seemed to have been piqued, for he looked at me intently as he took another sip of his brandy. "Who is the unsuitable gentleman?"

I lifted my glass and took a sip, waiting to feel the heat of it spread through my chest. "Mordecai Bennington. He proposed to me."

Patrick sat up. "You didn't accept. Surely, you wouldn't."

"Certainly not."

He sat back, shaking his head. "Then I propose to make you a better offer."

I looked into his eyes, bracing myself.

"Let me make you my wife, and I will tenderly care for you and give you a home and your son a father, a good father. And you will not be prey to lonesome men in pursuit."

I chuckled at the latter part, but he deserved a sober reply. "I am honored, Patrick, but I cannot accept. Not now."

I could tell my words stung him.

"I can wait as long as it takes, for my daughter has come to adore you..." He hesitated. "As have I."

The thought of little Emma becoming my own daughter made me smile, and Patrick was a man better than most.

"Might I have some time? It would not be fair to you that I marry you now, for there has not been a day that I have awakened without Sebastian on my mind. And then... my son. As good a father as you would be, he is an Ortega and a Cuban; it is in his blood and surely in his soul. If I marry you, in time he won't remember who he really is, and I won't forget that I took it from him. I must have time to think."

We sat in silence for a long moment.

"I will give you time," he said. "As for Diego, he would grow into privilege, knowing he is both an Ortega and a Warrick. The two worlds could be his for the taking."

CHAPTER TWENTY-TWO

St. Augustine, January 1770

Drinking Abbie's delectable coffee on a lazy afternoon would have been sheer pleasure had it not been for her clipped conversation.

"What is it?" I asked. "Something is churning in that head of yours, probably to my detriment."

I laughed, but she didn't.

"How long is Warrick to wait? He proposed months ago," Abbie said, lighting her cigar and shooting me a glance.

"Is there haste?"

"Men like Patrick only wait so long. Then they are gone. You are growing old."

I gasped. "You are without mercy!"

Patrick had been good to me these last months, although Mordecai resented his constant presence at the inn, and he rivaled Patrick for Diego's attention.

"Perhaps I should bring Diego back to Cuba."

Abbie turned to me. "You know you don't have the heart for it. Sebastian is dead, and he has been dead long enough for you to marry."

* * *

After a while, thoughts of Patrick and his proposal seeped into my every endeavor, tossing me from unease to hope, with equal resolve.

He deserved an answer.

As soon as I immersed myself in my ledgers, Mordecai was at the door. His fists were opening and closing as they did when he was perturbed about something.

"There you are," he said as if it were a surprise to him. "A word?"

"Certainly," I said, bracing myself for another of his lengthy explanations.

"It's rumored that the captain is waiting for you to accept a proposal," he said. "Would you consider it?"

"It is possible," I replied, seeing his eyes darken. "I haven't decided."

Why Mordecai and Abbie would choose the same day to probe this question had to be fate, for it felt like a tug.

"So, a common man is not good enough for you?" He glared at me. "You are no higher bred than me!"

I swallowed hard. "Mordecai! This is not your concern! I see nothing good coming from a union between us."

"I see, ma'am. But you do with Warrick. Why else would you allow that little daughter he has to follow you about like an adoring pup? Surely, she will grow to be as devious as her mother."

The look in his eyes could have unnerved me, and the tightening of his fists seemed suddenly threatening.

Although I wanted to get him out of my sight, I stepped closer. "Stop this, Mordecai. You—"

Rolling his eyes, he smirked. "When will the captain have your reply?"

I stepped back, weary from his unrelenting contention over the last weeks. "Soon! If it will silence you!" I said with more venom than I intended.

His jaw tightened. "Then you should like to have a wedding here at the inn while the weather is still cool?" He watched me with an unappealing haughtiness.

"I have made no decisions," I snapped back at him. "Leave me be."

As if he hadn't heard, he made no motion to excuse himself.

"But where else would you have a wedding suitable for your rank as a wealthy man's wife? It is not a small bit of work that will be needed to prepare for such an event."

I sighed.

"Then you are going to accept his proposal?" It was hardly a question.

"I didn't say that, Mordecai. You are being unpleasant."

"You think it is not unpleasant to have one's proposal dismissed with the flicker of a lash? At least spare me the humiliation of not having the time to prepare a worthy event, for my name would be tarnished if so much as one dish was served cold. I beg you at least for that kindness."

"Mordecai, I don't—"

Suddenly formal, Mordecai bowed. "I see. Well then, I will start to prepare what must be done," he said, backing away.

When Patrick arrived at the inn for dinner, I took extra care to prepare a special evening.

"Good God, this is exquisite, Anna!" Patrick said when I led him to the table.

"Please sit and let me pour your wine, Captain," I said, smiling coyly as Della appeared with a platter of grilled fish on a bed of roasted vegetables and rice.

"To what do I owe this honor? Have you news?" He raised a brow and looked at me with unmasked anticipation.

"I wanted to thank you."

Patrick looked puzzled, but I could tell he hoped for more. "For what are you thanking me, exactly?"

"I want to apologize as well."

He smiled quite endearingly. "You have done nothing to apologize for, or am I about to learn of your sins?"

I laughed. "No! I am completely without sins! You must know this!"

Patrick's blue eyes took on a deeper glow as he looked at me across the table.

"I want to thank you for being so kind, and I apologize for not being as grateful as I should have been, for you went to great length to secure the inn. But there is more…"

I looked into Patrick's questioning eyes, certain of my choice while ignoring the ache in my heart. I would have to live with that, but I would be my best for Patrick.

"What?" he asked, cocking his head.

"I accept your proposal. I would be honored to be your wife."

Patrick stood up and pulled me into his arms. My knees weakened as he kissed me and held me tenderly, surprising me more than him.

"You have made me a very happy man, Anna."

* * *

Sitting on her porch, Abbie blew pipe smoke into the air. "See, time does heal."

"It helps, but I still grieve," I said. "Part of me will always hope against hope that Sebastian could have survived."

"Have you no love for Patrick?"

I thought Abbie knew me better than that, but I didn't fault her.

"I do, but I love Sebastian. I can't change that?"

Abbie waited until I looked up at her before she spoke.

"You know Sebastian would want you to live well," she said as she took another puff and then released more smoky rings into the air.

"He would, certainly, but it's time I bring my boy back to the inn."

When I summoned Diego from where he had been playing near Abbie's aviary, we startled at the sound of a thunderous stampede of men with buckets running down the street.

"Where are they going?" I asked.

"And why...?" Abbie added.

Grabbing my son, who stood wide-eyed by my side, we slipped out to the street, pressing ourselves up against the garden gate, and watched men on foot and many with wagons and coaches roar past us, spraying us with dust and sand.

"Jonathan!" Abbie called out to a youth she recognized in their midst.

He turned to us, wild-eyed and panting, as he ran on. "The inn's burnin'! All men to the rescue!" he cried out without slowing down.

The men behind him started to chant the same: "The inn's burning! All men to the rescue!"

I gasped, feeling the smoke in the air. "Abbie, this can't be! Not the Matanzas!"

"God only knows," Abbie muttered, but her face mirrored the horror I felt.

In the street, we pressed forward with Diego between us as the crowd made their way to the inn with buckets in hand as fast as their feet could carry them. Gravel crunched underfoot and dust rose, making my mouth dry and leaving my chest aching.

As we turned the corner, the ray of hope I had been clinging to dimmed. Both stories of the inn's white wooden glory, behind dense, impenetrable smoke, were rapidly being devoured by flames lapping higher and higher. Soon all that would be left was smoldering embers.

"Oh, no! Dear God, no!" I cried out, grasping for Diego, who looked as dazed as I felt.

Unable to speak or to take another step, we took in the sight of fire ravaging the inn. Even from a distance, the heat was intense, and plumes of soot drifted up through the air while parts of the roof crashed down to the ground.

Men lining up from the well to the inn heaved bucket after bucket of water onto the flames, but to no avail. They might as well stop, for the fire was beyond their control, and several of the men looked to have been overcome by smoke and effort.

I tried to remember who would have been at the inn this evening.

"Mordecai!" I called out.

Surely, he would know, but he was nowhere to be seen.

"Did everyone get out?" I asked one of the nurses who ran past me. "Do you know? Have you seen Mordecai?"

She stopped, wiping soot and sweat from her face, but then she shook her head. "I haven't seen Mordecai. Captain Warrick is injured, but everyone else got out."

"Warrick? What was he doing here?"

"He must have thought you returned and went in for you," Abbie said, sending shivers through me.

"Where is he?"

"They are working on him by the tool shed. Just over there!"

I turned to Abbie, and our eyes met.

"Take care of Diego," I said.

Abbie nodded. "I will take him home with me. He has seen enough."

As I hurried on, a figure came toward me, and I recognized Mr. Blumford's sweaty face glistening in the light of the flames as he held out a hand for me to stop.

"The man did himself in, he did! He stood on the balcony, tempting the flames to take him once the blaze reached up there. Didn't do a thing to stop it," he said, holding on to me.

"Who, Mr. Blumford? What man?"

"Mordecai! Quite shocking!"

"Mordecai did this?" I asked, suddenly feeling stone cold.

Mr. Blumford leaned in. "One of the maids said he'd been angry lately, something about a woman. Didn't know who, but a woman can break a man."

I felt my jaw drop. *Me. He did this because of me!* He would rather the inn burn to the ground than see Patrick as its master again and wed to me.

As I sped forward, a carriage came to a halt at my side.

"He's here, Anna," Dr. Catherwood called out, reaching a strong arm out for me.

Patrick lay motionless in the front of the coach. In the dim light, I could hardly be certain it was him, for his face and the right side of his chest were covered in torn, wet linens, but he gripped my arm tightly when he heard my voice.

I sank down next to him, trying to avoid applying pressure to any part of his skin. He looked ashen from soot, and by now, we all smelled like cinders.

"Patrick! What were you doing here?"

"Thank God you are safe!" He groaned as the wheels of the carriage dipped into a hole as it sped away. "My leg!"

As Dr. Catherwood gave me the slightest nod, I noticed the makeshift splints tied to Patrick's right leg.

"He fell through the floor," he said, lowering his head.

Patrick tried to turn toward me, wincing from the effort. "I tried to get you out."

"Oh, Patrick, what trying to save me has cost you!"

He cleared his throat. "Seeing you is worth it. Diego?"

"With Abbie," I said. "He is well."

Patrick squeezed my hand and nodded, dislodging the cloth covering most of his blistered face. At the sight of it, I suppressed a gasp.

"Take Diego, go to my home, and order what you need. The Oglethorpes will care for you."

"I will, Patrick. Thank you. You saved me once again."

His lip curled, and his hand reached for my tear-drenched cheek. "I will take care of you," he said, his voice suddenly raspy.

I smiled down at him, hoping it would reassure him. "I will take care of you, Patrick, and… and as soon as you heal, there will be a wedding."

His eyes closed, and when I leaned in, I heard him say, "Then I had better heal quickly."

* * *

"We're here!" the coachman shouted when we reached the infirmary, and he pulled the horses to a halt by the double entry door.

Patrick had kept his eyes closed for the remainder of the winding passage through the town, to the square, and then to the infirmary beyond. Every now and then he had groaned, crying out as if the pain were agonizing. Then he would settle for a moment before it gripped him again.

As I jumped from the carriage, three attendants rushed out from the infirmary. Swiftly lifting Patrick from the coach, they whisked him away, into the building and down the hallway.

As soon as the attendants put Patrick on a treatment table, Dr. Catherwood started to bark out orders, and nurses came running with pots of water, reams of bandages, a pot of lard, and a whole jug of wine. While others unwrapped his legs and started to remove his clothing, Dr. Catherwood turned to me.

"It's best you leave. Attend to your boy. You can return tomorrow afternoon." He pointed at the door. "Give the man some time."

"No!" I said, louder than I intended. "Let me help! Please…"

Dr. Catherwood shook his head as he took my arm and led me away from Patrick. "Don't waste my time with him in an argument with you. Go."

I sighed. "Dr. Catherwood! I have salves for burns that may do him good! And—"

"Mistress Ortega."

From the look in his eyes, it was clear he was certain of his cause.

"Very well, then. Until tomorrow," I said.

Yanking my arm away from him, I walked back out into the street and headed to Abbie's cottage to collect my son.

CHAPTER
TWENTY-THREE

——

St. Augustine, March 1770

The inn was an eerie skeleton of charred wood, ash, and barely recognizable remnants of items from the Matanzas's interior. As I stood in front of the rubble, the view was now unobstructed. I could see the fort and the bay as I had seen them from the back porch, as if nothing was devastated at all.

Mordecai's body had been removed before I arrived. I could no more bear to look at his remains than I could have faced him had he survived his own evil. I couldn't think of a word to say that would fully convey my shock over his actions.

Patrick was the only one sorely injured, for somehow Mordecai had raised enough alarm and provided the staff and guests enough time to escape with their lives. Only Patrick rushed in, when everyone else rushed out.

Townsmen taking down teetering beams that threatened to fall wouldn't let me near the debris-scattered grounds. Many had worked all morning trying to uncover what was left in the rubble, stacking anything salvageable near the shed.

I found night pots sitting unscathed in the soot next to a mortar I had brought from England. Kettles and pots were stacked up alongside them, charred so black they were barely recognizable.

"Sorry for your troubles, Mistress Ortega. You've had more than your share as of late."

I turned to see Mr. Blumford's round face.

"Have you come with more penalties for me now?" I asked.

"Not this time, ma'am. You can rebuild should you choose."

"I am too weary to know what I will do," I said.

"Well, if you sell the land, the money will keep you well."

"I will keep that in mind," I said as he walked away.

"Ma'am?" Della was covered in soot, but she was smiling. "I know you'd want this, ma'am," she said, handing me Edmund's scorched medical bag and dropping his gold pocket watch into my hand. "I was fortunate to find it."

"Della! How can I ever thank you!"

"There is no need, Mrs. Ortega. I will ensure that everything is put in the shed by nightfall, so you need not trouble yourself looking at this mess."

I nodded. "I thank you. This is more than I can bear this morning."

* * *

When afternoon arrived, I started out to see Patrick, but in route I was stopped by many of the townspeople. They meant well, conveying their dismay over the loss of the inn, but their questions were draining. "Why would a fine man like Mordecai do such a thing?" "What woman broke his heart?" "Why did the captain rush into the fire?"

I couldn't speak of it without breaking into sobs, so they let me be, walking away with regretful expressions on their faces while I tried to dodge others who might approach me.

Thankfully, the infirmary was just around the bend.

"I'm here to see Captain Warrick," I told the attendant once I entered the building.

"Of course, Mistress Ortega," the man said. "I shall fetch his nurse. Please take a seat."

I waited for what seemed a long time but finally, I heard light footsteps hurrying toward me.

The nurse looked weary when she finally appeared and sat down next to me. "He feels better, but he is not faring well."

"What does that mean?" My mind started to race as if jolted awake.

"He is weak and at ill ease. Some of the burns are deep, and his leg will take long to heal. Pray pneumonia won't set in, for he already has a cough that is giving him fits."

I stood. "Can I see him?"

"I'm very sorry, ma'am. He has left strict instructions that he wants no visitors. Let him be for now."

Despondent, I sank back down. "But, surely—"

"It's for the best," she said. "He doesn't want you to see him like this."

"So be it, then. I will go, but tell him I will return, and I will see him."

* * *

Over the next few days, I spent most of my time with the children since Patrick still refused to see me, and, for once, I found no solace in my herbs.

Mrs. Oglethorpe seemed set on carrying out Patrick's request to care for me with exceptional diligence. Having brought in a tailor to measure me, she laid out seemingly endless lengths of fabric, asking me to make choices, but nothing seemed important compared to Patrick and his injuries.

"I don't know if I can pay for all of this, Mrs. Oglethorpe," I said, letting my fingers glide across a swatch of cream-colored satin.

"Nonsense, dear," she said. "The captain has ordered you a wardrobe to replace all you have lost. His intended can't be running about in a gown starting to tatter from all the rummaging you do in the debris of the Matanzas."

I started to realize why Patrick was so fond of his home's caretakers, for the Oglethorpes' were more like doting parents than servants.

"We don't question the captain, ever," Mrs. Oglethorpe said, suddenly looking at me with more sternness than I expected.

After the tailor had packed up his samples and left, I turned to Mrs. Oglethorpe. "The captain's generosity is astounding. But he still refuses to see me."

Mrs. Oglethorpe hesitated. "It's no secret, ma'am. He's as proud a man as any of 'em. He has not cared for anyone since Sofia died, but I'm not certain he cared as much for her as he does for you. You must have the good sense to obey him, without question, as a good woman should."

Sebastian would have laughed at that.

After a fortnight, I had more dresses than I had ever owned in my life, and Diego was dressed better than a prince.

Still, Patrick refused to see me.

"He is healing," Abbie said when I confided in her, "but I imagine his impatience. He has always been so agile and strong."

I hesitated. "I think I love him."

Abbie's eyes widened. "Do you?"

"How could I not love a man who has shown me such kindness?"

"Love and gratitude are not the same. Fortunately, good marriages don't have to spring from the throes of passion."

* * *

Days later, I awoke to the commotion of voices and the rumble of trunks being heaved onto a horse-drawn cart outside.

I stared out the window in disbelief. "Mrs. Oglethorpe! What has come about?"

She came into my room, holding a letter. "This came for you, along with a letter with instructions for Mr. Oglethorpe and me."

I tore it open.

My Darling Anna,

I hope your stay in my home has been comfortable and that the Oglethorpes have cared well for you. As of today, you and your son will be moved to another residence, which you can call your own. I will provide all that you need.

It is with great regret that I have decided we are not to be married, so please accept the provisions I make for you as my apology. I do not wish to see you, nor can you change my mind.

With my sincerest wishes for your happiness,
Patrick

I put the letter down, stunned to my core.

"What is the meaning of this?" I asked, glaring at Mrs. Oglethorpe.

"He wants to set you free, ma'am, not bind you to a man who may become disfigured or deformed." She wiped away the tears streaming down her cheeks.

I rushed to the window and looked down at the street below. "Those are my belongings?"

Mrs. Oglethorpe nodded.

"Take everything off that cart, and do not touch anything at all until I return," I said with a command that startled her. I dressed faster than she could gather herself to help me. Then I grabbed my hat and set out for the infirmary.

The guard looked up when I passed by, but he wasn't fast enough to stop me.

I made way down the hall, looking into each room before I found Patrick. As I entered his room, I braced myself, unsure of my welcome.

He lay in an iron bed with his splinted leg elevated by the use of a pulley, which he couldn't reach if he tried. His chest was bound in white cloth, his left arm was wrapped and tethered to his side, and part of his face was still covered. From the stench of him, I gathered that Dr. Catherwood was still treating the burns with lard and soaking the bandages in wine before applying them to his burns. I ached to tear them all off and let his wounded skin breathe, but I refrained and, instead, slipped into the chair at his side.

"You can't keep me away, Patrick," I said.

"You shouldn't have come. You are under no obligation to me," he said.

"I'm not leaving. I will not be dismissed so lightly," I said, making no effort to stand.

He groaned. "You are intolerable."

I smiled. "That will be your plight when I am your wife, for your wife, I will be."

"You can't mean that."

"I do." I smiled down at him. "I love you, Patrick Warrick."

"I've yearned to hear those words, but I may become a beast to behold and have a limp, at best. You might not love me then."

I reached for his hand and held it tight. "I will love you, limping beast or not. You are alive. That's all that matters."

"I will give you time to reconsider your folly," he finally said, not as cross as before. "Stay away until I send for you."

"I will go, but I will be back in the morning. I do not fare well with orders." I winked at him and turned on my heel, leaving his room without looking back.

* * *

Patrick never became the beast he imagined, for as soon as he was brought home to heal further, I washed his burned skin and left it to dry in the open air. His severely blistered face healed and only his right cheek bore signs of his injury, while the burns on his chest healed beyond my expectations. As for the limp, I had yet to see it, although he was not as eager to leap from his carriage as before or take the stairs two steps at the time.

We wed at St. Mary's Church on a beautiful June morning, and Diego and Emma attended us with great dignity for their young ages. With previous marriages behind us, Patrick and I were not thought ill of for wedding so privately.

I was fortunate to have this man at my side, and sometimes I wondered if Sebastian, or perhaps Edmund, had helped me find my way to this new life I was embarking on. Perhaps Sebastian somehow knew how similar Patrick's ideals were to his own.

Heading toward the Warrick house in an open carriage, I remembered how I had walked past it so many times when I had first come to St. Augustine, never imagining it would ever become my home—but then, there were so many things I had never imagined, least of all that I would ever marry Captain Patrick Warrick.

* * *

As I readied myself for our wedding night, I vowed I would not burden Patrick with my grief for Sebastian, but nothing could erase my memory of him, or my desire.

Putting on a lace night shift, I took one last glance in the mirror. Then I walked into the hallway and peeked into Emma and Diego's rooms, where they slept soundly, their nursemaids asleep on cots nearby.

Patrick's eyes lit when I slipped into our bedroom and closed the door behind me. He stood as I walked confidently toward him. Kissing me lovingly, he brought me to bed, but there was no urgency about him as he caressed me masterfully, exploring me until I could think of nothing but him. His touch excited me, and for the first time in a long time, I left Sebastian's world and stepped into my own, where I had become Patrick Warrick's wife.

* * *

Days after the wedding, I realized how much my life was about to change. There were luncheons, dinners, fetes, all attended by people I would never have known had they not stayed at the inn during their time in St. Augustine.

Many of the faraway visitors brought with them the plight of the colonies, and it had become a looming topic as they struggled to unite and free themselves from King George's tightening grip. The topic was a sore one for Patrick, for his loyalty was with the king, as I had always assumed mine was. But since East Florida had not become a colony, there was little need to take an unyielding stand and perhaps cause rifts where there was now friendship.

* * *

After three months of marriage, Patrick called me into his study and motioned for me to sit.

"This appears official, husband," I said. "I imagine I could think of far more amusing things to pass our time."

He smiled at me. "I believe you, but we are here for a very serious matter."

I startled. "What displeases you?"

"Nothing at all," he said. "I merely want to inform you of what I have provided for you."

"Patrick, we want for naught! I have more dresses than any woman in East Florida."

"Exactly!" Patrick said. "Dresses will not sustain you, my love. This document leaves everything I own to you, your son, and Emma, should anything befall me. Any children of our own will, of course, have an equal share."

"You would give my son the same share as the children we have together? Why would you?"

"Anna... I would because you love him no differently than you would a child of ours, and I will raise him as my own, just as you with Emma."

I sat back, more in awe of my husband than ever.

"There is also the matter of the plantations. All the workers are free Negroes, all with a stamped copy of the manumission documents. They are employed by their free will. Remember that."

I nodded, but I had to ask, "Patrick, why do you tell me of this now?"

He paused. "I can profess my love for all our days and raise your son as my own, but if I were to die without bequeathing my fortune to you, it would be a grievous death."

I sighed, and he continued.

"So, by assuring your future, I profess my love to you, Anna Warrick. May you never again be in need, and may you never surrender your independence unwillingly."

I rose, walked around my husband's desk, and slipped into his arms.

CHAPTER TWENTY-FOUR

St. Augustine, January 1774

"I was about to pay you a visit," Abbie said when I burst through her garden gate.

"I have news I can barely contain. Wonderful news!" I said, brushing by her and plopping down on her porch.

Abbie smiled and slipped into the seat next to me. "So, speak!"

"Abbie! I think I am with child! Patrick won't be back from Boston for weeks, but I'll go mad if I don't tell someone!"

Abbie's eyes widened. "Little wonder you are in such a flurry. For once, I'm without words." She took a deep breath, but her eyes darkened and filled me with sudden dread.

"Abbie? What is it?"

She looked away, rubbing her temples as if she were truly pained.

"Please, Abbie," I whispered, "It can't be so terrible that you can't tell me."

Abbie stood. "Come with me. I must show you. There is no other way."

* * *

We walked in silence until we were near the fort.

Leading me down a passageway that I had never noticed before, we entered the foyer to what seemed to be an abode furnished for a person of prominence.

"Wait here," she said.

"Why? Why must I?" I asked as she stepped back.

She appeared to look past me, but then she slipped out the door without another word.

"*Mi corazon...*" The voice coming from behind me was thick with emotion, but I knew it in an instant. Sebastian. *My* Sebastian.

Turning around, I looked into his luminous eyes, seeing him clearly yet not believing he was truly there.

As my hand went to his face, I was sure I was staring at a ghost, but the world started to spin, and I no longer trusted my senses. As I faltered, I felt myself lifted into his arms and thrust into a familiarity that was only mine and his, but as my world darkened, all I could hear was his rapid steps across the stone floor and the thundering beat of his heart against my ear.

When I came to, I was lying on a bed opposite a leaded glass window, in a room with stone walls and a tall domed ceiling. As I stirred, Sebastian sat down at my side.

"You—"

"I'm here, my beloved. I see you have not lost your habit of fainting."

His face was thinner and more chiseled than I remembered, but he was still my wildly handsome Sebastian.

"Where have you been?"

Half-smiling, he took my hand and kissed it. "Searching for you, Anna *mia*."

Pulling me into his arms, he kissed me, igniting an inferno no reason could tame. There could be no explanation, for he was mine and I was his, and the world melted away when we are together, leaving only us and a love that was indestructible.

I slipped my fingers under the linen of his shirt, easing it off him while he loosened my bodice. With clothing falling to our sides, the heat between us rose, melting any inhibition that could hinder the reunion of our bodies and returning us to the rapture we only found together.

Later, when we lay each other's arms, we were silent, and the air was laden with questions demanding answers that neither of us wanted to speak of, but we had to.

"Sebastian?"

He sighed and lifted himself on to one elbow as he reached out and tucked a lock of my hair behind my ear. "Mistress Warrick," he said, no longer smiling.

My jaw dropped. "Sebastian…" My eyes filled with tears, but he barely glanced at me as he got up and started to dress, leaving me stunned and silenced.

When he came toward me, the expression on his face sent shivers through me.

"Do not cry. Listen," he said, "do you know what it has taken me to come back for you?"

I shook my head. "Sebastian—" I started, but he held out a hand to stop my reply.

"Of course you don't, for you were the Lady of the Matanzas and Mistress Warrick, while I awoke shackled to the hull of a slaver, headed to the Bight of Benin to procure more cargo off the shores of Africa. Human cargo, Anna! I was forced to take part in filling the ship with women able to breed like mares, men for labor, and lost and confused children until there was barely a plank left for them to lie on. It would have been easier to die than to fight to stay alive, but then, I find you married. What became of our pledge and the proud, bold woman who made it with me? Have you forgotten, Anna? Do you not see that one of us without the other will never be whole? Would Mrs. Warrick come to my bed unless she knew she was truly mine? I think not!"

I gasped.

"I thought you were dead!" I screamed at him. "Diego needed a father, and I needed a husband. What was I to do?"

Sebastian raised his hands to the sky as if my words were unfathomable, but then he turned to me. "I couldn't exactly write!"

"So, how would I know? I wouldn't have married if I'd thought you were alive. I would never have stopped waiting."

Sebastian shook his head. "It matters not now. You are still mine, Anna! Mine! Look at that bed! Look at it! The woman rising from that bed is mine! Pretend what you will, but you lie if you deny it."

"Sebastian, please." I leapt out of bed, putting my arms around his waist and my cheek against his chest, standing motionless until his arms closed around me.

"Go now," he said. "Bring Diego here for my keeping while you do whatever you must do."

I sighed and pulled away from him. "Diego has a governess, a nursemaid, and house staff to look after him. Let him be for now."

Sebastian sauntered toward the window and looked out while my heart memorized his every movement as I indulged in the scent of him, which still lingered on my skin.

"I've seen him."

I sat up taller. "You have seen whom? Diego?"

My heart started to race.

He turned to me, but the look in his eyes made me uneasy. "I saw my son. A fine boy, he has become."

I gasped. "Did you speak to him? He would have told me, certainly..."

Sebastian shook his head. "I thought not to confuse him by claiming him before I claimed his mother."

The hair on the nape of my neck started to rise, and I felt as if I were unraveling. "Claim his mother..." I echoed flatly.

"I cannot blame you, but what happened while we were apart must be of no importance now. We would have been together still had we not so savagely been ripped apart."

My hand went to my belly and to my unborn, whose mere existence would change the course of my life and shatter hearts.

"I understand," I said, barely comprehending.

He stood and sauntered back to the window, glancing back at me. "*Nuestra Habana* will sail at week's end, for my only reason for being here is to bring you home. You must be ready to leave by then," he said, making me ache to forget the pain we had endured and to go back to who we had been and to us...

I stood, struggling to compose myself. "Where will you be? The ship is not at the docks," I asked, finally bringing a glow back to his eyes.

"I will stay here until we set sail, and you may come as you please, but when *Nuestra Habana* comes through the Matanzas Bay, we will leave St. Augustine with our son for good."

* * *

"Whatever is wrong, Mrs. Warrick?" Mrs. Oglethorpe stood over my bed, looking down at me, her brows tight with worry. Reaching out, she put a hand on my forehead. "Thank heavens you haven't caught the fevers! Shall I call for Dr. Catherwood?"

If it were only the fevers, there would be no decision to make.

"No, I just want to be alone. I'm in need of rest. There is nothing a doctor can do for me," I said, waving her away.

Memories of Sebastian had flooded my mind for such a long time, but he was no longer a memory, he was here.

Sebastian had called me Anna *mia*... It had always sounded like a melody to me, the sweetest of music. Even his outburst yesterday had only made me want me to hold him closer and shut out what had come between us.

Had I truly married you, Sebastian, the law would have made this choice for me, but we so boldly pledged ourselves to each other, believing our bond of love could never be broken.

"It's not broken, for I love you as much as I ever did," I whispered into the stillness.

It would be easier if I didn't.

And Patrick, how could I leave you? I have come to love you deeply, and I have never felt more tenderly cared for. I owe you so much, more than could be repaid in a lifetime.

I got up and walked to my bedroom window as a storm formed in the distance. I was still there when the rain came, for I watched it fall as I tried to push through the tangled thoughts in my head, but there was no reprieve.

Which heart must I break, along with my own? Which child is to be raised by a man who is not his father? Which man will I keep my pledge to, and which man will I force myself to forget, only to see him in my child's eyes until the day I die?

* * *

Abbie greeted me at the door, but at the sight of me, she pulled me inside and shut the gate behind me. "From the looks of you, you won't make it until *Nuestra Havana* returns. Sit." She gestured to one of the chairs on her porch.

I sat.

"Has he seen Diego?" she asked. "I didn't have a chance to ask."

"He watched him, but he didn't approach."

"What says your heart?"

I rolled my eyes. "My heart is in pain. It will shatter regardless of what I do. I have but to choose my poison and wait."

Abbie cleared her throat. "You are grim."

"Abbie, you know this. I am Sebastian's, the revered Lady of Casa Ortega, and I am Mrs. Patrick Warrick, one of the most respectable women of St. Augustine, but mostly I am neither. I'm just a woman, hopelessly torn and passionately in love. I don't know what the right choice is, but if I did, how could I live with it?"

Abbie faced me. "You can live with what is best for your children," she said, sending a dagger through me. "When the time comes, you will know in your heart what is right and trust that thinking of your children's best will lead you to your destiny."

* * *

Abbie's words left me in a daze as I started to walk home, but then I found myself turning toward the fort as if it were pulling me toward it.

Sebastian was bent over a table, studying maps as I entered, but he flashed a smile at me and reached toward me.

"Come here, woman, for I have missed you sorely in these short hours we have been apart."

My composure faltered as I took in the sight of him. Rushing into his arms, I yearned for him to hold me, just hold me until there was no need for a decision.

"What have we here?" he asked, looking down at my wet cheeks.

"This is difficult," I said. "I don't know how to do this! It is as if I am two people. I don't know who I am!"

He squeezed me, kissing the top of my head as if I were a child, but then I felt his hands encircling my waist and his lips hot against my neck.

"Perhaps I should remind you," he said.

"Sebastian…" I sighed, wanting to explain.

"Hush, my love," he whispered. "My angel, I will never take my eyes off you again."

After he unlaced my gown, I let it fall to my feet.

* * *

When the billowing sails of the *Nuestra Havana* crested the horizon, I could bear no more. The choice that would leave me cored would have to be declared, and I couldn't look back.

Sebastian was standing at the window when I burst into his room.

"You saw her too," he said, beaming at me. "We can leave at first light."

He gathered me into his arms, and for a moment we took in the majestic view of the ship forging through sea and sky to come for us.

I slipped out of his arms and steadied myself against the cold stone wall opposite him. "I can't go with you, Sebastian," I said, nearly choking on my words. "I can't stay with you."

He took a step back, looking at me in disbelief. "What say you?"

Every word I was to say would cost me dearly, but it had to be. "I can't leave."

He took a step closer. "You cannot stay."

I noticed his jaw starting to tighten as he stared at me.

"I th-thought you were d-dead, Sebastian," I stammered. "I shouldn't have come to your bed, but I couldn't resist you. I never could."

His stance shifted, and I could see him tense as the eyes that had been so loving glared at me.

"You've been my home, my shelter, my love. I'm so sorry, so dreadfully sorry for both of us."

"So, you choose Warrick."

"He cleared my name, Sebastian. Without him, I would have been hanged for murders I didn't commit! I'm the one who would be dead now."

I searched for a flicker of warmth in his eyes, but there was nothing.

"I had no choice. The inn burned to the ground, and he almost died to save me. I can't abandon him."

Sebastian's eyes filled with contempt as he looked at me. "Spare me his woes. You have a choice now."

"I don't have a choice, Sebastian. I am with child, my legally wedded husband's child."

I could see the shock in his eyes.

"Anna *mia*," he whispered, "you can hurt a man more than a thousand daggers."

He stood back, looking at me, studying me as intently as I did him. He was memorizing me, for we will likely never lay eyes on each other again.

He snuffed, shaking his head. "My son. I will not take him from his mother now, but I will be back for him."

The words stung.

"You can't take him," I said. "He won't know you."

"He has merely to look at me to know where he belongs, but I will never come back for you, Mrs. Warrick."

"Sebastian, I'm sorry..."

He lifted my chin and forced me to look at him. "You've chosen safety over love, my woman. You love me, your soul yearns for me, and you will never find peace for one day or one night, knowing I am alive and that we could have been together. You will burn in your own hell, as I will burn in mine."

He kissed me, his hands gripping me tightly, pulling me to him, awakening every inch of me to his touch as I melted into his arms. Then suddenly he let go, leaving me speechless to watch him turn back to the window.

"Be gone," he said.

I stood, motionless.

For a brief moment, he turned, and a final glance shot between us. Then I fled out the door.

* * *

"I am a stranger to him, Abbie. How do I stop loving someone who means so much to me?" I asked, once again finding refuge in our friendship.

"You don't stop loving him. You let him go, and you let yourself live."

I sighed. "I don't know how."

"You know now that Sebastian is alive, but you made your choice. You broke his heart as well as your own, but you live on for Diego, for Emma, for your unborn, and for the man who was willing to die for you."

CHAPTER TWENTY-FIVE

——

YEARS LATER

St. Augustine, February 1779

For years, I wondered if Sebastian would come back for me, despite what he had said that awful day. Looking at my son, I questioned whether I had made the right choice for him. He was fourteen now, as tall and strong as his father and with the same smoldering dark eyes, which never let me forget.

The child I was pregnant with when I last saw Sebastian was Ella Mia. She was five and as fair-haired as Patrick, with the same high cheekbones and artic-blue eyes. Like me, she has no qualms about speaking her mind, something that only sometimes amuses her father.

Still, these years have been good. Patrick and I are happy together, and there is more laughter in our home than most. We live quietly and rarely journey anywhere, in spite of our many properties. We have spoken of leaving St. Augustine for perhaps Boston, or even London, but whenever we speak of it, St. Augustine lures us to stay.

* * *

"If Diego has no military inclination, he should be sent to Harvard or Princeton as soon as they will take him," Patrick said one evening when we were sipping a brandy on the porch after supper.

"It's so far away, Patrick. I'm not ready."

He smiled and took my hand. "A mother is never ready, but the boy is. Don't stand in his way. He has a sharp mind."

I felt chilled at the thought.

"The inn," I said. "He is quite interested in running the Matanzas someday."

Patrick had taken great care in rebuilding the inn, but for now it was well run by Master Grayson from the Carolinas, and little was required of us.

"I was thinking he could run much more than that," Patrick said. "The country, perhaps, the way the colonies have united. It would be a travesty to keep the boy here."

I feared this would be a battle I wouldn't win, but my husband saw my dismay and reached out to take my hand, squeezing it reassuringly.

"Don't worry. Diego and I will talk man to man and come to the best agreement."

"Thank you, Patrick. You are so good to my son. I'm grateful."

"Our son, Anna."

I nodded.

"It will be a shock for Emma and Ella," I said. "For they will miss him sorely."

I had barely spoken the words when Diego and the girls burst out onto the porch.

"There is a gathering at the harbor to greet an arriving ship," Diego said, hesitating before he turned to me. "I'm almost certain of its ribbons, Mother."

My heart leapt. "What say you, Diego?"

"Diego thinks it is a Spanish ship," Ella said. "He thinks his father has come for him."

I noticed the stern look Diego gave his sister, who quickly bit her lip and looked away.

"It's an Archer vessel," Patrick said. "He is delivering goods to the fort from Charlestown."

Archer? A chill went through me.

"Not Angus Archer, or Emanuel?"

"Their interests have turned elsewhere," Patrick said, seeing my alarm. "They have no need of us."

"May we go to greet the ship?" Emma asked, casting a glance at her brother before she turned and smiled up at Patrick. "There are other children at the docks."

"It is already late. You had better go to your rooms and get ready for bed," I said.

Diego sighed in unison with Patrick as both turned to me.

"My dear, Diego can surely handle himself," Patrick said, winking at Diego, who beamed back at him.

"What about us, Papa?" Ella's eyes flushed with outrage, but I decided to intervene before she melted Patrick's resolve.

"No, girls, off to bed! Young girls should not be on the docks in the evening, even if they are with their brother."

The girls dutifully kissed us goodnight and turned to the stairs, taking long, wistful looks at their brother, who was about to leave.

"Thank you, Father," Diego said. "I won't be long."

He leaned down and kissed the top of my head, but I pulled him into an embrace that he promptly squirmed out of.

"I'll be fine, Mother," he said, flashing me a disarming smile.

Diego slipped out the gate, leaving me more ill at ease than I would admit.

Patrick lifted his glass. "So, where were we?"

"We were talking about our son and Harvard or Princeton."

"Indeed, but for now, let's just enjoy the still of the evening."

Within the hour, the grinding of the garden gate heralded Diego's return, and he came bounding toward us with a smile on his face.

"Look, sweetheart! There he is, just as I said he would be. He is most responsible!" Patrick smiled as Diego slowed down and walked up the final steps to the porch.

"Of course he is," I said, secretly relieved.

"Now, tell us," Patrick demanded. "What was there to see?"

"I met a ship's boy who challenged my dreams of sailing, for apparently, my fantasies should have included retching over the railing most of the time!"

"Remind me not!" I said, stifling a laugh. Strange to smile at it now, for it had been far from amusing then, when so many had succumbed to it on the *Penny Rose*.

* * *

There was a light tap on the door, rousing me from sleep. My eyes fluttered open just as Mrs. Oglethorpe stuck her head in.

She looked apologetic but persistent all the same. "Just wanted to let you know that I'll walk with the girls to the schoolhouse on the way to the market, but I left warm scones for you in the kitchen, and you have only to ask Cook for your tea."

I sat up, stretching leisurely. "Thank you, Mrs. Oglethorpe. And Diego?"

"Oh, ma'am, he's not in his room. I assume he went with the captain to the fort this morning."

"Yes, probably," I said. "Patrick might make a soldier out of him yet, as much time as he spends there."

"Indeed! We'll be off now."

She closed the door behind her, but it was flung open again within the minute when my daughters burst in, planting kisses on my cheeks before they dashed back down the stairs and slammed the front door shut behind them.

* * *

"Where to this morning, ma'am?" Mr. Oglethorpe asked.

"To Abbie. Then to the inn," I said, stepping into the carriage.

Abbie met us on the front porch with baskets overflowing with fruit.

"Take it all! Please! Even my birds are tired of mangos this week!"

"Little wonder your pigeons don't care to fly off, as well as you feed them," I chided as Mr. Oglethorpe carried the baskets to the carriage.

"They reward me for my efforts in their own way," she said. "But talk of birds made me nearly forget that I have the throat balm you asked for. Is Patrick ill again, or are you just having it on hand since his last throat malady pained him so?"

"More of the latter, but I think his throat is starting to give him grief again. Although when I tell him he sounds hoarse, he says he only strained his voice."

Abbie went inside and returned with a large bottle just as Mr. Oglethorpe came back to the porch.

"There is just a small space left for you should you want to be taken to the inn now, or I can come back for you."

"I'll come now. No need to make the trip twice," I said before turning back to Abbie. "Thank you! There will be much pie and marmalade to be made with all this fruit, and Patrick will be grateful for the balm!"

A quick smile passed between us as I dashed off and climbed back into the carriage.

The first thing I noticed on arriving at the inn was that there were no ships in the harbor. The docks looked swept and clear, and only a few people walked by, while the dock men wagered their hard-earned money on dice as they gathered in the shade.

I let out a deep sigh of relief. The *Mary Archer* was gone! There would be no need to argue with Diego about squandering his time at the docks, searching for any snippet he could hear about his colorful father. Perhaps it was high time I gave him answers to some of the questions that fed his imagination. I had thought it would be easier for him if he didn't know too much about Sebastian, whose life was so different than ours, but maybe I was wrong.

By the time I got home, the girls were practicing the piano. From the smells coming from the kitchen, I could tell it was close to supper time, and Mrs. Oglethorpe would soon be calling us to the table.

Patrick came through the door just as I was starting to wonder if we would have to eat without him and Diego because of whatever important matter was taking place at the fort.

Closing the door behind him, he peeled off his coat and came toward me.

I lifted my cheek as he bent down to kiss me. Then he picked up the day's mail, which was waiting for him on the desk.

"It smells divine in here," he said. "Mrs. Oglethorpe has apparently prepared a feast!"

"Yes, Diego's favorite," I said, looking toward the door. "Where is he?"

Patrick stopped and looked at me. "I just arrived. I wouldn't know."

"Was he not with you at the fort today?"

Patrick looked perplexed. "No. Why would he have been? Was he not at school?"

I felt my stomach flip as I stood.

"No... He wasn't in his bed this morning. We thought he left with you. Patrick..."

My fingers started to shake, and I clasped my hands together, but Patrick had already noticed.

"Anna, there has to be a logical explanation," he said.

I knew he was trying to calm me, but my son wouldn't leave without a word; he never had.

Patrick went to the staircase and looked up. "Girls, come down here at once!"

A door opened and shut, and within seconds the girls came rattling down the stairs and leaped into their father's arms.

"Papa!" Ella cried out, squeezing her cheek against his chest as he wrapped his arms around her.

"Did Diego tell you where he was going today?"

Emma looked from Patrick to me and then at Mrs. Oglethorpe, who had just come to the parlor door. She had heard what we were speaking of, and her worried look only made me feel more ill at ease.

"Wasn't he with you, Papa?"

I felt myself tremble, and I sank into my chair. "Patrick..."

"So, he has been gone since morning... or longer. And he said nothing about this?"

The girls shook their heads, watching us with big eyes.

Mrs. Oglethorpe sighed. "This is so unlike the boy. He is not one to stray or disobey."

I swallowed, suddenly unwell. "Patrick!" I gasped.

"What is it, Anna?" He let Ella slide out of his arms and turned to me.

"Patrick... Angus Archer..."

Patrick's eyes narrowed. Slowly he shook his head. "That's unlikely. Why on earth? How would he know...?"

I took a deep breath, praying this was all a nightmare and Diego would be on his way up the garden path as we spoke, but there was no grinding of gate hinges, nor did we hear the sound of his steps leaping onto the porch.

"Have you looked at Diego as of late? He is the image of his father, and Archer hates Sebastian," I said, trying to contain myself in front of our daughters.

"Aye, sir, ma'am! I should not have assumed he was with you this morning, Captain! I will not forgive myself!" Mrs. Oglethorpe said, wringing her hands.

"This is not your doing," I said, turning to her. "Please take the girls for their dinner while we speak."

"But, Mother—" Emma said, taking a step toward me.

"Have your supper, girls. Unless you remember something that your brother might have said?"

I looked into their tear-filled eyes, but neither said anything as they followed Mrs. Oglethorpe into the kitchen. When the door closed, I turned to Patrick.

"Diego went to look at the ship," he said, "but he returned not very impressed, with no word of having spoken to Archer or anyone but a ship's boy."

"The *Mary Archer* left early this morning!" I said, feeling my chest tighten. "What else could it be, Patrick? Where else could he be?"

My husband looked at me for a long time before reaching for the door. "I'm going to the harbor. The dockmaster must know something."

"And I'll go to Abbie. She might have seen him," I said, following him outside.

Before we parted ways, I looked up at Patrick. "I'm frightened, Patrick. Diego always lets me know where he is."

Patrick nodded. "Let's make haste, but try not to worry. There is probably an explanation that seemed quite agreeable to him but, perhaps, not to us."

Nothing he said was of any comfort.

* * *

Abbie came toward me as soon as I stepped onto her porch, her eyes questioning. Sometimes words were superfluous between the two of us.

"What has happened?" she asked, drawing a deep breath.

Blinking away tears, I couldn't find the words.

"Tell me," she said, looking into my eyes.

"Diego," I whispered.

"What about Diego?" Her eyes widened, and she seemed suddenly guarded. "Is it the fevers? What has happened?"

I shook my head, drawing a deep breath. "He's missing... since this morning... I thought he was with Patrick... Have you seen him? At any time today?"

It took her only a moment to reflect. "No. Not since yesterday, and he said nothing unusual then."

After I told her everything, we sat silent for a moment. Her first thought was Archer too, and like me, she wondered how he could have gotten to Diego without awakening anyone in the early morning.

Neither of us asked why. It was obvious. This was about Sebastian and Angus. The feud between them had endured for decades and was probably even more bitter now, after Sebastian's escape.

"I dare not think of what Archer could do to him," I said, trying to control my nerves.

Abbie turned to me. "They will likely ask for ransom, but with that, they should keep him sound and well fed... although terrified, poor boy."

CHAPTER TWENTY-SIX

———

St. Augustine, April 1779

The anguish of not knowing where Diego was felt like it was squeezing my innards to a pulp, barely allowing me to breathe.

There had been no word from him, no request for ransom, and not a word of gossip that had led to anything at all.

"Nothing," Patrick said when he came home just before supper. "Still nothing."

He kissed the top of my head absentmindedly, but his gaze went to our daughters, who waited for word as much as I did. There was barely a need for a "hello" anymore, for coming through the door, he knew to relay what he knew about Diego before so much as a greeting.

"Someone will speak up," he said to our daughters more than to me. "It's just a matter of time."

I nodded, not certain I believed him.

Before either of us could respond, there was a knock on the door. Mrs. Oglethorpe rushed to open it, making me realize that she had been nearby, as anxious to hear a word of hope from Patrick as the rest of us.

The man at the door looked like a dock man. His face was sun-darkened, his hair as unkempt as his clothing, and the distinctive smell of sea and tar followed him inside.

"Evenin', folks," he said. "I'm Samson Grimsby. A word, Captain?"

Patrick walked toward the man. "What's this about, Grimsby?"

Mr. Grimsby glanced at me, the girls, and Mrs. Oglethorpe as we all stared back at him.

"In private?"

"Is this about our boy?" Patrick towered over the man, but I could see his almost imperceivable nod.

Patrick turned to me. I knew that from the look on my face, he would not think to dismiss me, but his gaze settled on Mrs. Oglethorpe and the girls.

"We will talk in my study," he said.

Opening the door for Mr. Grimsby, he offered him a seat while he sat down at his desk. I stood, for my nerves were about to do me in, and sitting with any calm felt impossible.

"What do you know, Grimsby?" Patrick asked him.

Grimsby looked up at me as if he would have me leave.

"I am his mother. I am not leaving." My words came out sharper than I intended, surprising the man, but I didn't care.

Patrick nodded. "Out with it. We have no patience for opportunists."

Mr. Grimsby grinned. "I'm no such thing, Captain. I know who has your boy, and I'm here to talk of ransom."

I gasped. "Thank God! He is not hurt, is he?"

The man shot a glance at Patrick before he answered me. "Your son hasn't been harmed, Mrs. Warrick." He looked at me as if I should thank him. Instead, I exhaled and waited for him to speak.

"Archer's got him. Lured him in like a pup."

Patrick held a steely face, but I could tell he cringed at the thought, as did I.

"He's on the *Mary Archer*?"

"I didn't say that."

Mr. Grimsby sat back confidently, but my husband's impatience was evident. "I have no time for your amusement, Grimsby. Make yourself clear."

Samson Grimsby stifled a grin. "You will get your boy back, but Archer wants the *Luisa*, fully fortified, canons and all."

I gasped, and I saw that Patrick startled.

"Why does he think we can deliver that ship?" Patrick asked.

"I'm a messenger. Got good coin for telling you this. You are to tell me when you are ready to deliver."

"What happens then? How much time do we have?" Patrick asked without urgency.

Grimsby shrugged. "Dunno, sir. You are just to tell me when you got her. Guess it depends on when you want your boy back." He chuckled. "I'll be back from time to time to see how you are faring."

From time to time? The unpredictability of this link to my son's return rattled me.

"Surely, we must be able to find you?" I said.

I felt Patrick's gaze on me and stepped back.

"You can find me on the docks," Grimsby said, half-smiling at me. "I'm there when I'm not elsewhere."

"Tell Archer he will have what he asks as long as our son is unharmed," Patrick said.

Bidding Grimsby good night, Patrick led him to the door while I sank into a chair in the parlor, burying my face in my hands.

"At least there's some news," Patrick said, sitting down beside me and taking my hands in his.

"What they want is the *Cuervo*," I whispered, "but why do they think we have any influence over Sebastian?"

"Because they have his son. And they're right. We will go to any lengths."

Patrick seemed lost in thought as he paced with his fists digging into his sides and his eyes downcast.

"Sebastian should know of this—"

"What of Isabella?" he asked. "Would she surrender a ship like the *Cuervo* for a nephew?"

The question sounded almost odd to my ears.

"Isabella would surrender her life for Diego," I said with a certainty that seemed to surprise my practical husband. "If she knew of this, she would be hunting down Archer as we speak."

Patrick stopped and turned to me. "Perhaps she is."

"What?"

"How are we to know they haven't presented Sebastian with the same request for ransom? Diego could become a prize for the highest bidder."

I sank back into my seat. "That could also mean that Isabella and Sebastian are searching for him this very moment, and no one knows Archer's lairs better than Sebastian!"

I threw my arms around Patrick, reveling in a sudden moment of hope.

"You might be right," he said, smiling down at me. "Either way, by morning, every ship leaving this harbor will have an eye out for Angus Archer and any Ortega vessel."

"Yes! Thank you, Patrick. Thank you!"

Patrick smiled, although I still saw the worry on his face.

* * *

The following morning, I took one of several gold coins hidden in a secret compartment in my jewel box and slipped it into my pocket before I rushed out through the garden gate and headed to the docks.

Samson Grimsby saw me before I saw him and sauntered toward me with a wry smile on his face. "Mornin', ma'am. I didn't expect the captain's wife to come a lookin' for me."

I tried to look indifferent. "My husband doesn't know I am here. I want a word with you."

"Not much I can say, ma'am."

"Because you don't know, or because you don't dare?" I asked, looking into his eyes with a boldness that took him aback.

"I value my life, Mrs. Warrick. I already told you your boy is well."

I took a step closer. "Well, *where*, Mr. Grimsby?"

"Ma'am, I can't tell you."

We were standing uncomfortably close, but still, I lowered my voice. "Surely, you have the promise of being well paid, but I am a very wealthy woman, and I can pay you richly for your help... today."

A flicker of greed lit his eyes as he considered my words. "What are you offering?"

I pulled out the coin, holding it in the palm of my hand before I slipped it back into my pocket. "No one needs to know of this. If anyone should take note of this meeting, you can tell Archer we need more time."

His eyes narrowed as he studied me.

"You can trust me," I said, trying not to look as desperate as I felt.

He sighed. "He's being held on a ship off the southern-most island. On a good day, he can see Cuba."

He held out his hand, but I closed my fist around the coin, pressing it deeper into my pocket. "This island has a name?"

"The Spanish call it Cayo Hueso. That's all, ma'am. Now, give me that coin, for I've risked my life for it."

The coin fell into his hand as mine brushed over his.

"Thank you," I said. "You had better not have deceived me."

* * *

"There are Creeks near Cayo Hueso," Abbie said, ponder-ing my news. "It's the only deep harbor in that region where ships can come to port."

She took a deep puff from her pipe, blowing fragrant blue smoke into the air around us. "Getting there is a journey of several weeks," she said, "but we may have a remedy."

"What remedy?"

She got up and pulled parchment and an inkwell from a desk drawer. I watched as she wrote a few words along the top of the sheet. Then she blotted it, cut off a piece of the parchment, and rolled it into a scroll.

Winking at me, she said, "For our ally."

If this had not been of such dire importance, I would have thought her sudden glee was amusing, but now I was just perplexed.

We walked through the garden and stopped at her aviary. She seemed to be searching for a specific bird, but they looked identical to me. Finally, she reached in and pulled out the larger of several pigeons and tucked the bird under her arm before heading inside.

"Come along," she said to me without offering a bit of clarity.

As she carefully wrapped the strip of parchment around the pigeon's leg and tied it with a leather cord, I was slowly filled with a sense of hope.

"A messenger pigeon…"

"Yes. You didn't think I would send a smoke signal, did you?" The grin left her face as soon as she looked at me. "This may help, Anna. The bird will fly back to our tribe, far closer to Cayo Hueso than we are and faster than any ship can get there."

"Time to fly home, little friend," she whispered to the bird, and then she lifted her hands and released the bird into the sky. It took to its wings and was gone in an instant.

"Godspeed," we whispered in unison.

* * *

Patrick glared at me when I told him of the day's events.

"What comes over you, Anna! Do you not realize you could have put yourself in Archer's hands and I could be left searching not only for my son, but for my wife?"

I cringed. Patrick rarely raised his voice to me. I sat down and I waited for his anger to subside so we could talk. He would not put a hand to me—of that, I was certain, and blessed, compared to many women.

"Do you hear me, Anna?"

I looked up and nodded as dutifully as I could.

"I must know that you won't intentionally put yourself in danger when I am not with you."

"I just wanted to help," I said.

He stood. "You have, actually. You and Abbie are the most resourceful women I have ever known. May your efforts lead to Diego's safe return, but until we hear anything at all, our ships are patrolling the coast, and landowners from Charlestown southward will be aware of our quest."

"You will go to Cayo Hueso yourself?" I asked.

"Indeed, I will. At first light."

* * *

"Here's your tea, ma'am," Mrs. Oglethorpe said, placing a cup on the table as I entered the kitchen. "What can I serve you this morning?"

I sighed. "News from my husband, or Isabella, or even that Grimsby fellow. It's been weeks."

"At least there hasn't been any bad news," Mrs. Oglethorpe said. "Some oatmeal?"

I sighed. "No oatmeal. And, you're right about bad news. It does travel faster."

"I don't want oatmeal, either," Ella said, chiming in. "Can't I just have bread with peach jam?" She looked particularly cross this morning, pushing her bowl away as if it contained something foul.

Before Mrs. Oglethorpe could reply, I leaned over my daughter. "You don't know how fortunate you are, child! I was the one preparing breakfast of eggs and ham in my father's house from the time I was your age. You have but to wash, dress, and come down the stairs."

She looked up at me with big eyes. "Could I have eggs with ham, then?" she asked in a thin voice.

Mrs. Oglethorpe choked a chuckle as my example was lost on my daughter. "No. You cannot. That was not the point."

Our conversation ended with the screech of a carriage coming to a halt outside, followed by Patrick's voice.

Bolting out the door and into the rain, I flung myself into my husband's arms and felt them tighten around me.

"How I have missed you," he said.

"And I you," I said, planting a quick kiss on his lips. "Where is Diego?"

When he let me go, my heart sank as I realized Diego was not with him.

"Did you not find him?" I asked, barely daring to breathe.

"Diego has been rescued. He's safe," he said, leading me inside and out of the rain.

"Is there news?" Mrs. Oglethorpe asked carefully as Patrick scooped our daughters into his arms.

"He has been rescued," my husband said again.

"When is he coming home?" Ella asked, looking first at her father, and then at me.

Patrick removed his topcoat and sat down. Steepling his fingers, he sighed. "Ortega has taken him to Cuba. He has made it clear it's time his son stays with him."

As if I had been punched in the gut, I felt suddenly ill.

"He didn't," I barely whispered, sinking into the armchair across from him.

Patrick looked as grieved as I felt. "He did."

"You spoke to Sebastian?"

He nodded. "I did. He looks well," he said, sparing me the urge to ask. "There were no threats, no animosity. We granted each other safe passage, and we parted, but his words were clear."

Mrs. Oglethorpe sighed and retreated to the kitchen, blotting her eyes with her apron.

Emma buried her head in her hands while Ella slid down next to her father and wept.

"He can't do this, Patrick. Diego belongs here."

Tears stopped me from saying another word.

"Go to the kitchen, girls," Patrick said. "Your mother and I must have a word."

Reluctantly, the girls rose.

"You will make Diego's father give him back. Won't you, Papa?"

I could see that Ella's sweet plea tugged at Patrick's heart as much as it did mine. He nodded and gently steered her toward Emma, who turned into the hallway. When they were out of earshot, his gaze met mine.

"This is a painful turn of events, but we must find comfort in knowing that Diego is safe."

I slid to the edge of my seat. "That is not enough!"

Patrick sighed, watching me as I struggled to keep any composure. I had an intense desire to pick something up and hurl it at the wall, but instead I dug my hands into my lap and folded them.

Patrick was irritatingly calm, and worse, he spoke slowly to make himself clear to me as if I were no longer of sound mind. "Sebastian is Diego's father, and Diego has yearned to meet him, so—"

I stood, outraged at my husband's attempt at logic. "So, now they have met. He can bring him home! Diego has been raised English! He doesn't know a word of Spanish! And... we were speaking of Harvard, were we not?"

Patrick's smile was bittersweet. "I didn't realize you approved."

I wished I had, and I wished Sebastian were standing before me so I could make him give in to me like he always had when I wanted something. Then I remembered the last time I had seen him, when our hearts had been flayed open and he had said, "I won't be coming back for you, Mrs. Warrick."

The memory still hurt, and the realization that I could probably no longer sway Sebastian like I could when our love had meant everything in the world to us made it no better. To him, I was now someone from the past, someone who, long ago, had birthed the treasure that was now in his charge.

"I can't let this rest, Patrick. I must see him. Surely, Diego wants to come home. He can't just stay in Cuba."

"My darling, he is no longer in the hands of ruffians who kept him only for their gain. He is well, and he is with his father. The boy is fourteen—"

"He will be fifteen shortly," I said.

Patrick nodded. "Yes. He will soon be a man. Staying with his father for a while could be quite a benefit to the boy. Harvard can wait."

"Patrick! I thought you loved him!"

He looked at me with more patience than I probably deserved. "Anna. Think of the boy. This is an adventure for him, and Sebastian will cherish him. You lived there yourself, and quite well, from what you have told me."

"This pains me beyond reason, Patrick. Sebastian must have said more, how he came upon Diego and what his intentions are for him, did he not?"

Patrick pulled up a chair, so close to me that our knees touched.

"We arrived just as the *Mary Arch*er was sinking, but when Sebastian took note of us, he lingered in a small harbor, where we faced each other and talked between ships. Isabella, though, had already headed to Cuba with Diego on the *Incognita*. Apparently, the lure Archer had used to bring Diego aboard was that he possessed something of Sebastian's that he would have ready if Diego were to return later in the evening… Sadly, that something was to be Diego."

I gasped. "Good God, that evil man!"

Patrick nodded. "Sebastian and Archer agreed to meet in a bay near Cayo Hueso, where the ransom would be delivered and Diego freed. When Sebastian and Isabella arrived, Archer was already waiting, and Creeks were circling the ship in a fleet of canoes, as they often do, trading wares and relaying messages. Isabella's ship was the one Archer believed was the ransom, but when they came close, Sebastian stood midship with cannons pointed at the *Mary Archer* and called all his sailors on deck, causing Archer to do the same. Sebastian drew out the negotiations on how the exchange would take place until the Creek were able to open a hatch on Archer's vessel and retrieve Diego. Once they had him, they smuggled him through the array of canoes to the *Incognita*, where Isabella took him aboard, but before Archer realized that Isabella was taking the ship out to sea, Sebastian was signaled, and he sank the *Mary Archer* before they had a chance to attack."

I exhaled, not realizing that I had been holding my breath.

"Sebastian is brilliant," I said. "I shall try to be grateful to him, but I feel I am unraveling."

There was tenderness in Patrick's eyes as he looked at me, making me suddenly flush with shame over my selfishness.

"Husband, I do not want to seem ungrateful. I am more thankful for your efforts than words can express."

A subtle smile crossed Patrick's face. "You do not have to thank me. Diego will be back someday, but let him have this time with his father. It is something he has yearned for."

I nodded as my insides cringed.

"I miss him," I whispered, unable to stop a flood of tears for him, for me, for the madness of my life's events. Patrick wrapped his arms around me, and I clung to him as if he could ease my pain.

"We will all miss him," he said.

CHAPTER TWENTY-SEVEN

St. Augustine, June 1779

"Hm… pardon me," Mrs. Oglethorpe said, handing Patrick an envelope with a seal I recognized. "This was just delivered."

His eyes lit as he broke Sebastian's seal and opened the envelope. "I believe we have a letter from our son," he said, smiling at me.

I wanted to tear it from his hands, but instead, I sat down and waited for him to read it for me.

He cleared his throat and started.

"To My Beloved Parents,

At last, I have the ability to send you word, and my deepest, most heartfelt apology for my impulsive behavior, which has separated me from you all this time.

As you know, I am at Casa Ortega, and I have been reunited with my father. Aside from missing you and my sweet sisters, I am well and happier here than I ever expected to be.

My father and Tia Isabella have welcomed me into their lives, and I am learning much every day. Dalia, Father's lady, is quite jealous of Father's past, but when she is out of earshot, they both speak highly of you, Mother. Even the servants tell me about the years you spent here, including the day of my birth, which is more than I wished to know.

I have returned to my studies, and I am learning Spanish. My father is teaching me about the sea and sailing, and when there is time, we fish, hunt, and even dance. As you know, my father and Tia Isabella dance very well, and they say I have the rhythm of a Spaniard.

I don't know when I will see you again, but my thoughts are with you, and I pray for you every day. Please do not fret for me, and please be happy, because that is my wish for you.

Give my sisters a loving hug from me and extend my greetings to Abbie, the dear Oglethorpes, and the friends I left behind.

With respect and all my love,
Your son,
Diego"

Patrick grinned as he tossed the letter into my lap and sank into the seat next to me. "The boy is articulate! He writes with the finesse of someone beyond his years! And, he is well!"

I picked up the letter. Clutching it to my chest, I burst into tears.

"Anna! I thought this would please you!"

"It does," I said, sobbing.

I sensed that Mr. and Mrs. Oglethorpe had come into the room and were standing silently by the door.

"Is it about our boy?" Mr. Oglethorpe asked carefully.

"Yes, it's from Diego. He is well, but his dear mother is overcome by receiving word from him," he said while I wondered about this woman, Dalia, and where she fit into Sebastian and Diego's lives.

* * *

The following morning came with thunderstorms awakening us at an early hour.

Patrick cleared his throat, but I could tell something was amiss.

"You don't look well, Patrick," I said.

He shook his head, but his eyes were glassy, and there was a flush about him.

"It's just my throat again. I should curb my desire to correct the recruits at the fort as loudly as I do. It strains my voice."

I wasn't certain I believed him, but I indulged him. "You have high expectations but much is required should they aim to be anything like you."

He chuckled and cleared his throat again.

"It would do you well to spend the day in bed and let me give you a throat balm."

"This will pass quickly, as it has before."

"But, Patrick—"

"But naught," he said. "Stay with me for a moment before the day begins."

As I snuggled next to him, he caressed me with rising interest. Being flushed with fever seemed not to affect his desire for me, but I slipped away, chiding him.

"I will not surrender to you, Captain, unless you promise me you will abide by my medical instructions for the remainder of the day!"

"Unlikely," he said, pulling me down, and he took my breath away as I surrendered without further negotiations and no longer questioned his judgment.

* * *

Patrick came home early in the afternoon, pale and sweating profusely.

"I'll take the throat balm," he said in a barely recognizable voice.

Instinctively, I rushed to him and placed my fingers below his jaw, alarmed at the bulging glands in his neck.

"You should have listened to me, Patrick," I said, but I regretted it immediately, for this was no time for reproach.

"Mrs. Oglethorpe!" I called out, and she appeared in an instant, her eyes widening as she looked at Patrick.

"Good God! What has happened?" she asked. "What shall I fetch?"

"Your husband! He must help me get Patrick to bed, and please bring the throat balm and feverfew from the cabinet."

She nodded and hurried away. I loosened Patrick's cravat and helped him out of his jacket. His shirt was wet and stuck to his skin, and he shivered as I rolled up his sleeves.

"I've never seen you like this," I said. "You're so pale."

"I've never felt like this," he answered, clearly struggling to speak.

* * *

Dr. Catherwood arrived by suppertime, but after spending most of an hour with Patrick, he emerged with news that was of no surprise to me.

"What is it, Doctor?" I asked, rising to my feet, although I felt faint with worry.

Dr. Catherwood pinched his lips together and shook his head.

"Doctor?"

"Nothing I can do, Anna, dear. It looks like quinsy."

I sank down into my chair.

Patrick would die, and it would be a slow and painful death, where swallowing and breathing would be agonizing and taking in the slightest bit of fluid would be a struggle. His throat would gradually swell until it shut, not allowing him another breath, and then my beloved husband would be dead.

"I'm sorry," the doctor said, but I couldn't bear to look up at him.

I didn't notice Mrs. Oglethorpe come into the room until I felt her hand on my shoulder.

"Ma'am?" She looked from me to the doctor, her lower lip quivering, and she trembled, just as I did.

"I'm afraid it's bad news," Dr. Catherwood said. "Quinsy. The only thing I can offer is a good bleeding."

Mrs. Oglethorpe sank down beside me, bursting into tears and heart-wrenching sobs as we wrapped our arms around each other and wept.

Dr. Catherwood waited until we managed to collect ourselves. Mrs. Oglethorpe rose and stood next to me. I could feel she was willing herself once again to be the strong, motherly woman I so often depended on, while I sat, clutching the armrests of my chair to keep myself from shaking.

"Should I leave a tincture of Valerian for the two of you?" he asked, glancing from Mrs. Oglethorpe to me.

Mrs. Oglethorpe looked at me and shook her head, as did I.

"No thank you, Doctor," I said. "We have what we need, and I believe my husband will not want to be bled."

"Very well, then," he said. "I will return in the morning."

When the girls came home, we sat in the kitchen with Mrs. Oglethorpe.

"There must be some hope, Mama," Emma said after I told them. She shot to her feet and started to pace while Ella climbed into my lap, pressing her face against my chest and weeping bitterly.

"You can make another tonic! Abbie will have a remedy!" Emma insisted.

I shook my head, and Mrs. Oglethorpe's face showed no sign of agreement.

Ella looked up at me, wiping the tears from her cheeks. "Diego will never see Papa again, will he?"

Her question brought me to tears, and I held her tightly as I shook my head. "Probably not, darling child. Probably not."

* * *

By morning, Patrick was no better. After our daughters left for school, I sat at the foot of our bed while he sipped tea and struggled to swallow.

He no longer made an effort to speak, but instead, whispered.

"Send for Joshua Bridges. I must see him today," he said.

I froze. "The barrister? But why? Surely, it can wait until you are better," I said, hoping it would give him a modicum of hope.

He cocked his head, and from the look in his eyes, he did not have to say more.

"Very well, but you are being far too ambitious. You should rest."

"There will be time to rest," he said, unsettling me more.

Mr. Bridges arrived within the hour with ledgers and documents in hand. He reminded me of Mr. Blumford, hardly ever a bearer of good tidings and equally dull.

When Mrs. Oglethorpe showed him in, I rose to leave Mr. Bridges and Patrick to their business, but Patrick motioned me to sit and took my hand.

"Whatever is this about that cannot wait?" I asked while Mr. Bridges shuffled through his papers, making an effort to avoid my gaze.

"My will," Patrick said.

I rose from my seat, staring at them both. "Patrick! Surely, there is no need for this! You need your rest."

From the stern look on his face, I realized that any opposition would be a strain on him, so I sat.

"Mrs. Warrick," Mr. Bridges said, "since we are gathered here, perhaps it would be prudent to review these matters and hope that none of it will have to be taken into effect for many years."

I looked at them both and nodded.

"Patrick, old friend, please interrupt me should there be anything you would wish to change. Otherwise, I will review your wishes, as we have previously discussed." He turned to me. "Are you ready, Mrs. Warrick?"

"Oh, Joseph, we know each other well! Call me Anna, please. I have no patience for formality."

"As you wish, Anna. As you are aware, your husband owns this house, the cottage and the stables behind it, the Matanzas Inn, the plantation here, one n New Smyrna, another in Carolina, a house in Boston, a townhouse in London, a large estate in Surrey, and a smaller one in Kent. In addition, he owns livestock, fine riding horses, furnishings, silver plate, crystal, and fine china, art, exquisitely bound books, tapestries, a fine collection of jewels, and much gold."

I gasped when the list came to an end.

"It sounds so immense when it is all summarized in this manner," I said.

Joseph smiled. "It is. Your husband is a very wealthy man."

Patrick lifted his hand, interrupting him. "Tell her the plan," he whispered.

"Yes, indeed. On the day your daughter Ella Mia Warrick was born, this document was created. In the event of Patrick's death, all the property I have mentioned will be yours to do with as you choose. Secondary owners are Diego, Emma, and Ella, in equal parts, but they will not have the right to claim it before your death unless you consent to it."

I looked at Patrick as he nodded.

"This is to safeguard you and the children in the event of an unfortunate marriage where property could be lost to your respective husbands, but with joint ownership, the entire fortune cannot, at any time, be lost."

"Patrick… what great trust you have in me. I am honored."

"I love you," Patrick whispered.

"Patrick and I both have inventories of everything he owns, as well as copies of the will. Lawton and Harvey, in London, also have the same documents in their files, so should you need their assistance while in London, they know who you are."

I nodded, too numb to speak.

"You will also have an annual income, as will your children, in addition to the girls' dowries and monies for education."

"And my funeral?" Patrick asked.

"It is all here, in the will," Joseph said.

They turned to me, but I was dumbstruck. My husband was dying, my children would be without a father, and I would soon be a widow again, but these two had addressed everything with a calm that seemed impossible to me.

"Is our business concluded?" Joseph asked.

Patrick nodded and whispered, "Thank you. You've been a good friend, Joseph."

"As have you, Patrick, but I hope to have word of your full recovery within the week."

Patrick attempted a wry smile, and I stood, glancing at him before I walked Joseph downstairs. He attempted a smile, but I didn't.

"I have no words," I said, looking up at Joseph when we reached the door.

"Then just pray," he said. "I will."

* * *

Time passed so slowly that I felt a pause between the seconds.

My brave husband lay before me, so dreadfully pale that I could cry. The glands in his neck were bulging ominously, and his jaw was clamped shut as if a vice were gripping it.

Every now and then his eyes would flutter open, but I was not certain he saw me.

He hadn't said a word in days. He had also refused food and drink, though I would have gladly given him anything a drop at a time if he hadn't pushed me away with the little strength he had left.

This was the end, and he would leave me. This wonderful man would be no more. His smile would no longer light up a room, his subordinates would no longer hear the voice that made them snap to attention, our children would only have memories of their father, and I would be without the man I had come to love so tenderly.

I would be a widow thrice over, but this was the first time I sat at my husband's bedside and watched as death approached a moment at a time.

At three o'clock every afternoon, Dr. Catherwood called on us, and I wondered if it was more for my sake than Patrick's, for there was nothing he could do. A malady like quinsy was an ominous foe.

The doctor had become an old man since I'd first come to St. Augustine. My Edmund had spoken highly of him, and now, in particular, I knew why.

"How are you faring, Mrs. Warrick?" he asked me after he had examined Patrick.

I shrugged. What was I to say, that I was numb because my husband was dying, or should I say I was grateful that I still had this time with him?

When our daughters came home from school, they sat at the foot of their father's bed, chatting with him as if he were awake, but I saw they were watching him as if they were memorizing his every feature. I thought back to the day we'd met during my first days in St. Augustine, when he'd leaped from his carriage with that enchanting grin on his face. Never would I have imagined I would be the wife who would sit vigil at his deathbed, nor would I have imagined how much I would come to love him.

Patrick took his last breath as the girls and I sat there with him, dying quietly, without a sound or a movement. In one instant, he stopped breathing and was gone, leaving me dumbfounded, as if I hadn't known what was to come.

I gathered my girls into my arms, and the tears we had tried to hide from him fell freely while our hearts shattered. I wished I could spare them this grievous part of life, and more than anything, I wished I could wrap my arms around Diego when he learned that his papa had died.

"Say goodbye to your father," I whispered. "It's time."

* * *

Patrick's funeral was held the following Sunday. Emma and Ella sat in the first pew, between Abbie and me, and I couldn't help but think of the time before when I had been here with my husband's wooden casket only feet from me.

The church was full, with the governor, all the members of the royal council, the officers from the fort, and, from what I could see, the rest of the town in attendance.

After the service, which I remember nothing about, Emma held her sister's hand and walked with Abbie and me to the graveyard.

The governor had offered me his arm, and without lowering his voice an octave, he praised Patrick for his bravery, strategic military acumen, his integrity, good sense of humor, and love of his family, but to me, it was a merciless drone. All I wanted was to be left alone to grieve within the confines of my own home.

When I looked down into the open grave into which Patrick's casket would be lowered, I trembled as I fought the unimaginable thought that my husband would be put into such darkness. It was as if I were burying Edmund all over again. I felt the governor's arm tighten around me as I stumbled, and Abbie gripped my arm to keep me standing.

"It won't be much longer," the governor said. "A good pour of rum awaits."

The Governor hosted a wake after the burial, where we gathered for food and drink in honor of Patrick. I sank into a chaise with my girls next to me while everyone talked, but thankfully, most of their chatter was among themselves. There was no longer speculation about what would become of me, for I was wealthier than most of them. It was an odd thought, and something I never expected to be in my own right. Soon solicitors, accountants, and suitors would be at my door, but Patrick had schooled me well in managing what needed to be done. There would be no need for any of them.

CHAPTER TWENTY-EIGHT

———

St. Augustine, March 1781

"I've always known the day would come," Abbie said as we sorted herbs from my garden. "But it's too soon."

I tried to smile, but Abbie kept her gaze on the rosemary leaves she was plucking from their stems.

"I will miss you, Abbie, but we can't remain. Patrick left us so much, and our daughters should see that there is a world beyond East Florida and these united colonies."

"But London?"

I nodded. "I have grieved my husband for two years. Everything here reminds me of him, and Sebastian…." I sighed. "It's settled Abbie. You could come with us."

Abbie chuckled. "You jest. The frigid weather tempts me not."

I could hear Mrs. Oglethorpe's footsteps approaching us. She wasn't pleased with my decision either, but she and Mr. Oglethorpe would be well provided for.

"Ma'am, I believe you have a letter from Diego," she said, handing me an envelope with a familiar seal.

I felt a shiver the moment I opened it, for Sebastian's handwriting was unmistakable.

Anna,

I must tell you that Diego was thrown from his horse in full gallop. We were not able to awaken him for days, and although he is of sound mind now, it will take months before he is fully healed, for he has several broken bones.

Isabella will come to St. Augustine this spring, and from the depth of my heart, I ask that you return to Cuba with her to see our son.

As you are his mother, I welcome you and wish you a safe passage.

Sebastian

My heart raced as I folded the letter. Our son would fully recover, Sebastian had said. I had to trust that he was right.

* * *

A few weeks later, the *Incognita* approached St. Augustine.

Watching Isabella's ship sail into the bay made my heart skip. It seemed an eternity until the *Incognita* docked and the gangway was in place, but it was no surprise that Isabella was the first off the ship. Without a word, we fell into each other's arms, both laughing and sobbing.

"Isa," I said, "it has been so long! Too long!"

The lines on her bronzed face were deeper, as were mine, but the love between us had not changed.

"Sister," she said, "seeing you pleases me more than you know. It is time you come home."

My heart sank. I was so far from the woman I had been when I was Sebastian's, but the sight of her filled me with a joy I hadn't felt in a long time, as if in some manner I still belonged in the Ortega world.

My daughters took to her in an instant, thrilled to have such an exotic visitor. When Abbie joined us later that evening, I realized they would become ladies with different views than many of the English girls they had grown up with. They were enthralled by these two unusual women, and secretly, I was pleased.

"When are we leaving on your ship, Captain Isabella?" Ella asked when we had retired to the porch after dinner.

Isabella grinned. "As soon as you can be ready," she said, sending my daughter to her room in a flurry of excitement.

* * *

The weather was remarkably good during our voyage, with winds perfect for the sail, and my daughters took to sailing with unexpected delight.

We would be in Havana sooner than we anticipated, but as we came nearer, my stomach made a habit of clenching.

One evening, when Isabella and I sat in the captain's quarters, sipping rum, I couldn't keep my apprehension to myself anymore. "How do you think Sebastian will receive me? We haven't seen each other since that dreadful day I tore our hearts to shreds."

Isabella swirled her goblet and glanced into its contents as if the rum held an answer before she looked up at me with those magnificent Ortega eyes. "I believe he prefers not to think of that day. He has a woman now, Dalia Escobar. She is nothing like you, and if anyone were to distress you, it would likely be her rather than Sebastian."

Dalia. Diego had mentioned her in his letters. Silently I scolded myself for the jab that struck my heart. I had been married for over a decade; certainly, I had no right to feel anything at all about Sebastian's lovers, if they were only lovers.

"Are they not married? You said he has a woman, not a wife."

Isabella chuckled. "She is already married to Captain Alfonso Escobar, but he is in love with the Duchess of Altarosa, so my brother finds Dalia an amusing pastime he can rid himself of when he pleases."

I took a deep breath, trying to imagine Sebastian and my son with her. "And how is it that this Dalia is nothing like me?"

Isabella hesitated, studying me as if it had never occurred to her to compare the two of us. Knowing my Isabella, she could do so with a glance. "Hm... She is Spanish, with dark and alluring looks, and unlike you, my dear English sister, she has music in her soul, because we know you were not blessed with rhythm."

We both chuckled at that, but still, I couldn't resist comparing. "So, she is everything I am not?"

Isabella paused for a moment. "Dalia has an unflattering propensity for drama, which Sebastian abhors. She cannot match your intelligence or grace... and unlike you, I don't think she ever captured Sebastian's heart."

Tears filled my eyes, but blinking them away was futile. "I can't remember a day I didn't love him, Isabella. I just haven't allowed myself to remember the sound of his voice, his laughter, or the way he looked at me."

Isabella reached out and patted my hand, making her gold bangles clang and fill a rare moment of silence between us. "If it helps, I'm certain that he has been as troubled as you are."

"Has he not remained angry with me?" I felt childish and silly for asking, but I couldn't bear to think there would be hostility between us, not now, when our son needed us both.

Isabella smiled. "He might not know this, but I believe he has very deep feelings for you, and they are not anger."

* * *

When Cuba was within view, I knew Sebastian would be preparing for our arrival. Rooms would be readied, food would be prepared, and surely, a carriage would be sent for us. While my daughters were dizzy with anticipation, I was not certain of what I felt. The thought of Diego lifted my spirits, while meeting Sebastian could tear open deep wounds that might never have fully healed.

"Remember to breathe now and then," Isabella chided as I stood beside her at the helm.

Today was the day we would dock in Havana. I would return to what had once been my home, to my son, to the man I loved beyond reason but who now had another woman in his life who perhaps, offered him something I never could.

My girls would expect me to be their steadfast mother, but I felt I was coming undone. For them, I would have to be their St. Augustine mother, not the Lady of Casa Ortega or the mistress of the most sensuous man I had ever met.

* * *

The ship came to port midday, and when we heard the festive sound of music drifting over from the dock, we rushed to the railing to catch sight of who would be waiting for us.

"This is nothing at all like St. Augustine!" Emma exclaimed. "The buildings are exquisite! And look, Mama! I can't imagine such a thing at home!"

My daughters watched wide-eyed, taking in the sight of the musicians playing, while young girls danced without inhibition and peddlers shouted over each other to sell their wares.

I smiled at their excitement. "There will be much that you haven't seen at home, my darlings," I said, giving them both a squeeze.

"There he is!" Ella screamed, pointing down to the pier. "Diego is here! He is here!"

Emma and I looked in the direction Ella had indicated, and suddenly tears sprang from my eyes, and my heart attempted to burst, for there he was! My beloved Diego was there, waving up at us!

"Oh, God! How handsome he is!" Emma gushed. "Mama! Look at his hair!"

He did have Sebastian's lush hair, but as I looked down at my boy, I couldn't help but see he wasn't a child anymore, but a man who would never again be the boy I had lost. But still, my son was here, and within the hour I would be able to put my arms around him.

Behind him, I caught sight of Jane and Malcolm on the perch of a carriage drawn by four beautiful black horses. Malcolm held the reins, but both were waving wildly, which warmed my heart.

As soon as we stepped off the gangway, Diego came toward us. Although his gait was guarded, he still had much of Sebastian's swagger and exuded the same charisma, and as he came closer I noticed one of Sebastian's medallions about his neck.

Ella tugged at my sleeve. "How tall he is! He's as tall as Papa!"

The comparison to Patrick felt like a dart to my side, but my gaze was fixed on my boy, and our eyes were already locked in an embrace. I ran into his arms, and he caught me with the strength of a full-grown man.

"My son! My beloved son... I am glad to see you so well, my darling boy! How I have missed you."

"Mother, awaiting your arrival gave me the strength to rise from my bed," he said as our tear-wet cheeks met, and I dared to breathe. "It has been too long. I am so deeply sorry, Mother. I wanted to be there with you when Papa—" He hesitated. "There is so much I want to tell you."

I placed a finger to his lips. "Shush, my dear child. We will have time," I assured him. "Lots of time."

* * *

My stomach twisted as we approached Plaza de Catedral and the imposing villa that was Casa Ortega.

As I took a long look at the magnificent building that had once been my home, I saw Sebastian watching us from the balcony. The years had left their mark, but it was my Sebastian who I looked up at. Just as our eyes met, a beautiful woman stepped up behind him, draping her arm around him, and my heart startled. Sebastian took her hand and kissed it, but his eyes were on me, sending shivers through me.

Moments later, he strode out through the courtyard to greet us. The woman was at his side, clattering along the cobbles in her little satin shoes with her hand tucked under Sebastian's arm, and I noticed he fondled it absentmindedly.

"Welcome," he said, giving us a subtle bow. "As my son's mother, you will always have a home here."

The oddity of the greeting disturbed us both. I could see it in his eyes, and I felt the tension build, but I could say nothing about it.

"Thank you, Sebastian," I said, looking up at him. "You are most gracious."

"May I present Senora Dalia Escobar," he said, but if he said anything after that, it was lost to me.

The vixen at his side had shining dark eyes and olive skin that didn't fold into crow's feet around her eyes when she smiled. Her long black hair was held in place with jeweled pins that competed with the strands of pearls around her neck, and the emeralds set in gold rings on her fingers shimmered in the afternoon sun.

"Delighted to meet you, Mrs. Warrick," she said. "Diego speaks highly of you."

She was too pleasant for my mood, and it suddenly bothered me that she would probably welcome us into the house that I had never stopped thinking of as mine.

"Thank you. You are most kind," I replied, offering all I could manage.

With an uneasiness brewing inside me, I wondered if I had the right to feel disdain for her. She had stepped into my world in her tiny shoes, but it was I who needed to remind myself that I had chosen to stay with Patrick and had no right to judge her.

I noticed Sebastian watching my exchange with his mistress, and when we locked eyes, the rhythm of my heart burst into disarray as if it were screaming at the oddity of it all. He was studying me, and my habit of memorizing everything about him added to the madness I was feeling. There had never been a time when he and I hadn't sought each other, and each other only, but now he was here with her... a jewel box of a woman who couldn't possibly know my Sebastian—or suit him.

My Sebastian. The years disappeared, and I remembered everything that was so good about us. I felt as if I could leap into his arms, and he would catch me and we would be us again, but then he looked away, as if I were just some ordinary woman, and something inside me sank.

Diego shifted at my side, bringing me back to the moment. *I am a widow and grateful to be reunited with my son. I came here for him.*

My daughters gushed when they saw Sebastian for the first time, dazzled by the smile that must remind them of Diego, but they also marveled over Dalia, her magnificent jewels, and the way everything about her glittered as she moved.

Trinkets, I thought, hating myself as she snuggled closer to Sebastian.

"You must be Ella," Sebastian said, bowing to her as if she were a grown lady.

She giggled and turned crimson.

"Ella Mia Warrick. How do you do, sir?"

Everyone smiled, but when Sebastian's eyes met mine, I knew what he was thinking. She was the child I had been carrying when we were last together, and he knew I had named her Mia because of the cherished memory that name carried.

Anna *mia*, he used to call me, and I still carried it in my heart, but I doubted he would ever call me that again.

I watched as Emma introduced herself to him, and he kissed her hand, making her blush too.

Thankfully, Isabella joined us, and her boisterousness lightened the mood. "What are you all standing here for? I, for one, am in search of a bath and a meal!"

"It's waiting for you, all of you!" Dalia said, taking Isabella's arm and leading the way into Casa Ortega. The two of them were already lost in a lively conversation, and I felt my lips tighten at the realization of their familiarity and that Isabella had a history with Dalia as true as the one Isabella had with me, but I caught myself before my unwelcome dismay could become obvious.

Diego offered me his arm, and behind us Sebastian was in the midst of an animated conversation with my daughters. I couldn't hear his words, but I could hear the girls giggle and was again struck by the oddity of the moment.

Before we walked into the open foyer of Casa Ortega, I turned to greet the servants who had lined up by the door.

Some of them were more than familiar faces. Their features showed the passing of time, but they had fared well, and it was good to see them.

As we climbed the grand staircase from the courtyard to the second-floor mezzanine, I wondered which rooms we would be given. Before I could say a word, Isabella turned to us. "My room awaits! I shall see all of you at supper!"

With a smile, she turned the corner, and within a moment a door closed behind her.

Dalia led us down the hall to a room close to the one that was Diego's from the time he was an infant.

Two maids were waiting for the girls with a bath and towels prepared, and my daughters gushed with delight.

"Mother!" Emma exclaimed, looking around. "Have you ever seen a room so beautiful?"

I smiled, remembering how Sebastian and I had labored over the details of this room, from the ornate windowsills and door frames to the pleasing colors of the walls and the rich brocade of the curtains. It looked unchanged, except for the dresses strewn across the beds, which Ella was already examining. To her surprise, she found a doll among the layers of fabric.

"Is all this for us?"

"It is," Sebastian said as he and Dalia came up behind Emma and Ella.

The girls glanced at each other and turned to curtsy to Sebastian and Dalia.

"Thank you so much, sir, ma'am," they said almost in unison.

Sebastian and his woman smiled, and I was secretly relieved they hadn't said "Captain" and "Mrs. Ortega."

I took a deep breath. I had to stop this pettiness, this looming jealousy, even if I could conceal it. Many years had passed, and I had no right to feel this way.

Leaving the girls to their newfound treasures, Diego led me to the double doors farther down the hall, and like the perfect gentleman, he opened them for me and bade me enter. I hesitated, looking back at Sebastian, but he was smiling at Dalia, who seemed to be telling him something amusing.

Surely, they didn't expect me to sleep here. This was the room where Sebastian and I had slept, and as I peered into it, I recognized our bed. This was the bed where Diego had been conceived, the bed that had been our sanctuary, where the depths of our passion had found no boundaries.

"Where do they sleep?" I whispered to my son, tilting my head toward Sebastian and Dalia.

He gestured to the doors at the far end of the mezzanine. "They have the entire east side to themselves," he whispered.

This didn't comfort me, but as I entered the room, I tried not to let the memories overtake me.

"I think this is the most beautiful of the bedrooms," Diego said. "I hope you like it. But, Mother…"

He suddenly became serious, and as his eyes filled with tears, I reached up and wiped them away before they could roll down his cheek. *My darling boy…*

"Mother, I am so glad you are here," he said. "I have desperately prayed for this, but Papa… he died before I could beg his forgiveness, and I'll never see him again."

My heart hurt as I listened to him.

"Sweet boy," I said, fighting back the tears, "there is nothing to be forgiven for. Patrick loved you, and he never blamed you."

"But I shouldn't have been at the docks, so eager to learn more about my father. I will never forgive myself!"

"That would displease him to hear," I said. "It is I who is at fault, for I should have told you more and not shielded you from Sebastian."

A faint smile lit my boy's face. "It is not too late. While you are here, you can tell me the stories my father hasn't," Diego said, smiling down at me.

My heart sank, as I realized that he had no intention of leaving Cuba.

CHAPTER TWENTY-NINE

———

Havana, Cuba, May 1781

A young lady stood next to Diego when I entered the dining room with my daughters. She was as beautiful as Dalia, and no doubt her daughter, but my heart startled when I noticed how Diego looked at her and how she smiled up at him as they whispered something to each other.

Seeing us, Diego came toward us, and the girl followed him.

"Mother, sisters, may I present Dalia's daughter, Esmeralda Escobar, my intended."

Esmeralda curtsied, while my jaw dropped.

"Your intended?"

"Indeed," Esmeralda said, beaming at me. "We hope to be married while you are here."

"I don't know what to say," I stammered. "I—"

"Say you are happy for us, Mother."

My son is a man, no longer a boy. I hid my thoughts behind a smile, but Sebastian saw my qualms and came to my side.

"They are well suited, Anna," he said. "They might as well marry, for one can't seem to breathe without the other."

I remembered a love like that, but I didn't look up at Sebastian. Somehow, I managed to congratulate my son and his lady, realizing I would lose my son to this girl, but he was no longer the boy who was taken from me years ago.

Emma and Ella were delighted by Esmeralda, who asked they attend her at the wedding and took great joy in telling them she would be their sister for the rest of their lives. Before I could stop them, they tried on Esmeralda's jewels, and oddly, the three of them acted like long lost friends who had found each other again.

Ella tugged at my skirt. "Mother! Look what she gave us!"

Ella held up a string of small pearls, and as I glanced at Emma, I saw Esmeralda placing a similar necklace around her neck.

My daughters were already smitten by this girl whom my son loved.

"You must thank her. It is a lovely gift," I said, trying to not look weary.

For a moment, I missed Patrick more than I had in a long time. I missed the quiet, easy days in St. Augustine and the life we had with our children when all I felt was contentment and love. I had suddenly become a jealous, envious woman, something I detested, but these possessive feelings had taken me by surprise. My Sebastian, my Diego... both living their lives without me. I should have been pleased, but all I wanted was to be in the center of their world and not a spectator on the outside, looking in.

Dinner was announced when Sebastian and Dalia came down the grand staircase to lead us to the dinner table. As I took in her gown of emerald-green satin, the jewels about her slender neck, and her hair, expertly coiffed to frame her beautiful face, I felt sorely underdressed in my pale blue silk, but I doubted anyone noticed. Isabella, as usual, had dressed as she pleased in a billowing blouse and a colorful skirt. She looked more like a dancer than a sea captain or a woman of means.

"Please be seated," Dalia said when Sebastian held out a chair for her.

«This is delightful," Sebastian said, looking at all of us gathered around the table. When he met Dalia's gaze, he lifted his glass in a toast. "I am thankful tonight for Isabella's safe return and that she brought my son the gift of his beloved mother and sisters. He has missed you sorely, and as I said when you arrived, Anna, you and your daughters will always be welcomed at Casa Ortega."

"Thank you, Sebastian," I said. "We are most grateful."

Dalia took a sip of wine and nodded. "Sebastian is a wonderful host, is he not? He wouldn't turn anyone away, would you, *mi amor?*"

"There is no reason to," Sebastian said. "*Buen Provecho.* Everyone, enjoy!"

Dinner was a familiar medley of delicacies from the sea with saffron rice. Wine flowed freely and, thankfully, numbed my senses.

"This puts the fare on the *Incognita* to shame," Isabella moaned. "You should lend me a cook, brother."

Sebastian raised his goblet to her. "Then how would I lure you home?"

"I don't have to be lured, Sebastian. I know where I belong."
She smiled at him, but I was the one who caught his eye.

"I hope you found your rooms comfortable," Dalia said,
turning to me. "Surely, yours must feel familiar, Anna.
Unfortunately, Sebastian hasn't let me do a thing to that
side of the building, so it isn't quite to my standards yet."

I looked into Sebastian's eyes and wondered if he ever
thought of me in that bed and if that was why he kept this
sparkling woman on the far side of the building.

Ella gushed and answered before I could. "Oh, yes! Our
room is grand, but Mother's rooms are even grander! She
will feel like a queen in that large bed!"

As everyone laughed, I watched Dalia glancing up
at Sebastian.

"Thank you, Dalia. The rooms are lovely," I said, not wanting to elaborate or say it had been Sebastian's and mine to
begin with—or that Sebastian had left it untouched because,
perhaps, it mattered to him.

Sebastian smiled and turned to my children. "Your
mother and I fought more than you can imagine while we
were finishing that particular room. It was something to
behold!" he said, making me want to sink through my chair.
"Do you remember, Anna?"

"I couldn't forget," I said with a nod before quickly chang-
ing the subject. "This wine is divine, Sebastian. Is it from
your vineyard? I should like some more."

Without taking her eyes off Sebastian, Dalia snapped
her fingers at a servant hovering nearby, and my glass was
immediately filled.

"It is," he said. "Do you recall how we argued about which
color the walls should be painted? After a while, there were
twenty different colors on one wall alone!"

"Sebastian! Surely, it wasn't more than twelve. You jest!" I said, trying to be serious.

Isabella nearly choked on her food as she burst into laughter, leaving Sebastian to act quite indignant, but he laughed too.

"The color of the walls was of the utmost importance," he said.

I lifted my glass to him. "That's why we had them painted white," I said dryly, drawing a laugh around the table.

Sebastian shook his head. "Fortunately, we agreed on the furnishings. The bed was specially commissioned..." He paused, looking at me. "Our initials are still in the frame."

"I didn't notice," I said, avoiding his gaze. "But you've kept Casa Ortega as beautiful as I remembered, and it pleases me that you have kept Malcolm and Jane in your employ. They seem to be thriving here."

"I think they have missed you. They've often said through the years that you were a kind mistress to serve."

Dalia shrugged. "You were told that by a man who doesn't speak? I've never gotten any sense out of him."

Sebastian shook his head. "Sometimes words are not necessary, my dear."

"Then you shouldn't use so many of them on a topic as dull as paint, on beds commissioned so long ago that it doesn't matter." Dalia peered at Sebastian over the gold rim of her glass. "I could think of far more interesting things for us to talk about."

Sebastian shook his head, smiling, but when he looked up at me, I felt a quiver, as if even my body was telling me how wrong it was that this jewel box of a woman was at his side and not me.

* * *

After dinner, Jane collected Ella to take her upstairs to get her ready for bed. Diego wandered away with Emma on one arm and Esmeralda on the other, while Sebastian and Isabella excused themselves to discuss a matter regarding a ship. This left Dalia and me alone together on the terrace.

"I'm pleased we have a chance to talk," I said, trying to be gracious. "You have been most kind to receive us."

Dalia signaled for more wine and leaned toward me with a smile that reminded me of Sofia Warrick. "Dear woman, have no worries. Diego's rapid recovery has astounded us all, so now there is no need for you to delay your plans."

Before I could say a word, her eyes lit.

"It has been quite interesting to make your acquaintance, for frankly, I never heard Sebastian mention you until Diego came to us. I could be mistaken, but perhaps it's because nothing from your distant past together matters now," she said, smiling. "With the exception of Diego, of course; he is practically a son to both of us."

"Do not delude yourself, Dalia. My son knows to whom he belongs."

Dalia seemed surprised, but my calm facade was wearing thin.

She shifted in her seat. "Well, since you are our guest, you will not have a quarrel from me. What I do recall is that Sebastian spoke much more of the woman he found after you. From what I understand, they had quite the go of it. I even heard she insisted he burn your portraits to prove his love for her."

Her smile was smug.

I swallowed hard. "And did he burn my portraits?"

She took a long sip of her wine and gave me a wide-eyed look dripping in innocence. "Well, I don't see them anywhere, do you?"

I gasped. I would have to ask Isabella about the portrait-burning woman, but the one across from me was certainly no more than a bejeweled viper. Good God, what had become of Sebastian to take up with the likes of her, beautiful or not?

After droning on without her anticipated reactions from me, Dalia emptied her glass. "It is late, Anna dear, and I will take my leave of you. I must prepare myself for bed before Sebastian comes to our rooms."

It took great effort not to roll my eyes. "Yes. Certainly, he would not wish you to lose even a wink of your beauty sleep," I said as sweetly as I could muster. "Good night, dear."

When she left, I escaped to the highest of the loggias, where I sat, trying to calm my mind by slowly breathing in the salty sea air. I couldn't even bear to speak to Isabella tonight, and somehow she must have known this, for she hadn't sought me out.

When the house had quieted down, I heard footsteps on the winding staircase leading toward me. They were slow and steady, and with each step my insides tightened. I was nearly breathless by the time Sebastian stood before me with two glasses of rum in his hands.

He looked magnificent, a sight my eyes had sorely missed, but I couldn't help feeling unnerved by his presence.

"I thought we should have a word," he said.

We should have much more than a word, but I tried to look less disturbed than I felt.

"I suppose," I said as I took the glass of rum he handed me, hoping I sounded unfazed, but my heart was about to undo me.

He slipped down into the chair beside me, and I couldn't help drawing in the scent of him. I held my glass with both hands, willing my gaze from drifting over every inch of him.

"The years have been kind to you, for you are as beautiful as I remember," he said, studying me.

"Thank you, but I never forgave myself for what I did to us," I said, already doubting my timing.

"Tell me," he said, becoming my Sebastian again.

I sighed. "I saw you in Diego's face every day and every night. Not a day passed that I didn't think of you."

He smiled, but there was something bittersweet about his expression. We looked away from each other, and I could tell that he, like me, looked out to the sea to seek a comfort that neither of us felt.

"Everything could have been different, Anna," he said, not looking at me. "I searched for the kind of love we had, but it has eluded me."

I felt pained, but there was nothing I could do to take back the years. The thought of Patrick tugged at me too, for our life together had been precious, and I didn't regret being his wife.

We sat in silence for long minutes before he gathered himself and turned to me.

"It is good to have you here, truly."

"Thank you, Sebastian," I said. "I feel I have been forgiven, and that is a comfort."

He looked at me, and for a moment I thought he was going to kiss me, but instead, he reached out and put a hand on my shoulder, letting it slide down my arm.

"You never have to seek my forgiveness," he said. "You are my son's mother, and…"

We were sitting so close, making my yearning to touch him almost unbearable, but instead of giving in to my desires, I spun the rum in my glass and looked down into it as if it could give me a wisdom or a calm I didn't possess.

"You have cared well for our son," I said. "He appears to thrive."

He smiled, and a light appeared in his eyes as he looked out over the bay. "As have you, Anna. He was brave and fearless in his ordeal, although it has pained him to be separated from you and his sisters."

And Patrick, I thought, but I was certain Sebastian would not say his name. Diego loved Patrick, and having lost him forever pained him greatly, although he looked to have hidden this from Sebastian.

"Dalia tries to be a mother to him, but he is a man now. The only mother he needs is you."

I felt my hair rise at the mention of Dalia's efforts with my son. "If she seeks to mother our son and you allowed her to fill this house with monstrously gilded pieces and excess, why haven't you married her?"

He glanced at me quickly. I saw that I had startled him, and I was not certain if it had been merely to torment myself that I had asked or because I wanted to hear the words from his lips.

"There is no need for marriage, I was once told." He smiled genuinely as he looked at me, and we both remembered our bold pledge, but then the smile ebbed. "I asked you to be my wife, and I will not ask another."

I nodded but wondered what I would say if he asked me again.

What a fool I was. I knew what my answer would be, but at that moment, the pain of his nearness and the oddity of being a guest in what had once been my home was unnerving. Certainly, we could not stay here for long, for it would undo me.

London would give me and my daughters a better life, and perhaps I could lure Diego to spend some time there.

I rose slowly, making certain my feet would not falter, and handed my glass back to him. "It is late. I will retire to my room."

He rose and looked down at me. "It pleases me that you have come home at last."

I didn't trust myself to look up at him. "Good night, Sebastian," I whispered, gathering my skirts and moving toward the stairs.

"Good night, Anna," he said.

Looking over my shoulder, I saw him bring my glass to his lips and empty it, reminding me that Havana without Sebastian at my side could never again be my home.

CHAPTER THIRTY

Havana, July 1781

Awakening to a commotion, I rushed to the window, surprised to see a carriage being loaded with trunks and boxes.

Stifling a gasp, I watched Dalia burst through the front door heading toward the carriage, just as Esmeralda ran across the cobbles and flung herself into her mother's arms.

Esmeralda wept, but Dalia looked to be in a rage, spewing out words with such haste that I couldn't catch the gist of them.

It appeared she was leaving, for she wore a travel cape over her billowing mauve gown, but I couldn't recall a word spoken of any departure, other than Isabella taking Ella and Emma with her to buy new riding horses in Jaruco later today.

Suddenly, Dalia glanced up at me. I ducked, hoping she hadn't seen me, but when I peeked out the window again, she had quieted. Sebastian stood motionless between the entry to Casa Ortega and Dalia. He appeared weary, but he made no effort to move toward Dalia and her daughter.

Dalia released herself from Esmeralda's embrace and took a long look at Sebastian before she turned and stepped up into the carriage and signaled the coachman, leaving me agape and uncertain of what I had witnessed.

Is she gone for good? Did they quarrel, or had Sebastian dismissed her as Isabella said he would do when he tired of her?

Sebastian wasn't at breakfast when I came downstairs and seated myself across from my son and a red-eyed Esmeralda.

I tried to give her a reassuring look. "I saw that your mother left this morning."

Esmeralda nodded, as her eyes filled with tears. "She could not compete with Sebastian's love for you," she whispered. "From the time she and Sebastian were first together, she felt you were a shadow standing between them. My mother is no fool, she knew he would never love her as he loved you, but she never thought you would return."

"How can that be? She told me he never spoke of me."

Esmeralda laughed, sadly.

"My father spoke of you often, as if you were in every fiber of Casa Ortega," Diego said, taking Esmeralda's hand. "Anna's lantern, Anna's chair, Anna chose this, Anna chose that. That is why she wanted to change everything here, to remove every shred of your presence."

"I didn't know," I said, genuinely surprised.

"It's true. She knew she was defeated the moment you came through the gates," Esmeralda said.

Diego watched me, his eyes narrowing like Sebastian's. "You have no fault in this. It is not your doing."

Esmeralda nodded. "Believe him. You have been nothing but kind since you arrived, but my mother feared you from the moment Sebastian wrote to you."

"Where is he now?" I asked, taking a long sip of the tea that Jane put in front of me.

"He left to oversee work on the new ships, but he'll be home for supper," Diego said. "Would you be at ease if we leave with Tia Isabella and my sisters as well? Esmeralda is in need of a distraction, and what better way to please her than to buy her a new horse?"

Diego smiled at her, and she seemed comforted, leaning into him.

"We'll be back by tomorrow afternoon," he said.

I shook my head. "Have no worries about me. I should like to go through the things that were left behind all those years ago. It seems I will have the time for it today, unless my things are no longer here."

The sound of footsteps heralded Isabella's approach. She was dressed in riding clothes and appeared to be in high spirits. "There are trunks in the storage room across from Sebastian's study in the high tower," she said, sitting down next to me.

When Esmeralda and Diego excused themselves, I turned to Isabella, but before I could say a word, she put up her hand to silence me.

"She is gone, and she won't be back," she said.

I could feel my brows furrow. "How can you be sure?"

"I know my brother." There was suddenly a mischievous glimmer in Isabella's eyes. "While you are in the tower, you might take a look into his study. He allows no one there, but the key is behind the sconce next to the door, should you fall into temptation. Just don't let anyone see you enter."

"It sounds like you have," I said. "What would I find if I dare enter?"

"You'd be surprised," she said, standing up just as my daughters bolted into the room with Esmeralda and Diego in tow.

"We're ready for Jaruko," Ella said, beaming up at me. "Sebastian said we could have our own horses."

* * *

Finishing my tea, I found that I was more intrigued than I wanted to be.

The door to Sebastian's study was on the top landing of a spiral stone staircase, and the key was where Isabella said it would be. For a moment, I held it in my hand, fighting the voice inside my head that told me to put it back and search my own trunks instead, but Isabella had made me curious.

I put the key in the lock, and when the door creaked open, I slipped inside.

I remembered the oak desk, his beautifully carved chair, and the Ortega crest filling the wall behind it. Light filtered in from two windows, casting light on a map spread across his desk, but that was hardly anything that would surprise me.

What had Isabella thought I might find of interest here? Looking around, I turned to the opposite wall and gasped. Standing there, I felt my knees weaken and couldn't help my jaw from dropping.

Steadying myself on the desk, I couldn't take my eyes off the painting that covered most of the wall. The image was of a woman with a small child on her hip, and it was more than five feet tall, almost as tall as I am in life. The woman in the painting was me, and the child was certainly Diego.

The likeness was of a younger me, and Diego was but a toddler. My hair, so much longer then, was loose and billowed around me. A breeze had picked up the hem of my white dress that was cinched at the waist by a lavender sash. The top slipped off my left shoulder, as I recall it often did, but it was my face that startled me. My gaze was deep and haunting and painted so that no matter where Sebastian would move in this room, my eyes would follow him, as would the eyes of our cherub-cheeked Diego, who was perched on my hip with my arms around him. We were both barefoot, and I was walking on sand with the sea and sky behind me.

It was beautiful, and I wondered how my likeness was captured so well when I didn't sit for it. What startled me more was that Sebastian had kept the image of us here in front of him, in his private study, where even the servants knew not to tread.

I stared at the painting for a long time. When did he have it commissioned? Would he have my face in front of him here if he didn't still yearn for me, if he didn't still love me?

Turning away, I grabbed the key and slipped out the door, locking it behind me.

"Thank you, Isabella," I whispered as I entered the storage chamber to find my trunks.

* * *

I would be late for dinner. Lingering in my bath longer than usual was particularly pleasing this evening. Jane had scented the water with fragrant oils of citrus, ginger, and rosehips, soothing my senses and making my skin feel silken and supple.

Stepping out of the water, I caught my reflection in the mirror of my armoire. I was still lithe and strong, still young, or at least not old, but probably not young enough to ever bear another child and live.

I smiled, surprised at my thoughts of another child. It has been years since I'd had such a yearning, but tonight I would make years melt away, as if I myself had found the fountain of youth and taken my fill of it.

As my skin absorbed the oils I rubbed into it, I brushed my hair until it felt like silk between my fingers. I dabbed the slightest touch of rouge to my cheeks, and it brought a glow to my face. When I was done, I was pleased with what I saw in the mirror.

Taking a deep breath, I ignored the impatience of my heart and dressed without haste before putting on soft satin slippers and descending the grand staircase.

Sebastian rose as I entered the terrace and pulled out a chair for me. Surely, he recognized the dress I'd recovered from the trunks in the tower. It fit as well as it had all those years ago. Lifting my bosom and cinching my waist with its lavender sash, it allowed the voluminous skirt to swirl about me as I walked with a bearing even a noblewoman could not fault.

My hand drifted across his as I slipped into my seat, and he adjusted my chair before settling down next to me.

"Anna," he started, then hesitated. "You look magnificent."

"Thank you," I said, casting him a side glance.

"As if the years melted away," he said, seeming oddly disturbed.

I smiled, trying to appear aloof a little longer. He knew I'd found my way to the tower chamber, where he'd kept my image sheltered in secret all these years. It told me he loved me still, and wearing this dress tonight was my reply.

For once, I barely noticed the paella we were served or the wine I usually found so pleasant. Oddly, I was without words. I knew he was waiting for me to speak, but I wouldn't, not this time.

"Anna *mia*," he said, melting my heart. Those were words that echoed inside me through the years, that whispered to me in moments of silence, and the sound that calmed me in moments of turmoil. I thought I'd never hear them flow from Sebastian's lips again, but then I never thought I'd feel the thrill of the tension mounting between us that used to drive us to madness. It reminded me of that magical night we danced in the moonlight on the deck of the *Nuestra Havana,* long before we were lovers, not knowing where our journey would take us.

Turning to look into his eyes, I saw my Sebastian, the man I loved beyond reason, and who loved me back.

"Dalia—" he said, but I put a finger to his lips.

"She is gone," I said, rising from my chair.

He stood, and we kissed deeply, passionately, as if we'd found each other for the first time, but to me it felt like coming home.

"Come back to me," he said, his voice thick with emotion, as he planted featherlight kisses on my neck, making me dizzy with desire as he murmured my name.

Taking his hand, I drew him toward the stairs leading to our sanctuary.

"I have always been yours," I told him.

The glow in his eyes returned. "This time you will marry me."

It was not a question, although I knew he intended it to be. I knew him as well as I knew myself.

"I will," I whispered. "This time I will."

ACKNOWLEDGMENTS

—

This book has been long in the making. In spite of multiple versions, even an attempt to turn it into a trilogy, and at times feeling my characters had become completely different people than I first intended them to be, I couldn't put it away.

My first thanks go to New Degree Press and my publisher, Brian Bies. Also, my wonderful editors, Lauren Sweeney, Colin Lyon, and Anne Belott, who made the NDP experience fun; and of course, Venus Bradley and Christy Mossburg; author coaches Kyra Ann Dawkins, Stephen Howard, John Saunders, and Haley Newlin; designer Gjorgji Pejkovski; and last but not least, Professor Eric Koester of Georgetown University and the Creator Institute, who started this all.

This book wouldn't be what it is without my insightful beta readers. Thank you so much, Dr. Mai Saif, Julia Smith, Doretta Bree, Dr. Nancy Whitham, and Faye Ellen Gaetz.

A special thanks goes to Captain Roger Howell for giving me insight to what a storm would be like on a 1760s sail-ship.

What is a writer without readers? I am immensely grateful for the support of:

Dr. Piedade Silva, Dr. Mai Saif, Dr. Linda Veraja, Dr. Carmen Chinea, Dr. Olivia Richman, Dr. Ellen Hoefer-Hopf,

Louise Wigglesworth, Melanie Payne, Michael McNally, Edel Haugrønningen, Katie Craig, Cynthia Renee Marquez, Kathy Kuser,

Dr. Judy Sicilia, Dr. Laura Streyffler, Dr. Denise Billen Mejia, Deborah Spyker, Paula Harper, Mickie Suzanne, Richard Claire, Diane Grytzelius, Christopher Probst, Linda Parras, Natalie Richman, Dr. Joanna Carioba, Fay Ellen Graetz, Isabel Watson,

Dr. Nancy Whitham, Wenche Watson, Kenneth Tuschoff, Dory Bennett, Julian Cabrera, David John Huber, Shannon Nelson, John Eiseman, Sheena Johnson, Gudrun Marie Jonsdottir, Eirikur Hrafnsson, Nicole Vranjican, Ingrid Vranjican, Lindsay Mitchell, Natalie Micciulli, Shifra Schacher, James Twining, Jean Setering, Lori Kokich, Ana Aborlleile, Janet E. Koharik, Mary Mazzotta, Bonnie Gallo, Barbara Vranjican, Elizabeth Bernstein, Eva Nappi, Katherine Feigin, Felicia Huffman, E. Burns, Shelby Eiford, Kayla Atkins, Hanna Bree, Dtrimyer, Depenaob, Morten Sissener, Deborah Deschene, Debra Almeida, Kelly Arsenault, Sherri Marquez, Anne Sissener, Josette Mangione, Rob Soper, Kelsey Mark, Rebekah Sell, Dilla Trimyer, Melissa Lepe, and of course, my family.

WHAT'S NEXT

——

WHAT WE CAN'T FORGET
By
Linda Saether

This WWII novel grew from my memory of family dinners where wine flowed freely and tongues loosened to tell stories of events that were usually left unspoken.

Today I wish I had asked deeper questions and tried harder to understand that we aren't any different than the people who lived during the war. They were of flesh and blood as we are and felt as deeply as we do, but they had to endure events so unimaginable that we prefer not to.

Based on these true stories and extensive research, I have created *What We Can't Forget*, the story of two Serbian twins and a Norwegian woman who find themselves thrust into the horrors of WWII and are haunted by it in the aftermath when the world around them no longer wants to remember what they can't forget.

This book will be published in Spring 2022.